Oregon Pharmacy Law
An MPJE Study Guide

First Edition

Authored by:
Kristen Bossert, Pharm.D., MBA, BCPS

RxPharmacist, LLC

ISBN: 9781093422382

COPYRIGHT

© 2019 Oregon Pharmacy Law: An MPJE® Study Guide
First Edition
Copyright© 2019 RxPharmacist®, LLC | Published May 2019, Edited December 2019
Authors: Kristen Bossert, Pharm.D., MBA, BCPS
Maryam Khazraee, Pharm.D., BCPS

All rights reserved. No part of this publication may be reproduced, distributed, or transmitted in any form or by any means, including photocopying, recording, or other electronic or mechanical methods, without the prior written permission of the publisher, except in the case of brief quotations embodied in critical reviews and certain other noncommercial uses permitted by copyright law. For permission requests, write to the publisher, addressed "Attention: Permissions Coordinator," at help@rxpharmacist.com. All trademarks are trademarks of their respective owners and some marked with a registered trademark symbol to notify, with no intention of infringement of the trademark.

DISCLAIMER: The MPJE® and NABP® marks are federally registered trademarks owned by the National Association of Boards of Pharmacy (NABP®). RxPharmacist LLC and the authors, Kristen Bossert and Maryam M. Khazraee, are not associated with the NABP®, and its products or services have not been reviewed or endorsed by the NABP®.

TERMS OF USE

The work is provided "as is". RxPharmacist and its licensors make no guarantees or warranties as to the accuracy, adequacy, or completeness of or results to be obtained from using the work, including any information that can be accessed through the work via hyperlink or otherwise, and expressly disclaim any warranty, express or implied, including but not limited to implied warranties of merchantability or fitness. RxPharmacist®, LLC and its licensors are not engaged in rendering medical, legal, accounting, or other professional service. If medical or legal advice, or other expert assistance is required, the services of a competent professional should be sought. If any errors are found, please report them via email to: help@rxpharmacist.com.

RxPharmacist®, LLC and its licensors do not warrant or guarantee that the functions contained in the work will meet your requirements or that its operation will be uninterrupted or error free. Neither RxPharmacist®, LLC nor its licensors shall be liable to you or anyone else for any inaccuracy, error or omission, regardless of cause in the work or for any damages resulting therefrom. RxPharmacist®, LLC has no responsibility for the content of any information assessed through the work. Under no circumstances shall RxPharmacist®, LLC and/or its licensors be liable for any indirect, incidental, special, punitive, consequential, or similar damages that result from the use of or inability to use the work, even if any of them has been advised of the possibility of such damages. This limitation of liability shall apply to any claim or cause whatsoever whether such claim or cause arises in contact, tort or otherwise.

This guide was created with the help of recent pharmacy student graduates and parts of their work have been reproduced by their permission.

Printed in the United States of America. This publication does <u>not</u> contain actual exam questions but we sure do try to give you a real taste of what to expect! All pictures are from Unsplash.com and the photos are free to use and can be used for commercial, personal projects, and for editorial use.

FOREWORD

We understand how it feels being a pharmacy student or professional looking forward to an exciting journey in getting licensed in another state or your home state! We can relate to the high stresses of studying for the MPJE exam as well. Having very little resources or guides out there, almost all being outdated, and the monstrous list of raw laws can be overwhelming! We want to thank all the recent pharmacy graduates who were involved to help us review and write this guide. We hope this guide serves you well in passing the MPJE exam with flying colors! Be sure to review the test bank questions to test your knowledge and skills.

Best of luck!

How to use this guide

This guide is separated into a basic contents section and then question section that further helps to expand your knowledge. It's important to review the links provided for the different statutes and review the questions and explanations to further study for your MPJE exam.

Table of Contents

INTRODUCTION 6
   What is the MPJE? 6
   Quick Test-Taking Tips 7
FEDERAL PHARMACY LAW REVIEW PART 1 9
INVESTIGATIONAL NEW DRUG (IND) APPLICATION 11
NEW DRUG APPLICATION (NDA) 13
FEDERAL PHARMACY LAW REVIEW PART 2 15
PRESCRIPTION DRUG USER FEE ACT (PDUFA) 15
PHASE IV AND POST-MARKETING SURVEILLANCE 18
OVER-THE-COUNTER (OTC) REGULATIONS 18
REGULATING MARKETING 20
VIOLATIONS AND ENFORCEMENT 20
FEDERAL PHARMACY LAW REVIEW PART 3: OVERVIEW OF FEDERAL ACTS 22
FEDERAL PHARMACY LAW REVIEW PART 4: CONTROLLED SUBSTANCES LAWS 37
FEDERAL LAWS AND REGULATIONS GOVERNING PHARMACIES, PHARMACISTS AND PRESCRIPTIONS 37
DRUG ENFORCEMENT ADMINISTRATION (DEA) REGISTRATION 39
PRACTIONERS 39
PRESCRIPTION BASICS 40
PRESCRIPTION LABELING 42
PHARMACY REQUIREMENTS 43
DRUG ENFORCEMENT ADMINISTRATION (DEA) FORMS 44
SCHEDULE LISTED CHEMICAL PRODUCT (SLCPS) 45
Poison Prevention Packaging 47
Specific Labeling Requirements 48
Health Insurance Portability and Accountability Act (HIPAA) 50
FEDERAL PHARMACY LAW EXAM 53
ANSWERS TO FEDERAL PHARMACY LAW EXAM 77
OREGON PHARMACY LAW REVIEW 102
OREGON PHARMACY LAW PART 1: INSIDE THE PHARMACY 104
OREGON PHARMACY LAW PART 2: LICENSES, REGISTRATIONS, OPERATIONS 142
OREGON PHARMACY LAW PART 3: GENERAL REGULATIONS 147
OREGON PHARMACY LAW EXAM 148
ANSWERS TO OREGON PHARMACY LAW EXAM 174
OREGON PHARMACY LAW REFERENCES 188

Introduction

What is the MPJE?

The Multi-Prudence Jurisdiction Examination (MPJE) is a 120-question computer-based exam that uses adaptive testing response questions to test your knowledge on both federal and state pharmacy laws. For example, if you keep getting questions wrong then the computer will provide you questions that are statistically deemed "easier". It's important to note that of the 120-questions on this exam, only 100 are used to calculate your final score. The remaining 20 questions are pretest questions that won't count into your MPJE score, but you won't be able to tell which ones are pretest questions and which ones are not. The total testing time is two hours with NO breaks during the testing session so it's important to take note of time.

The passing scaled score is 75 with the minimum score being zero and maximum 100. The exam is divided into three major sections:
- Pharmacy Practice- 83%
- Licensure, registration, certification, operational requirements- 15%
- General Regulatory Processes- 2%

Some major points to remember:
- All questions are answered in order so there's no going back
- Lots of situational questions
- Online registration costs $250.00 per examination
    - $100 non-refundable application fee + $150 examination fee
- Best to be prepared and bring two forms of **unexpired** IDs at Pearson Vue:
    - At least one picture ID with signature (i.e. Driver's License) is needed
    - Other can be a credit card with signature
- 120 questions, 100 count towards your score
- MUST complete 107 questions for examination to be scored
- If you do fail, you must wait 30 days to retake
- Examination doesn't distinguish between state and federal laws, but...
    - Answer each question based on what is the more restrictive law
- Any misconduct or inkling of misconduct is grounds for failure
- Arrive at least 30 minutes early
- Ensure to read EVERY SINGLE WORD!

They will try to trick you so make sure to answer the question they ask, and lookout for unusual words as triggers. We recommend reviewing the nabp.net/programs/examination/mpje site and reading over the NAPLEX/MPJE registration bulletin.

They provide a more specific overview of the exam, scheduling requirements, and a list of core competencies for you to understand. While you may use the core competencies as a guide to ensure your studies are complete, we do not recommend to spend too much time on the core competencies, but more on understanding the laws, as there are many situational type questions.

Quick Test-Taking Tips

There are practice questions included in this review to help you prepare for the MPJE. Note that the practice questions in the Oregon specific section, like on the MPJE need to be answered as if you were working as a pharmacist in Oregon. That is, you will have to think about both state and federal law for all questions to determine what to do in the scenario.

Some practice questions will be easy, and test the law in a very literal sense such as the following example: "How many CE's must a pharmacist complete every renewal cycle?"

Other questions will require you to think about the law and interpret it in a practice setting. A simple example would be:

> You receive a faxed prescription from an internet-based provider for Zolpidem 10mg. You should do the following:
> A. Fill the prescription
> B. Call the internet-based provider to verify a patient-provider relationship before filling the prescription.
> C. Refuse to fill the prescription because it is a controlled substance.
> D. Refuse to fill the prescription.

The answer in this case under Oregon law would be D., as Oregon law does not consider internet-based practices a setting that fulfills the patient-provider relationship requirement. It has nothing to do with the fact that it is a controlled substance.

Some of the practice questions contained in this book provide harder examples of this type of question, and it is easy to confuse the right answer after looking at the possible choices. When you encounter these questions, we recommend first thinking of the exact laws that govern in the situation. For example, in the sample question above, remembering Oregon law states internet-based practice sites do not fulfill the patient provider relationship requirement will assist in answering this question. Therefore, you cannot fill the prescription, regardless what it is for. You can pick answer choice D. without looking at the other answer choices. If the question does list a medication and you have to consider it in your answer, first determine if it is a Schedule II (**CII**), Schedule III- V (CIII-V), legend, or over the counter (OTC) medication. Think about what specific laws apply to the schedule of medication and then narrow your options down one by one.

Because the questions on the test can trick you, it is of the utmost importance that you read and answer the question that is written on the test- not the question you in your head! You will need to find a middle ground between impulsively picking an answer and debating between the answer choices for too long. For the test you don't need to know everything but you do need to learn how to cut down to two answer choices to improve your odds of getting it right. And obviously, it will help your odds immensely if you prepare by both studying the law and completing mock-exams, such as the two included in this book.

The general outline for any test question is the following:

Stem- This is the meat of the question

Lead-In- This is the bones on the meat for the question, the actual question that you need to answer

In any test question for any exam, they are going to have 'distractor' answer choices to steer you away and try to make you pick the answer choice. One way to not fall into this trap is first look at the question being asked in a patient case question, then read through the case to pick out the pertinent information, and last try to answer the question before looking at the answer choices.

Usually your gut feeling is the right answer choice so we recommend not to change your answer unless you really feel certain that it is not right compared to the first answer you chose. When going through these practice exams in this study guide, we recommend you go back and ask yourself why you missed that question. Was it not reading the question carefully? Was it answering the question in your head and not the actual question? Was it just a lack of understanding or knowledge of the law? These are all important steps for you to improve your test taking abilities.

Lastly, be sure to analyze yourself and how well you test. Are you a slow test-taker? If so, you would want to work on your endurance and time yourself while you are taking these practice exams in this guide. Are you a fast test-taker? We would recommend to slow down since you may mis-read the question or jump to an answer that is a distractor and fall into a test-taking trap.

Both the Federal-specific and Oregon-specific Pharmacy MPJE Mock exams are 120 questions, imitating the number of questions on the actual MPJE. You may consider completing these in a timed setting to help in your preparations.

FEDERAL PHARMACY LAW REVIEW PART 1

You may have remembered some of these concepts during your law course in pharmacy school, but it's important to remember our country's regulation policy as much of our industry is highly regulated!

In the United States, all food, drugs, cosmetics, and medical devices, for both humans and animals, are regulated under the authority of the Food and Drug Administration (FDA). The FDA and its laws were created by government bodies in response to promoting and protecting the safety of the public when it comes to food, medicines, and medical devices. We highly recommend participating in an FDA rotation despite being highly competitive and costly for a budget-minded student, it is well worth the experience! Our pharmacists that have had this opportunity speak very highly of the rotation.

This introduction to federal pharmacy law discusses the FDA's regulatory oversight and that of other agencies, the drug approval and development process, the mechanisms used to regulate manufacturing and marketing, as well as various violation and enforcement actions taken by the FDA to ensure pharmaceutical and corporate industry companies are maintaining compliance.

PHARMACEUTICALS

The main responsibility for the regulation of pharmaceuticals and the pharmaceutical industry is the Food and Drug Administration (FDA), its headquarters is located in Silver Springs, MD. The FDA formed in 1931 and is one of several branches within the US Department of Health and Human Services (HHS). The "sister" agencies to the FDA that also work in HHS are the Centers for Disease Control and Prevention (CDC), National Institute of Health (NIH), and the Healthcare Financing Administration (HCFA). These sites are harder to get rotations during pharmacy school, but a lot of information can be found on their websites. Other agencies that fall under HHS also include the Agency for Healthcare Research and Quality (AHRQ), Centers for Medicare and Medicaid Services (CMS), Substance Abuse and Mental Health Services Administration (SAMHSA), and the Indian Health Service (IHS). Our main focus will be the FDA as they are the agency that solely regulates the drug industry.

The FDA is organized into a number of offices and centers headed by a commissioner. It is a scientifically based law enforcement agency whose mission is to protect the public health and ensure fairness between health-regulated industries (i.e., pharmaceutical, device, biological, and the consumer). The vast number of tasks done at the FDA is more than you think. It licenses and inspects manufacturing facilities to ensure they follow Good Manufacturing Practices (GMP); tests products on a smaller scale; evaluates claims and prescription drug advertising to ensure there is no false marketing done; monitors research and reviews clinical trial methods; and creates regulations, guidelines, standards, and policies.

It does all of this through its Office of Operations, which contains component offices and centers such as the Center for Drug Evaluation and Research (CDER), the Center for Biologics Evaluation and Research (CBER), the Center for Devices and Radiological Health (CDRH), the Center for Food Safety and Applied Nutrition (CFSAN), the Center for Veterinary Medicine (CVM), the Office of Orphan Products Development, the Office of Biotechnology, the Office of Regulatory Affairs, and the National Center for Toxicological Research. It's definitely a lot! The main office where pharmacists work is in CDER. Each of these offices and centers has a defined role to play, but sometimes they overlap on their work. For example, if a pharmaceutical company submits a drug that is delivered to a patient during therapy by a medical device, then the CDER and CDRH may need to coordinate that product's approval. Although CDER is the main center that reviews prescription drugs, any other center or office may become involved with its review depending on the circumstances. One of the most significant resources to industry and consumers is the FDA's web site www.fda.gov. We highly recommend taking some time in reviewing their site, which also has links to the other offices and centers.

It's important to note that the FDA is not the only agency within the US government that plays a role in pharmaceutical issues. The Federal Trade Commission (FTC) has authority over general business practices in general, such as deceptive and anticompetitive practices (i.e., false advertising). In addition, the FTC regulates the advertising of over-the-counter (OTC) drugs, medical devices, and cosmetics. Also, the United States Pharmacopoeia (USP) plays a role in regulating natural supplements, over-the-counter (OTC) drugs, and dietary products. When you think of USP, you may think of those big red "USP-NF" reference standard books during your Dosage Forms and Pharmaceutical Compounding courses. However, they play a big role in offering a voluntary third-party auditing and testing system with all dietary supplements and products. Next time you go out to the pharmacy, see if you can spot an USP stamp of approval on an OTC bottle in the aisles. Despite many of these federal and private associations, it's important to note that the FDA plays a main role in drug regulation.

NEW DRUG APPROVAL AND DEVELOPMENT

A drug is a substance that puts an action on the structure or function of the body by chemical action or metabolism, and is intended for use in the diagnosis, cure, mitigation, treatment, or prevention of diseases. A new drug is defined as one that is not recognized as safe and effective use for the indications stated by the manufacturer. "New drug" could also refer to a drug product already in existence, although never approved by the FDA for marketing in the United States. This also spans to new therapeutic indications; a new dosage form; a new route of administration; a new dosing schedule; or any other significant clinical differences than those approved. Make sure to understand that this differs from a new chemical entity. Essentially, any chemical substance intended for use in humans or animals with medicinal purposes "aka pharmaceuticals" is not safe or effective until proper testing and FDA approval are met. For non-FDA approved drugs such as over-the-counter (OTC) or nonprescription medications contain the disclaimer statement, "This statement has not been evaluated by the Food and Drug Administration. This product is not intended to diagnose, treat, cure, or prevent any disease". OTCs are only regulated by FDA through the OTC Drug monographs. OTC drug monographs are a kind of "recipe book" covering acceptable ingredients, doses, formulations, and labeling. Monographs will continually be updated adding additional ingredients and labeling as needed. Products conforming to a monograph may be marketed without further FDA clearance, while those that do not, must undergo separate review and approval through the "New Drug Approval System."

PRECLINICAL INVESTIGATION

Before any manufacturer starts human testing on a new drug, they must provide evidence that the drug can be used safety in humans. This phase is called the preclinical investigation. The basic goal of preclinical investigation is to assess therapeutic effects of the substance on living organisms and to gather enough data to determine the reasonable safety of the new drug in humans through laboratory and animal experimentation. The FDA does not require any prior approval for investigators, manufacturers, or pharmaceutical industry sponsors to begin a preclinical investigation on a drug. However, investigators and sponsors must follow Good Laboratory Practice (GLP) regulations. GLPs govern laboratory facilities, personnel, equipment, and operations. Compliance with GLPs involves procedures and documentation of training, study schedules, processes, and status reports. These documents are submitted to facility management and included in the final study report to the FDA. As far as a timeline, usually preclinical investigation takes 1 to 3 years to complete. If at that time enough data is gathered to reach the goal of a therapeutic effect and reasonable safety, the product sponsor must notify the FDA to pursue further testing on humans. This phase is also very important for the sponsor or investigator to test the drug of any viability. You'll see when reading pharmaceutical news articles of many companies that decide to stop investigation of a drug from the preclinical phase and sometimes up to phase III trials due to safety concerns or lack of therapeutic efficacy.

INVESTIGATIONAL NEW DRUG (IND) APPLICATION

The FDA starts getting highly involved in the Investigational New Drug (IND) application phase. Because a preclinical investigation is designed to gain data of safety and efficacy of the drug, the IND phase is the clinical phase where all activity is used to gather evidence on safety and efficacy information about the drug in humans. Clinical trials in humans are heavily scrutinized and regulated by the FDA to protect the health and safety of human test subjects as well as ensuring the strength and ethics of the clinical data. Numerous meetings between both the agency and sponsor occur during this time. The negotiations don't usually take much time, but the investigation phase for the sponsor may take up to 12 years to complete! Only one in five drugs tested may actually show clinical effectiveness and safety to reach the pharmacy shelves.

Once done with preclinical trials, the sponsor submits the IND to the FDA. The IND must contain information on the drug proposed itself and information of the study and how it was conducted. At FDA, there is a defined difference of types of applicants which can be either sponsors, or sponsor-investigators. Sponsors take responsibility for and initiates a clinical investigation. A sponsor can be an individual, pharmaceutical company, governmental agency, academic institution, private or other organization. An investigator is the individual who actually conducts the investigation. A sponsor-investigator is an individual that both initiates and conducts an investigation, and as an investigator oversees the direction of the investigational drug administered or dispensed.

All INDs must have the following components for sponsors:
- Cover Letter
- Form 1571
- Form 1572
- Form 3674
- Table of Contents
- Introductory Statement and General Investigational Plan
- Chemistry, Manufacturing, and Control Information
- Pharmacology, Toxicology Information
- Investigator's Brochure
- Clinical Protocol(s)
- Summary of Previous Human Experience with the Investigational New Drug

For sponsor-investigators, they should include the same components as the sponsors above except for the investigator's brochure as this is not required. The reason why is there are instances a sponsor-investigator may not be required to submit an IND such as for a study of a lawfully marketed drug if the criteria for an IND exemption is met. The sponsor-investigator should always submit their IND application to FDA for consideration to determine IND exemption.

After submission, the sponsor company or sponsor-investigator must wait 30 days to commence clinical trials. Thus, this gives the FDA 30 days to respond to the sponsor. If there is no contact from the FDA after this 30-day period, the sponsor has a right to start the clinical trial testing in humans unless notified by FDA through a clinical hold or other correspondence. The exceptions to this general rule are for emergency individual, single-patient, or intermediate IND applications where the sponsor or sponsor-investigator could start the trial sooner. For example, for emergency use the sponsor or sponsor-investigator may contact the appropriate FDA division and once getting a study may proceed via e-mail, telephone, or other correspondence can start the trial as long as they report to their responsible Investigational Review Board (IRB) within 5 working days of initiation of treatment. For non-emergency use, similarly the sponsor or sponsor-investigator must contact FDA and receive correspondence of a study may proceed, the treatment use of the drug can start when the IND goes into effect (FDA grants a study may proceed to activate the IND) and IRB approval has been obtained. Lastly, for intermediate or expanded access INDs, these are INDs that go beyond one patient in patient trial size. An expanded access IND goes into effect 30 days after FDA receives the IND and can start unless the FDA notifies the sponsor that they are on a clinical hold.

Before the actual start of the clinical trial, there are some ground rules to follow. The sponsor needs to have a clinical study protocol that's reviewed by an Institutional Review Board (IRB). An IRB is required and is a committee of medical and ethical experts designated by an institution, such as a university medical center, where the trial will take place. The purpose of the IRB is to oversee the research to ensure that the rights of human test subjects are protected, and rigorous medical and scientific standards are maintained. An IRB must approve the proposed clinical study and monitor the research as it progresses to ensure ethics and rights are protected during the trial. It must develop written procedures of its own regarding its study review process and reporting changes to the IRB board. The IRB must also review and approve informed consent documents before starting the clinical study. Regulations require that participants are informed adequately about the risks, benefits, and treatment alternatives before participating in experimental research. Usually the committee is composed of a diverse number of individuals to review the study in a community, legal, and professional standards point of view. All of the IRB activities must be documented, as they are open to FDA inspection. As soon as the IRB board approves the study, the clinical trial phase starts! It's composed of three phases.

PHASE I

A Phase I study is small, consisting of less than 100 subjects and brief usually lasts less than a year. Usually these subjects are healthy individuals who don't have the disease being studied. Its purpose is to determine toxicology, safety, metabolism, pharmacologic actions, and any early evidence of effectiveness. The results of the Phase I study are used to develop phase II.

PHASE II

Phase II studies are the first controlled clinical studies using several hundred subjects who have the disease being studied. Phase II is to determine the compound's effectiveness against the targeted disease and its safety in humans. Phase II could be divided into two subparts depending on how the sponsor decides the conduct the trial: Phase IIa is a pilot study that is used to determine efficacy, and Phase IIb uses controlled studies on several hundred patients. At the end of the Phase II studies, the sponsor and FDA will usually meet to discuss the data and plans for Phase III.

PHASE III

Phase III studies are considered "pivotal" trials that are designed to collect all of the necessary data to meet the safety and efficacy regulations governed by FDA. Phase III studies usually consist of several thousands of patients in multiple study centers with a large number of investigators who conduct long-term trials over several months or years. Usually it's testing the current "gold standard" against the drug that is being studied. However, this does depend on the disease state being studied. If there is a rare disease state being studied, there only may be twenty patients. Phase III studies also set up the final formulation, marketing claims and product stability, packaging, and storage conditions. Once phase III is complete along with all the safety and efficacy data being analyzed, the sponsor is ready to submit the compound to the FDA for market approval! This process begins with submission of a New Drug Application (NDA).

NEW DRUG APPLICATION (NDA)

An NDA is a regulatory tool that is designed to give the FDA sufficient information to make an evaluation of a new drug. All NDAs must contain the following: preclinical laboratory and animal data; human pharmacokinetic and bioavailability data; clinical data; methods of manufacturing, processing, and packaging; a description of the drug substance; a list of relevant patents for the drug; its manufacture or claims; and any proposed labeling. In addition, an NDA must provide a summary of the application's contents and a presentation of the risks and benefits of the new drug. Traditionally, NDAs consisted of hundreds of volumes of information, in triplicate, all cross referenced. Since 1999, the FDA has issued final guidance documents that allow sponsors to submit NDAs electronically in a standardized format. These electronic submissions facilitate ease of review and possible approval. If you're interested to see how an NDA should look like, you can access this guidance document:

http://www.fda.gov/downloads/Drugs/DevelopmentApprovalProcess/FormsSubmissionRequirements/ElectronicSubmissions/UCM163187.pdf

Once accepted, the FDA then determines the application's completeness. If complete, the agency considers the application filed and begins the review process within 60 days. This starts the mad dash of reviewers such as those in the office of pharmacology or the office of pharmacokinetics who receive piles of documents to read and sift through. Despite much paperwork and review, from the FDA's perspective it's necessary to ensure that the new drug meets the criteria to be "safe and effective." Safety and effectiveness are determined through the Phase III studies based on evidence gained from a controlled clinical study. As there's no absolute safe drug, the FDA needs to review the new drug's efficacy as a measure of its safety. It weighs the risks versus benefits of approving the drug for use in the US marketplace as well as if the drug would help serve a rare disease population, which would place it as an orphan designation- I will go into this later in the book.

The NDA must be clear about the manufacture and marketing of the proposed drug product. The application must define and describe manufacturing processes, validate Current Good Manufacturing

Practices (CGMPs), provide evidence of quality, purity, strength, identity, and bioavailability (a pre-inspection of the manufacturing facility is conducted by the FDA). Finally, the FDA reviews all products packaging and labeling for content and clarity. Statements on a product's package label, package insert, media advertising, or professional literature must be reviewed. It's also important to know that "labeling" refers to all of the above and not just the label on the product container.

The FDA is required to review the application within 180 days of filing. At the end of that time, the agency is required to respond with an "action letter." There are three kinds of action letters that FDA may issue out for a New Drug Application:
- Approval Letter
- Complete Response
- Refuse-to-File

An Approval Letter signifies that all substantive requirements for approval are met and that the sponsor company can begin marketing the drug as of the date on the letter.

An Approvable Letter signifies that the application substantially complies with the requirements but has some minor deficiencies that must be addressed before an approval letter is sent. Generally, these deficiencies are minor in nature and the product sponsor must respond within 10 days of receipt. At this point, the sponsor may amend the application and address the agency's concerns, request a hearing with the agency, or withdraw the application entirely.

A Complete Response Letter signifies that the FDA has major concerns with the application and will not approve the proposed drug product for marketing as submitted. The available remedies a sponsor can take for this type of action letter are similar to those in the "Approvable Letter."

Lastly, a Refuse-to-File is when the sponsor withdraws the application from review or when the application is not considered acceptable and complete.

REFERENCES:
1. NAPLEX/MPJE Registration Bulletin. 2015 National Association of Boards of Pharmacy. Accessed on Nov 1st, 2015. http://www.nabp.net/programs/examination/mpje

2. Strauss S. Food and Drug Administration: An overview. In: Strauss's Federal Drug Laws and Examination Review, 5th edition. Lancaster, PA: Technomic Publishing Co., 1999:323.

3. FDA. 2015 U.S. Food and Drug Administration. http://www.fda.gov/

FEDERAL PHARMACY LAW REVIEW PART 2

PRESCRIPTION DRUG USER FEE ACT (PDUFA)

The new drug application (NDA) review has changed by both the Prescription Drug User Fee Act (PDUFA) and the FDA Modernization Act (FDAMA) in our federal government system. PDUFA allows the FDA to collect fees from sponsor companies who submit applications for review. The fees are used to update facilities and hire and train reviewers. To give you an idea, it's an average of a hundreds of thousands of dollars if not millions just to submit an NDA at the FDA. PDUFA usually is renewed and currently we are at PDUFA VI.

Here is the fee schedule based off PDUFA:

Program	Fiscal Year 2019	Fiscal Year 2018
PDUFA VI		
Applications:		
Requiring clinical data	$2,588,478	$2,421,495
Not requiring clinical data	$1,294,239	$1,210,748
Program fee	$309,915	$304,162

If you would like to learn more regulatory information and review the fees for the other acts such as the Generic Drug User Fee Amendments (GDUFA II) to help fund review of generic drugs, the Biosimilar User Fee Amendments (BSUFA II) to help fund review of biosimilar drugs, or the Medical Device User Fee Amendments (MDUFA IV) to help fund review of medical devices, you can visit the Regulatory Affairs Professional Society (RAPS) at the following link: https://www.raps.org/news-and-articles/news-articles/2018/7/fda-fy2019-user-fee-table.

This is a why many pharmaceutical companies stress on having a strong regulatory affairs department to ensure acceptance of their drug into market, not just for profitability, but also avoiding the hassles of a delayed approval. In addition, PDUFA requires the FDA to speed up their approval time and is expected by industry due to increased fees to file an NDA. Luckily, the results of the PDUFA legislation were significant; approval rates have increased from approximately 50% to near 80% and the review times have decreased to less than 15 months for most applications.

You'll notice that every couple of years, FDAMA reauthorizes PDUFA which is where the numbers come in after the name (i.e. currently we are on PDUFA VI). It waives the user fee to small companies who have fewer than 500 employees and are submitting their first application. It allows payment of the fee in stages and permits some percentage of refund if the application is refused. Also, it exempts applications for drugs used in rare conditions (orphan drugs), supplemental applications for pediatric indications, and applications for biological used as precursors for other biologics manufacture. In addition, FDAMA permits a "fast-track" approval of compounds that demonstrate significant benefit to critically ill patients, such as those who suffer from AIDS, hepatitis C, and other specialty disease states. The intricacies and complexities are much more than what is reviewed in this guide and may not be needed to study for your MPJE exam.

BIOLOGICS

Biologics are defined as substances derived from or made with the aid of living organisms, which include vaccines, antitoxins, serums, blood, blood products, therapeutic protein drugs derived from natural sources (i.e., anti-thrombin III), or biotechnology (i.e., recombinantly derived proteins). As with the more traditionally derived drug products, biologics follow virtually the same regulatory and clinical testing schema with regard to safety and efficacy. A Biologics License Application (BLA) is used rather than an NDA, although the official FDA Form is designated the 356h and is one and the same. The sponsor merely indicated in check box if the application is for a drug or a biologic. CBER (Center for Biologics Evaluation and Research) reviews these compounds and may work together with CDER depending on the association.

ORPHAN DRUGS

An orphan drug is defined under the Orphan Drug Act of 1993, a drug used to treat a "rare disease" that would not normally be of interest to commercial manufactures in the ordinary course of business. A rare disease is defined in the law as any disease that affects fewer than 200,000 persons in the United States, or one in which a manufacturer has no reasonable expectation of recovering the cost of its development and availability in the United States. The Act creates a series of financial incentives that manufacturers can take advantage of. For example, the Act permits grant assistance for clinical research, tax credits for research and development, and a 7-year market exclusivity to the first applicant who obtains market approval for a drug designated as an orphan. This means that if a sponsor gains approval for an orphan drug, the FDA will not approve any application by any other sponsor for the same drug for the same disease or condition for 7 years. The time-frame begins from the date of the first applicant's approval and certain conditions must be met, such as an assurance of sufficient availability of drug to those in need or a revocation of the drug's orphan status. Pharmaceutical companies have also placed high price tags on these orphan drugs.

ABBREVIATED NEW DRUG APPLICATIONS

Abbreviated New Drug Applications (ANDAs) are used when a patent has expired for a product that has been on the US market and a company wishes to market a copy. In the United States, a drug patent is 20 years. After that time, a manufacturer is able to submit an abbreviated application for that product provided that they certify that the product patent in question has already expired, is invalid, or will not be infringed.

The generic copy must meet certain other criteria as well. The drug's active ingredient must already have been approved for the conditions of use proposed in the ANDA, and nothing has changed to call into question the basis for approval of the original drug's NDA. Sponsors of ANDAs are required to prove that their version meets with standards of bioethical and pharmaceutical equivalence.

Bioequivalence

The FDA publishes a list of all approved drugs called, Approved Drug Products with Therapeutic Equivalence Evaluations, also known as the "Orange Book" because of its orange cover. It lists marketed drug products that are considered by the FDA to be safe and effective and provides information on therapeutic equivalence evaluations for approved multi-source prescription drug products monthly. The

Orange Book rates drugs based on their therapeutic equivalence. For a product to be considered therapeutically equivalent, it must be both pharmaceutically equivalent (i.e., the same dose, dosage form, strength), and bioequivalent (i.e., the rate and extent of its absorption is not significantly different than the rate and extent of absorption of the drug with which it is to be interchanged).

Realizing that there may be some degree of variability in patients, the FDA allows pharmaceuticals to be considered bioequivalent in either of two methods. The first method studies the rate and extent of absorption of a test drug that may or may not be a generic variation with a reference or brand name drug under similar experimental conditions.

Bioequivalence of different formulations of the same drug substance involves equivalence with respect to the rate and extent of drug absorption. Two formulations whose rate and extent of absorption differ by 20% or less are generally considered bioequivalent. The use of the 20% rule is based on a medical decision that, for most drugs, a 20% difference in the concentration of the active ingredient in blood will not be clinically significant. Both must have similar dosing schedules where the test results do not show significant differences.

The second approach uses the same method and from which the results determine that there is a difference in the test drug's rate and extent of absorption, except that the difference is considered to be medically insignificant for the proper clinical outcome of that drug.

The FDA's Orange Book uses a two-letter coding system that is helpful in determining which drug products are considered therapeutically equivalent. The first letter, either an A or a B, indicates a drug product's therapeutic equivalence rating. The second letter describes dose forms and can be any one of a number of different letters.

The A codes are described in the Orange Book as drug products that the FDA considers to be therapeutically equivalent to other pharmaceutically equivalent products (i.e., drug products for which):
- There are no known or suspected bioequivalence problems. These are designated AA, AN, AO, AP, or AT, depending on the dose form.
- Actual or potential bioequivalence problems have been resolved with adequate *in vivo* and/or *in vitro* evidence supporting bioequivalence. These are designated AB

The B codes are a much less desirable rating when compared to a rating of A. Products that are rated B still may be commercially marketed; but they may not be considered therapeutically equivalent. The Orange Book describes B codes as follows:
- Drug products that FDA at this time, does not consider to be therapeutically equivalent to other pharmaceutically equivalent products, i.e., drug products for which actual or potential bioequivalence problems have not been resolved by adequate evidence of bioequivalence. Often the problem is with specific dosage forms rather than with the active ingredients. These are designated BC, BD, BE, BN, BP, BR, BS, BT, or BX.
- The FDA has adopted an additional subcategory of B codes. The designation, B* is assigned to former A-rated drugs "if FDA receives new information that raises a significant question regarding therapeutic equivalence." Not all drugs are listed in the Orange Book. Drugs obtainable only from a single manufacturing source, drugs listed as Drug Efficacy Study Implementation (DESI) drugs or drugs manufactured before 1938 are not included. Those that do appear are listed by generic name.

PHASE IV AND POST-MARKETING SURVEILLANCE

Pharmaceutical companies that successfully gain marketing approval for their products are not exempt from further regulatory requirements. Many products are approved for market on the basis of a continued submission of clinical research data to the FDA. This data may be required to further validate efficacy or safety, detect new uses or abuses for the product, or determine the effectiveness of labeled indications under conditions of widespread usage. The FDA also may require a Phase IV study for drugs approved under FDAMA's "fast-track" provisions.

Any changes to the approved product's indications, active ingredients, manufacture, or labeling require the manufacturer to submit a supplemental NDA (sNDA) for agency approval. Also, adverse drug reports are required to be reported to the agency. All reports must be reviewed by the manufacturer promptly, and if found to be serious, life-threatening, or unexpected (not listed in the product's labeling), the manufacturer is required to submit an alert report within 15 days working days of receipt of the information. All adverse reaction thought not to be serious or unexpected must be reported quarterly for 3 years after the application is approved, and annually thereafter.

OVER-THE-COUNTER (OTC) REGULATIONS

The 1951 Durham-Humphrey Amendments of the FDCA specified three criteria to justify prescription-only status. If the compound is habit forming, requires a prescriber's supervision, or has an NDA prescription-only limitation, it requires a prescription. The principles used to establish OTC status (no prescription required) are a wide margin of safety, method of use, benefit-to-risk ratio, and adequacy of labeling for self-medication. For example, injectable drugs may not be used OTC with certain exceptions such as insulin such as Human Insulin that can be obtained without a prescription but after speaking to a pharmacist as it is still considered 'behind the counter'. Over-the-counter market entry is less restrictive than that for prescription drugs and do not require premarket clearance. Pose many fewer safety hazards than prescription drugs because they are designed to alleviate symptoms rather than disease. Easier access far outweighs the risks of side effects, which can be addressed adequately through proper labeling.

OTC products underwent a review in 1972. Although reviewing the 300,000 + OTC drug products in existence at the time would be virtually impossible, the FDA created OTC Advisory Panels to review data based on some 26 therapeutic categories. Over-the-counter drugs are only examined by active ingredient within a therapeutic category. Inactive ingredients are only examined if they are shown to be safe and suitable for the product and not interfering with effectiveness and quality.

This review of active ingredients results in the promulgation of a regulation or a "monograph," which is a "recipe" or set of guidelines applicable to all OTC products within a therapeutic category. Over-the-counter monographs are general and require that OTC products show "general recognition of the safety and effectiveness of the active ingredient." Over-the-counter products do not fall under prescription status if their active ingredients (or combinations) are deemed by the FDA to be "generally recognized as safe and effective" (GRASE). The monograph system is public, with a public comment component included after each phase of the process. Any products for which a final monograph has not been established may remain on the market until one is determined.

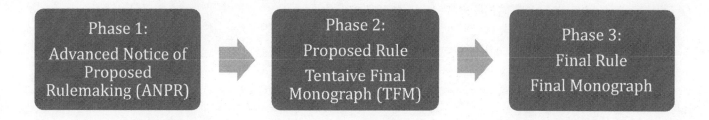

There are three phases in the OTC monograph system. In Phase 1 of the public rulemaking process, an expert panel is selected to review data for each active ingredient in each therapeutic category for safety, efficacy, and labeling. This is FDA's 'call for data' from industry where this expert panel's recommendations to FDA are made and they cover the active ingredient and labeling requirements. The classification of active ingredients could be the following:
- Category 1- GRASE
- Category 2- Affirmatively not GRASE
- Category 3- Insufficient evidence to make a determination of categories 1 or 2

In Phase 2, the expert panel from Phase 1 publish in the Federal Register with a 'proposed monograph' to provide advanced notice of the proposed rulemaking and seeking comments from the public. A public comment period of 30 to 60 days is permitted and supporting or contesting data are accepted for review. FDA then reviews the public comments for any new data, and then after publishes a 'tentative final monograph' (TFM). The TFM is a proposed regulation and sets forth the active ingredients, indications, warnings, and directions (Category 1).

Finally, in Phase 3 the FDA again reviews comments, objections and any new data. A final order is issued called the 'final regulation' setting forth the new requirements and monographs are typically effective 1 year after publication where non-compliant products are then subject to regulatory action. Following the effective date of the final monograph, all covered drug products that fail to conform to its requirements are considered misbranded and or an unapproved new drug.

The monograph panels are no longer convened, many current products are switched from prescription status. A company who wishes to make this switch and offer a product to the US marketplace can submit an amendment to a monograph to the FDA, who acts as the sole reviewer. They may also file an SNDA provided that they have 3 years of marketing experience as a prescription product, can demonstrate a relatively high use during that period, and can validate that the product has a mild profile of adverse reactions.

The ways an OTC monograph can be amended are the following:
- FDA amends the monograph by itself (21 C.F.R. 330.10(a)(12)(i)
- Petition requesting amendment through a Citizen's Petition
    - Can be used to amend an OTC drug monograph at any stage but is limited to pre-1975 marketing conditions (active ingredient, dosage form, indication, etc.).
- Petition requesting amendment through a time and extent application (TEA)
    - Effective 2002 under 21 C.F.R. 330.14, a TEA can be used to amend an OTC drug monograph for products marketed under an approved NDA after OTC drug review began, or products outside the U.S.

- As the name suggests, it must also meet the material time and material extent requirements which are at least 5 continuous years in the same country, and 10s of millions of dosage units sold

REGULATING MARKETING

The FDA has jurisdiction over prescription drug advertising and promotion. The basis for these regulations lies within the 1962 Kefauver-Harris Amendments. Essentially, any promotional information, in any form, must be truthful, fairly balanced, and fully disclosed. The FDA views this information as either "advertising" or "labeling." Advertising includes all traditional outlets in which a company places an ad. Labeling includes everything else, including brochures, booklets, lectures, slide kits, letters to physicians, company-sponsored magazine articles, and so on. All information must be truthful and not misleading. All material facts must be disclosed in a manner that is fairly balanced and accurate. If any of these requirements are violated, the product is considered "misbranded" for the indications in which it was approved under its NDA.

The FDA is also sensitive to the promotion of a product for "off-label" use. Off-label use occurs when a product is in some way presented in a manner that does not agree with or is not addressed in its approved labeling. Also, provisions of the Prescription Drug Marketing Act (PDMA) of 1987 apply. The Act prohibits company representatives from directly distributing or reselling prescription drug samples. Companies are required to establish a closed system of record keeping that can track a sample from their control to that of a prescriber in order to prevent diversion. Prescribers are required to receive these samples and record and store them appropriately.

VIOLATIONS AND ENFORCEMENT

The FDA has the power to enforce the regulations for any product as defined under the FDCA. It has the jurisdiction to inspect a manufacturer's premises and records. After a facilities inspection, an agency inspector issues an FDA Form 483s, which describes observable violations. Response to the finding as described on this form must be made promptly. A warning letter may be used when the agency determines that one or more of a company's practices, products, or procedures are in violation of the FDCA. The FDA district has 15 days to issue a warning letter after an inspection, and the company has 15 days in which to respond. If the company response is satisfactory to the agency, no other action is warranted. If the response is not, the agency may request a recall of the violated products. The FDA has no authority to force a company to recall a product, but it may force removal of a product through the initiation of a seizure.

Recalls can fall into one of three classes. A Class I recall exists when there is a reasonable possibility that the use of a product will cause either serious adverse effects on health or death. Class II recall exists when the use of a product may cause temporary or medically reversible adverse effects on health or when the probability of serious adverse effects on health is remote. A Class III recall exists when the use of a product is not likely to cause adverse health consequences. Recalls are also categorized as consumer level, in which the product is requested to be recalled for the consumer's homes or control; a retail level, in which the product is to be removed from retail shelves or control; and a wholesale level, in which the product is to be removed from wholesale distribution. Companies who conduct a recall of their products are required to conduct effectiveness checks to determine the effectiveness of recalling the product from the marketplace.

If a company refuses to recall the product, the FDA will seek an injunction against the company. An injunction is recommended to the Department of Justice (DOJ) by the FDA. The DOJ takes the request to federal court, which issues an order that forbids a company from carrying out a particular illegal act, such as marketing a product that the FDA considers a violation of the FDCA. Companies can comply with the order and sign a consent agreement, which specifies changes required by the FDA in order for the company to continue operations or litigate.

The FDA also may initiate a seizure of violative, misbranded, or adulterated products. A seizure is ordered by the federal court in the district where the products are located. The seizure order specifies products, their batch numbers, and any records determined by the FDA as violative. United States Marshals carry out this action. The FDA institutes a seizure to prevent a company from selling, distributing, moving, or otherwise tampering with the product.

The FDA also may debar individuals or firms from assisting or submitting an ANDA, or directly providing services to any firm with an existing or pending drug product application. Debarment may last for up to 10 years.

FEDERAL PHARMACY LAW REVIEW PART 3: OVERVIEW OF FEDERAL ACTS

We recommend to understand the concepts and rules that the acts provided to our current laws in place today. This information is taken directly from the Food and Drug Administration's publicly available website labeled, "Milestones in U.S. Food and Drug Law History" which can be accessed at:
https://www.fda.gov/aboutfda/history/forgshistory/evolvingpowers/ucm2007256.htm

1820
- Eleven physicians meet in Washington, D.C., to establish the U.S. Pharmacopeia, the first compendium of standard drugs for the United States.

1848
- Drug Importation Act passed by Congress requires U.S. Customs Service inspection to stop entry of adulterated drugs from overseas.

1862
- President Lincoln appoints a chemist, Charles M. Wetherill, to serve in the new Department of Agriculture. This was the beginning of the Bureau of Chemistry, the predecessor of the Food and Drug Administration.

1880
- Peter Collier, chief chemist, U.S. Department of Agriculture, recommends passage of a national food and drug law, following his own food adulteration investigations. The bill was defeated, but during the next 25 years more than 100 food and drug bills were introduced in Congress.

1883
- Dr. Harvey W. Wiley becomes chief chemist, expanding the Bureau of Chemistry's food adulteration studies. Campaigning for a federal law, Dr. Wiley is called the "Crusading Chemist" and "Father of the Pure Food and Drugs Act." He retired from government service in 1912 and died in 1930.

1897
- Tea Importation Act passed, providing for Customs inspection of all tea entering U.S. ports, at the expense of the importers.

1898
- Association of Official Agricultural Chemists (now AOAC International) establishes a Committee on Food Standards headed by Dr. Wiley. States begin incorporating these standards into their food statutes.

1902
- The Biologics Control Act is passed to ensure purity and safety of serums, vaccines, and similar products used to prevent or treat diseases in humans.
- Congress appropriates $5,000 to the Bureau of Chemistry to study chemical preservatives and colors and their effects on digestion and health. Dr. Wiley's studies draw widespread attention to the problem of food adulteration. Public support for passage of a federal food and drug law grows.

1906

- The original Food and Drugs Act is passed by Congress on June 30 and signed by President Theodore Roosevelt. It prohibits interstate commerce in misbranded and adulterated foods, drinks and drugs. The Meat Inspection Act is passed the same day.
- Shocking disclosures of insanitary conditions in meat-packing plants, the use of poisonous preservatives and dyes in foods, and cure-all claims for worthless and dangerous patent medicines were the major problems leading to the enactment of these laws.

1907
- First Certified Color Regulations, requested by manufacturers and users, list seven colors found suitable for use in foods.

1911
- In U.S. v. Johnson, the Supreme Court rules that the 1906 Food and Drugs Act does not prohibit false therapeutic claims but only false and misleading statements about the ingredients or identity of a drug.

1912
- Congress enacts the Sherley Amendment to overcome the ruling in U.S. v. Johnson. It prohibits labeling medicines with false therapeutic claims intended to defraud the purchaser, a standard difficult to prove.
- Mrs. Winslow's Soothing Syrup for teething and colicky babies, unlabeled yet laced with morphine, killed many infants.

1913
- Gould Amendment requires that food package contents be "plainly and conspicuously marked on the outside of the package in terms of weight, measure, or numerical count."

1914
- In U.S. v. Lexington Mill and Elevator Company, the Supreme Court issues its first ruling on food additives. It ruled that in order for bleached flour with nitrite residues to be banned from foods, the government must show a relationship between the chemical additive and the harm it allegedly caused in humans. The court also noted that the mere presence of such an ingredient was not sufficient to render the food illegal.
- The Harrison Narcotic Act requires prescriptions for products exceeding the allowable limit of narcotics and mandates increased record-keeping for physicians and pharmacists who dispense narcotics.

1924
- In U.S. v. 95 Barrels Alleged Apple Cider Vinegar, the Supreme Court rules that the Food and Drugs Act condemns every statement, design, or device on a product's label that may mislead or deceive, even if technically true.

1927
- The Bureau of Chemistry is reorganized into two separate entities. Regulatory functions are located in the Food, Drug, and Insecticide Administration, and nonregulatory research is located in the Bureau of Chemistry and Soils.

1930
- McNary-Mapes Amendment authorizes FDA standards of quality and fill-of-container for canned food, excluding meat and milk products.
- The name of the Food, Drug, and Insecticide Administration is shortened to Food and Drug Administration (FDA) under an agricultural appropriations act.

1933
- FDA recommends a complete revision of the obsolete 1906 Food and Drugs Act. The first bill is introduced into the Senate, launching a five-year legislative battle.

1935
- U.S. Government begins publication of the Federal Register.

1938
- The Federal Food, Drug, and Cosmetic (FDC) Act of 1938 is passed by Congress, containing new provisions:
    - Extending control to cosmetics and therapeutic devices.
    - Requiring new drugs to be shown safe before marketing-starting a new system of drug regulation.
    - Eliminating the Sherley Amendment requirement to prove intent to defraud in drug misbranding cases.
    - Providing that safe tolerances be set for unavoidable poisonous substances.
    - Authorizing standards of identity, quality, and fill-of-container for foods.
    - Authorizing factory inspections.
    - Adding the remedy of court injunctions to the previous penalties of seizures and prosecutions.
- Under the Wheeler-Lea Act, the Federal Trade Commission is charged with overseeing advertising associated with products otherwise regulated by FDA.

1939
- First Food Standards issued (canned tomatoes, tomato purée, and tomato paste).

1940
- FDA transferred from the Department of Agriculture to the Federal Security Agency, with Walter G. Campbell appointed as the first Commissioner of Food and Drugs.

1941
- Insulin Amendment requires FDA to test and certify purity and potency of this lifesaving drug for diabetes

1943
- In U.S. v. Dotterweich, the Supreme Court rules that the responsible officials of a corporation, as well as the corporation itself, may be prosecuted for violations. It need not be proven that the officials intended, or even knew of, the violations.

1944
- Public Health Service Act is passed, covering a broad spectrum of health concerns, including regulation of biological products and control of communicable diseases.

1945
- Penicillin Amendment requires FDA testing and certification of safety and effectiveness of all penicillin products. Later amendments extended this requirement to all antibiotics. In 1983 such control was found no longer needed and was abolished.

1948
- Miller Amendment affirms that the Federal Food, Drug, and Cosmetic Act applies to goods regulated by the Agency that have been transported from one state to another and have reached the consumer.

1949
- FDA publishes guidance to industry for the first time. This guidance, "Procedures for the Appraisal of the Toxicity of Chemicals in Food," came to be known as the "black book."

1950
- In Alberty Food Products Co. v. U.S., a court of appeals rules that the directions for use on a drug label must include the purpose for which the drug is offered. Therefore, a worthless remedy cannot escape the law by not stating the condition it is supposed to treat.
- Oleomargarine Act requires prominent labeling of colored oleomargarine, to distinguish it from butter.
- Delaney Committee starts congressional investigation of the safety of chemicals in foods and cosmetics, laying the foundation for the 1954 Miller Pesticide Amendment, the 1958 Food Additives Amendment, and the 1960 Color Additive Amendment.

1951
- Durham-Humphrey Amendment defines the kinds of drugs that cannot be safely used without medical supervision and restricts their sale to prescription by a licensed practitioner.

1953
- Federal Security Agency becomes the Department of Health, Education, and Welfare (HEW).
- Factory Inspection Amendment clarifies previous law and requires FDA to give manufacturers written reports of conditions observed during inspections and analyses of factory samples.

1954
- Miller Pesticide Amendment spells out procedures for setting safety limits for pesticide residues on raw agricultural commodities.
- First large-scale radiological examination of food carried out by FDA when it received reports that tuna suspected of being radioactive was being imported from Japan following atomic blasts in the Pacific. FDA begins monitoring around the clock to meet the emergency.

1955
- HEW Secretary Oveta Culp Hobby appoints a committee of 14 citizens to study the adequacy of FDA's facilities and programs. The committee recommends a substantial expansion of FDA staff and facilities, a new headquarters building, and more use of educational and informational programs.
- The Division of Biologics Control became an independent entity within the National Institutes of Health, after polio vaccine thought to have been inactivated is associated with about 260 cases of polio.

1958
- Food Additives Amendment enacted, requiring manufacturers of new food additives to establish safety. The Delaney proviso prohibits the approval of any food additive shown to induce cancer in humans or animals.
- FDA publishes in the Federal Register the first list of substances generally recognized as safe (GRAS). The list contains nearly 200 substances.

1959
- U.S. cranberry crop recalled three weeks before Thanksgiving for FDA tests to check for aminotriazole, a weedkiller found to cause cancer in laboratory animals. Cleared berries were allowed a label stating that they had been tested and had passed FDA inspection, the only such endorsement ever allowed by FDA on a food product.

1960
- Color Additive Amendment enacted, requiring manufacturers to establish the safety of color additives in foods, drugs and cosmetics. The Delaney proviso prohibits the approval of any color additive shown to induce cancer in humans or animals.
- Federal Hazardous Substances Labeling Act, enforced by FDA, requires prominent label warnings on hazardous household chemical products.

1962
- Thalidomide, a new sleeping pill, is found to have caused birth defects in thousands of babies born in western Europe. News reports on the role of Dr. Frances Kelsey, FDA medical officer, in keeping the drug off the U.S. market, arouse public support for stronger drug regulation.
- Kefauver-Harris Drug Amendments passed to ensure drug efficacy and greater drug safety. For the first time, drug manufacturers are required to prove to FDA the effectiveness of their products before marketing them. The new law also exempts from the Delaney proviso animal drugs and animal feed additives shown to induce cancer but which leave no detectable levels of residue in the human food supply.
- Consumer Bill of Rights is proclaimed by President John F. Kennedy in a message to Congress. Included are the right to safety, the right to be informed, the right to choose, and the right to be heard.

1965
- Drug Abuse Control Amendments are enacted to deal with problems caused by abuse of depressants, stimulants and hallucinogens.

1966
- FDA contracts with the National Academy of Sciences/National Research Council to evaluate the effectiveness of 4,000 drugs approved on the basis of safety alone between 1938 and 1962.
- Child Protection Act enlarges the scope of the Federal Hazardous Substances Labeling Act to ban hazardous toys and other articles so hazardous that adequate label warnings could not be written.
- Fair Packaging and Labeling Act requires all consumer products in interstate commerce to be honestly and informatively labeled, with FDA enforcing provisions on foods, drugs, cosmetics, and medical devices.

1968
- FDA Bureau of Drug Abuse Control and Treasury Department Bureau of Narcotics are transferred to the Department of Justice to form the Bureau of Narcotics and Dangerous Drugs (BNDD), consolidating efforts to police traffic in abused drugs.
- Reorganization of federal health programs places FDA in the Public Health Service.
- FDA forms the Drug Efficacy Study Implementation (DESI) to implement recommendations of the National Academy of Sciences investigation of effectiveness of drugs first marketed between 1938 and 1962.
- Animal Drug Amendments place all regulation of new animal drugs under one section of the Food, Drug, and Cosmetic Act-Section 512-making approval of animal drugs and medicated feeds more efficient.

1969
- FDA begins administering Sanitation Programs for milk, shellfish, food service, and interstate travel facilities, and for preventing poisoning and accidents. These responsibilities were transferred from other units of the Public Health Service.
- The White House Conference on Food, Nutrition, and Health recommends systematic review of GRAS substances in light of FDA's ban of the artificial sweetener cyclamate. President Nixon orders FDA to review its GRAS list.

1970
- In Upjohn v. Finch the Court of Appeals upholds enforcement of the 1962 drug effectiveness amendments by ruling that commercial success alone does not constitute substantial evidence of drug safety and efficacy.
- FDA requires the first patient package insert: oral contraceptives must contain information for the patient about specific risks and benefits.
- Drug Abuse Prevention and Control Act replaces previous laws and categorizes drugs based on abuse and addiction potential compared to their therapeutic value.
- Environmental Protection Agency established; takes over FDA program for setting pesticide tolerances.

1971
- PHS Bureau of Radiological Health transferred to FDA. Its mission: protection against unnecessary human exposure to radiation from electronic products in the home, industry, and the healing arts.
- National Center for Toxicological Research is established in the biological facilities of the Pine Bluff Arsenal in Arkansas. Its mission is to examine biological effects of chemicals in the environment, extrapolating data from experimental animals to human health.

- Artificial sweetener saccharin, included in FDA's original GRAS list, is removed from the list pending new scientific study.

1972
- Over-the-Counter Drug Review begun to enhance the safety, effectiveness and appropriate labeling of drugs sold without prescription.
- Regulation of Biologics--including serums, vaccines, and blood products--is transferred from NIH to FDA.

1973
- The U.S. Supreme Court upholds the 1962 drug effectiveness law and endorses FDA action to control entire classes of products by regulations rather than to rely only on time-consuming litigation.
- Low-acid food processing regulations issued, after botulism outbreaks from canned foods, to ensure that low-acid packaged foods have adequate heat treatment and are not hazardous.
- Consumer Product Safety Commission created by Congress; takes over programs pioneered by FDA under 1927 Caustic Poison Act, 1960 Federal Hazardous Substances Labeling Act, 1966 Child Protection Act, and PHS accident prevention activities for safety of toys, home appliances, etc.

1976
- Medical Device Amendments passed to ensure safety and effectiveness of medical devices, including diagnostic products. The amendments require manufacturers to register with FDA and follow quality control procedures. Some products must have pre-market approval by FDA; others must meet performance standards before marketing.
- Vitamins and Minerals Amendments ("Proxmire Amendments") stop FDA from establishing standards limiting potency of vitamins and minerals in food supplements or regulating them as drugs based solely on potency.

1977
- Saccharin Study and Labeling Act passed by Congress to stop FDA from banning the chemical sweetener but requiring a label warning that it has been found to cause cancer in laboratory animals.

1979
- Introduction of the Bioresearch Monitoring Program as an agency-wide initiative ensures the quality and integrity of data submitted to FDA and provides for the protection of human subjects in clinical trials by focusing on preclinical studies on animals, clinical investigations, and the work of institutional review boards.
- In the hours following the Three Mile Island nuclear emergency of March 28, 1979, FDA contracted with firms in Missouri, Michigan, and New Jersey to prepare and package enough doses of potassium iodide to protect those threatened with thyroid cancer if exposed to radiation. Nearly one quarter of a million bottles-enough for every household in the area-were delivered to Harrisburg, Pennsylvania within 72 hours.

1980
- Infant Formula Act establishes special FDA controls to ensure necessary nutritional content and safety

1981
- FDA and the Department of Health and Human Services revise regulations for human subject protections, based on the 1979 Belmont Report, which had been issued by the National Commission for the Protection of Human Subjects of Biomedical and Behavioral Research. The revised rules provide for wider representation on institutional review boards and they detail elements of what constitutes informed consent, among other provisions.

1982
- Tamper-resistant Packing Regulations issued by FDA to prevent poisonings such as deaths from cyanide placed in Tylenol capsules. The Federal Anti-Tampering Act passed in 1983 makes it a crime to tamper with packaged consumer products.
- FDA publishes first Red Book (successor to 1949 "black book"), officially known as Toxicological Principles for the Safety Assessment of Direct Food Additives and Color Additives Used in Food.

1983
- Orphan Drug Act passed, enabling FDA to promote research and marketing of drugs needed for treating rare diseases.

1984
- Fines Enhancement Laws of 1984 and 1987 amend the U.S. Code to greatly increase penalties for all federal offenses. The maximum fine for individuals is now $100,000 for each offense and $250,000 if the violation is a felony or causes death. For corporations, the amounts are doubled.
- Drug Price Competition and Patent Term Restoration Act expedites the availability of less costly generic drugs by permitting FDA to approve applications to market generic versions of brand-name drugs without repeating the research done to prove them safe and effective.
- At the same time, the brand-name companies can apply for up to five years additional patent protection for the new medicines they developed to make up for time lost while their products were going through FDA's approval process.

1985
- AIDS test for blood approved by FDA in its first major action to protect patients from infected donors.

1986
- Childhood Vaccine Act requires patient information on vaccines, gives FDA authority to recall biologics, and authorizes civil penalties.

1987
- Investigational drug regulations revised to expand access to experimental drugs for patients with serious diseases with no alternative therapies.

1988
- Food and Drug Administration Act of 1988 officially establishes FDA as an agency of the Department of Health and Human Services with a Commissioner of Food and Drugs appointed by the President with the advice and consent of the Senate, and broadly spells out the responsibilities of the Secretary and the Commissioner for research, enforcement, education, and information.

- The Prescription Drug Marketing Act bans the diversion of prescription drugs from legitimate commercial channels. Congress finds that the resale of such drugs leads to the distribution of mislabeled, adulterated, subpotent, and counterfeit drugs to the public. The new law requires drug wholesalers to be licensed by the states; restricts reimportation from other countries; and bans sale, trade or purchase of drug samples, and traffic or counterfeiting of redeemable drug coupons.
- Generic Animal Drug and Patent Term Restoration Act extends to veterinary products benefits given to human drugs under the 1984 Drug Price Competition and Patent Term Restoration Act. Companies can produce and sell generic versions of animal drugs approved after October 1962 without duplicating research done to prove them safe and effective. The act also authorizes extension of animal drug patents.

1989
- FDA issues a nationwide recall of all over-the-counter dietary supplements containing 100 milligrams or more of L-Tryptophan, due to a clear link between the consumption of L-tryptophan tablets and its association with a U.S. outbreak of Eosinophilia Myalgia Syndrome (EMS), characterized by fatigue, shortness of breath, and other symptoms. By 1990 the Centers for Disease Control and Prevention confirm over 1,500 cases of EMS, including 38 deaths, and FDA prohibits the importation of l-tryptophan.

1990
- Responding to increasing illicit traffic, Congress passes the Anabolic Steroid Act of 1990, which identifies anabolic steroids as a class of drugs and specifies over two dozen items as controlled substances. In addition, a four-part definition of this class is established to permit new, black market compounds to be assigned to this category, and thus subject to regulation as controlled substances.
- Nutrition Labeling and Education Act requires all packaged foods to bear nutrition labeling and all health claims for foods to be consistent with terms defined by the Secretary of Health and Human Services. The law preempts state requirements about food standards, nutrition labeling, and health claims and, for the first time, authorizes some health claims for foods. The food ingredient panel, serving sizes, and terms such as "low fat" and "light" are standardized.
- Safe Medical Devices Act is passed, requiring nursing homes, hospitals, and other facilities that use medical devices to report to FDA incidents that suggest that a medical device probably caused or contributed to the death, serious illness, or serious injury of a patient. Manufacturers are required to conduct post-market surveillance on permanently implanted devices whose failure might cause serious harm or death, and to establish methods for tracing and locating patients depending on such devices. The act authorizes FDA to order device product recalls and other actions.

1991
- Regulations published to Accelerate the Review of Drugs for life-threatening diseases.
- The policy for protection of human subjects in research, promulgated in 1981 by FDA and the Department of Health and Human Services, is adopted by more than a dozen federal entities involved in human subject research and becomes known as the Common Rule. This rule issues requirements for researchers who obtain and document informed consent, secures special protection for children, women, and prisoners, elaborates on required procedures for institutional review boards, and ensures that research institutions comply with the regulations.

1992
- Generic Drug Enforcement Act imposes debarment and other penalties for illegal acts involving abbreviated drug applications.
- Prescription Drug User Fee Act requires drug and biologics manufacturers to pay fees for product applications and supplements, and other services. The act also requires FDA to use these funds to hire more reviewers to assess applications.
- Mammography Quality Standards Act requires all mammography facilities in the United States to be accredited and federally certified as meeting quality standards effective Oct. 1, 1994. After initial certification, facilities must pass annual inspections by federal or state inspectors.
- Nutrition facts, basic per-serving nutritional information, are required on foods under the Nutrition Labeling and Education Act of 1990. Based on the latest public health recommendations, FDA and the Food Safety and Inspection Service of the Department of Agriculture recreate the food label to list the most important nutrients in an easy-to-follow format.

1993
- A consolidation of several adverse reaction reporting systems is launched as MedWatch, designed for voluntary reporting of problems associated with medical products to be filed with FDA by health professionals.
- Revising a policy from 1977 that excluded women of childbearing potential from early drug studies, FDA issues guidelines calling for improved assessments of medication responses as a function of gender. Companies are encouraged to include patients of both sexes in their investigations of drugs and to analyze any gender-specific phenomena.

1994
- Dietary Supplement Health and Education Act establishes specific labeling requirements, provides a regulatory framework, and authorizes FDA to promulgate good manufacturing practice regulations for dietary supplements. This act defines "dietary supplements" and "dietary ingredients" and classifies them as food. The act also establishes a commission to recommend how to regulate claims.
- FDA announces it could consider regulating nicotine in cigarettes as a drug, in response to a Citizen's Petition by the Coalition on Smoking OR Health.
- Uruguay Round Agreements Act extends the patent terms of U.S. drugs from 17 to 20 years.
- Animal Medicinal Drug Use Clarification Act allows veterinarians to prescribe extra-label use of veterinary drugs for animals under specific circumstances. In addition, the legislation allows licensed veterinarians to prescribe human drugs for use in animals under certain conditions.

1995
- FDA declares cigarettes to be "drug delivery devices." Restrictions are proposed on marketing and sales to reduce smoking by young people.
- A series of proposed reforms to reduce regulatory burden on pharmaceutical manufacturers is announced, including an expansion of allowable promotional material on approved uses of drugs that firms can distribute to health professionals, streamlining certain elements in the documentation of investigational drug studies, and a reduction in both environmental impact filings and pre-approval requirements in tablet manufacture.

1996
- Federal Tea Tasters Repeal Act repeals the Tea Importation Act of 1897 to eliminate the Board of Tea Experts and user fees for FDA's testing of all imported tea. Tea itself is still regulated by FDA.
- Saccharin Notice Repeal Act repeals the saccharin notice requirements.
- Animal Drug Availability Act adds flexibility to animal drug approval process, providing for flexible labeling and more direct communication between drug sponsors and FDA.
- Food Quality Protection Act amends the Food, Drug, and Cosmetic Act, eliminating application of the Delaney proviso to pesticides.

1997
- Food and Drug Administration Modernization Act reauthorizes the Prescription Drug User Fee Act of 1992 and mandates the most wide-ranging reforms in agency practices since 1938. Provisions include measures to accelerate review of devices, regulate advertising of unapproved uses of approved drugs and devices, and regulate health claims for foods.

1998
- FDA promulgates the Pediatric Rule, a regulation that requires manufacturers of selected new and extant drug and biological products to conduct studies to assess their safety and efficacy in children.
- Mammography Quality Standards Reauthorization Act continues 1992 Act until 2002.
- First phase to consolidate FDA laboratories nationwide from 19 facilities to 9 by 2014 includes dedication of the first of five new regional laboratories.

1999
- ClinicalTrials.gov is founded to provide the public with updated information on enrollment in federally and privately supported clinical research, thereby expanding patient access to studies of promising therapies.
- A final rule mandates that all over-the-counter drug labels must contain data in a standardized format. These drug facts are designed to provide the patient with easy-to-find information, analogous to the nutrition facts label for foods.

2000
- The U. S. Supreme Court, upholding an earlier decision in Food and Drug Administration v. Brown & Williamson Tobacco Corp. et al., ruled 5-4 that FDA does not have authority to regulate tobacco as a drug. Within weeks of this ruling, FDA revokes its final rule, issued in 1996, that restricted the sale and distribution of cigarettes and smokeless tobacco products to children and adolescents, and that determined that cigarettes and smokeless tobacco products are combination products consisting of a drug (nicotine) and device components intended to deliver nicotine to the body.
- Federal agencies are required to issue guidelines to maximize the quality, objectivity, utility, and integrity of the information they generate, and to provide a mechanism whereby those affected can secure correction of information that does not meet these guidelines, under the Data Quality Act.
- Publication of a rule on dietary supplements defines the type of statement that can be labeled regarding the effect of supplements on the structure or function of the body.

2002

- The Best Pharmaceuticals for Children Act improves safety and efficacy of patented and off-patent medicines for children. It continues the exclusivity provisions for pediatric drugs as mandated under the Food and Drug Administration Modernization Act of 1997, in which market exclusivity of a drug is extended by six months, and in exchange the manufacturer carries out studies of the effects of drugs when taken by children. The provisions both clarify aspects of the exclusivity period and amend procedures for generic drug approval in cases when pediatric guidelines are added to the labeling.
- In the wake of the events of September 11, 2001, the Public Health Security and Bioterrorism Preparedness and Response Act of 2002 is designed to improve the country's ability to prevent and respond to public health emergencies, and provisions include a requirement that FDA issue regulations to enhance controls over imported and domestically produced commodities it regulates.
- Under the Medical Device User Fee and Modernization Act, fees are assessed sponsors of medical device applications for evaluation, provisions are established for device establishment inspections by accredited third-parties, and new requirements emerge for reprocessed single-use devices.
- The Office of Combination Products is formed within the Office of the Commissioner, as mandated under the Medical Device User Fee and Modernization Act, to oversee review of products that fall into multiple jurisdictions within FDA.
- An effort to enhance and update the regulation of manufacturing processes and end-product quality of animal and human drugs and biological medicines is announced, the current good manufacturing practice (cGMP) initiative. The goals of the initiative are to focus on the greatest risks to public health in manufacturing procedures, to ensure that process and product quality standards do not impede innovation, and to apply a consistent approach to these issues across FDA.

2003

- The Medicare Prescription Drug Improvement and Modernization Act requires, among other elements, that a study be made of how current and emerging technologies can be utilized to make essential information about prescription drugs available to the blind and visually impaired.
- To help consumers choose heart-healthy foods, the Department of Health and Human Services (HHS) announces that the FDA will require food labels to include trans-fat content, the first substantial change to the nutrition facts panel on foods since the label was changed in 1993.
- An obesity working group is established by the Commissioner of Food and Drugs, charged to develop an action plan to deal with the nation's obesity epidemic from the perspective of FDA. In March 2004 the group releases "Calories Count: Report of the Obesity Working Group," which addresses issues connected to the food label, obesity therapeutics, research needs, the role of education, and other topics.
- The National Academy of Sciences releases "Scientific Criteria to Ensure Safe Food," a report commissioned by FDA and the Department of Agriculture, which buttresses the value of the Hazard Analysis and Critical Control Point (HACCP) approach to food safety already in place at FDA and invokes the need for continued efforts to make food safety a vital part of our overall public health mission.
- The Animal Drug User Fee Act permits FDA to collect subsidies for the review of certain animal drug applications form sponsors, analogous to laws passed for the evaluation of other products FDA regulates, ensuring the safety and effectiveness of drugs for animals and the safety of animals as foodstuffs.

- FDA is given clear authority under the Pediatric Research Equity Act to require that sponsors conduct clinical research into pediatric applications for new drugs and biological products.

2004

- Project BioShield Act of 2004 authorizes FDA to expedite its review procedures to enable rapid distribution of treatments as countermeasures to chemical, biological, and nuclear agents that may be used in a terrorist attack against the U. S., among other provisions.
- Passage of the Food Allergy Labeling and Consumer Protection Act requires the labeling of any food that contains a protein derived from any one of the following foods that, as a group, account for the vast majority of food allergies: peanuts, soybeans, cow's milk, eggs, fish, crustacean shellfish, tree nuts, and wheat.
- A ban on over-the-counter steroid precursors, increased penalties for making, selling, or possessing illegal steroids precursors, and funds for preventive education to children are features of the Anabolic Steroid Control Act of 2004.
- FDA publishes "Innovation or Stagnation? -- Challenge and Opportunity on the Critical Path to New Medical Products," which examines the critical path needed to bring therapeutic products to fruition, and how FDA can collaborate in the process, from laboratory to production to end use, to make medical breakthroughs available to those in need as quickly as possible.
- Based on recent results from controlled clinical studies indicating that Cox-2 selective agents may be connected to an elevated risk of serious cardiovascular events, including heart attack and stroke, FDA issues a public health advisory urging health professionals to limit the use of these drugs.
- To provide for the treatment of animal species other than cattle, horses, swine, chickens, turkeys, dogs, and cats, as well as other species that may be added at a later time, the Minor Use and Minor Species Animal Health Acts passed to encourage the development of treatments for species that would otherwise attract little interest in the development of veterinary therapies.
- Deeming such products to present an unreasonable risk of harm, FDA bans dietary supplements containing ephedrine alkaloids based on an increasing number of adverse events linked to these products and the known pharmacology of these alkaloids.

2005

- Formation of the Drug Safety Board is announced, consisting of FDA staff and representatives from the National Institutes of Health and the Veterans Administration. The Board will advise the Director, Center for Drug Evaluation and Research, FDA, on drug safety issues and work with the agency in communicating safety information to health professionals and patients.

2009

- President Obama signs the Family Smoking Prevention and Tobacco Control Act into law. The Tobacco Control Act gives FDA authority to regulate the manufacture, distribution, and marketing of tobacco products to protect public health.
- FDA Center for Tobacco Products established.
- FDA announced a ban on cigarettes with flavors characterizing fruit, candy, or clove.

2011

- FDA Food Safety and Modernization Act (FSMA). FSMA provides FDA with new enforcement authorities related to food safety standards, gives FDA tools to hold imported foods to the same standards as domestic foods, and directs FDA to build an integrated national food safety system in partnership with state and local authorities.

2012
- Food and Drug Administration Safety and Innovation Act (FDASIA). Expands FDA authorities to collect user fees from industry to fund reviews of innovator drugs, medical devices, generic drugs and biosimilar biological products; promotes innovation to speed patient access to safe and effective products; increases stakeholder involvement in FDA processes, and enhances the safety of the drug supply chain.
- Medical Device User Fee and Modernization Act (MDUFMA III). As part of FDASIA, reauthorizes user fees from industry to fund reviews of medical devices in exchange for FDA to meet certain performance goals.
- In 2012, an outbreak of fungal meningitis linked to a contaminated compounded drug product resulted in the loss of 64 lives and caused more than 751 illnesses. In response, Congress enacted the 2013 Drug Quality and Security Act (DQSA) that insures greater regulatory oversight of facilities creating compounded drugs.

2013
- Pandemic and All-Hazards Preparedness Reauthorization Act (PAHPRA). Establishes and reauthorizes certain programs under the Public Health Service Act and the Food, Drug, and Cosmetic Act with respect to public health security and all-hazards preparedness and response.
- Drug Quality and Security Act. Following an outbreak in 2012 of an epidemic of fungal meningitis linked to a compounded steroid, Congress enacted the Drug Quality Safety and Security Act (DQSA). Among other provisions it outlines steps for an electronic and interoperable system to identify and trace certain prescription drugs throughout the U.S.

DRUG RECALLS

Drug Recalls involve a manufacturer's voluntary removal or correction of a marketed product in violation of a law with each recall having a recall strategy from the manufacturer.

Class I: There is a reasonable probability that the use or exposure to the product will cause serious adverse health or death.
Class II: The use or exposure to a product may cause temporary or medically reversible adverse health or where the probability of serious adverse health consequences is remote.
Class III: The use or exposure to a product is not likely to cause adverse health consequences.

DIFFERENCE BETWEEN MISBRANDING AND ADULTERATION

MISBRANDING
- Label is false or misleading
- Label is missing name, active ingredients of drug, quantity
- Prescription or OTC label missing required information
- Drug made in a non-registered facility
- Not in compliance with laws or regulations
- Packed without regard to Poison Prevention Packaging Act
- Think "label"

ADULTERATION
- Contains any unapproved, unsafe substance
- Exposed to unsanitary conditions or lack of certified Good Manufacturing Practices (cGMPS)
- Strength, purity, or quality substandard
- Used in substitution of another substance
- Think "drug"

REFERENCES
1. Fundamentals of Regulatory Affairs. Regulatory Affairs Professions Society, 1999:200.

2. Strauss S. Food and Drug Administration: An overview. In: Strauss's Federal Drug Laws and Examination Review, 5th edition. Lancaster, PA: Technomic Publishing Co., 1999.

3. FDA. 2019 U.S. Food and Drug Administration. *http://www.fda.gov/*

4. Milestones in U.S. Food and Drug Law History. February 2018. Food and Drug Administration: *https://www.fda.gov/aboutfda/history/forgshistory/evolvingpowers/ucm2007256.htm*

FEDERAL PHARMACY LAW REVIEW PART 4: CONTROLLED SUBSTANCES LAWS

FEDERAL LAWS AND REGULATIONS GOVERNING PHARMACIES, PHARMACISTS AND PRESCRIPTIONS

The Federal Controlled Substances Act (CSA) of 1970 is the basis for all practice-oriented drug law and regulations. It's important to note that this is a closed-loop system that goes from manufacturer through administration or dispensing to the patient. Each controlled substance dosage is carefully recorded and tightly controlled. A nightmare of any pharmacist is missing controlled substances or wrong counts.

The CSA was brought about to regulate the manufacturing, distribution, dispensing, and delivery of drugs that have a potential for physical and/or mental abuse. CSA is regulated by the Drug Enforcement Agency (DEA) with a federal registration of all persons in the chain of manufacturing, distribution, and dispensing except the ultimate user- people or their caregivers don't have their very own DEA number to track. The DEA registration number must be renewed every 3 years and specific forms are used to order. All records should be maintained for at least four (4) years. However, federal facilities like veteran administration (VA) hospitals don't fall under the state laws of CSA as it is a federal level of practice. These potentially abusive drugs were termed "controlled substances" and broken down into five schedules. These medications have a "C" on their stock bottles.

The five schedules are based off of medical use and potential for abuse and dependence outlined below. Be sure to know what medications are listed in each of these schedules!

Note: Some states have specific rules such as medical marijuana which is becoming popular nationwide. Be sure to follow the more stringent law when answering questions on the MPJE unless they specify a focus on state.

C-I
High potential for abuse drugs have no currently accepted medical use (i.e. Heroin) in the treatment in the United States, and there is also little data on the accepted safety for use of the drug under medical supervision. These drugs may not be prescribed, administration, or dispensed for medical use, but they may be ordered for research and investigational use. This controlled substance class can be ordered using DEA 222/CSOS. Examples: Marijuana, Heroin, LSD, Peyote, Salvia.

C-II
These medications have a high potential of abuse but also have an accepted medical use. It's important to know that no refills or transfer are allowed for this controlled substance class. Patients are able to have multiple fillings of this class as long as they have multiple prescription blanks, the actual date of prescribing, and the earliest date to fill with a 90-day total. So, if Sally brings in a prescription for OxyContin, she is allowed to make three fills with three separate prescriptions but will need to see her prescriber after the 90-day supply is done. Oral prescriptions are allowed only if it's an emergency and written prescription arrives within 7 days. A central fill is not permitted in emergency situations. Facsimile prescriptions are not allowed of CIIs except in these situations:
- Home infusion/IV parenteral therapy if for pain
- Long Term Care Facility (LTCF) residents

- Registered hospice facility

Partial fills are allowed within 72 hours if the pharmacist doesn't have the supply needed to fill the entire prescription, but the prescription must have the amount dispensed noted. If the total amount of the prescription is not completed within 72 hours, then the remainder amount is void and the prescriber should be contacted to get a new supply. In a LTCF, partial fills are allowed with the prescription valid for 60 days from the date it was written; however, the pharmacist must note the date of fill, quantity dispensed and remainder along with a signature. DEA form 222/CSOS is required either typewritten or handwritten with one drug per line. Make sure to take time and accuracy on these forms as any ill markings or misspellings will make the form void. DEA form 222 can also be used by pharmacies to ship drugs back to a reverse distributor or other pharmacy that is in short supply. In this case, the pharmacy acting as a supplier, maintains copy 1 with the reverse distributor disposing the drug using form 41. Examples: Dilaudid, OxyContin, Demerol, Sublimaze, etc.

C-III AND C-IV

These controlled substances also have a potential for abuse but are not as high as CIIs. Patients are able to get five refills in six months from the date the prescription was written, and one transfer allowed unless the organization has a shared database (CVS to CVS, or Walgreens to Walgreens) they may transfer as many times as needed. Prescriptions in this class may be written, verbal or electronic and partial fills are allowed as long as the total quantity or six-month duration isn't breached. A DEA form 222/CSOS is not required for this controlled substance class.
Example for Schedule III: Buprenorphine, Anabolic steroids, Suboxone, Tylenol 3 (Tylenol with codeine), etc. Example for Schedule IV: Benzodiazepines, Lunesta, and Tramadol.

C-V

This is the last class with the lowest risk of abuse. Federally there is no limit for refills with one transfer permitted unless, again, if the chain shares a common database. Most CV drugs don't need a prescription such as cough or antidiarrheal (Imodium) as long as it contains less than 200 mg of codeine or per 100 mLs if a liquid preparation. The catch is dispensing these non-prescriptions need to be done by a pharmacist, and the buyer needs to be at least 18 years old, have a valid ID, and a log book must be kept of each transaction that includes:

- Name and address of buyer, name and quantity purchased along with date, and pharmacist name that dispensed the product

As you will notice when you review the Oregon-specific controlled substance section, Oregon has stricter laws involving these medications and most require a prescription. When a patient has a prescription for these products they do not need to be entered into a log-book. Please be careful and always go with the stricter law which in this case will be Oregon.

Central fill pharmacies are not allowed to dispense controlled substances at the retail level if someone wants to buy. Partial fills are allowed for CVs as long as total amount or six-month duration is not breached and no DEA 222/CSOS form is needed. Example: Lyrica (requires Rx), Phenergan with Codeine, Robitussin AC, etc.

DRUG ENFORCEMENT ADMINISTRATION (DEA) REGISTRATION

As mentioned before, every practitioner involved in the chain needs to have a DEA registration number except those that are federal (VA, US Public Health Service, Bureau of Prisons (BOP), etc.). A DEA registration number for a practitioner begins with the letter A or B. Registration numbers issued to mid-level practitioners begin with the letter M. The first letter of the registration number is followed by the first letter of the registrant's last name (i.e. T for Tanner or M for Munoz), and then a computer-generated sequence of seven numbers (such as MT3614511). So how can pharmacists check if this is a valid DEA number? The computer system generates these numbers based off a formula.

Add the sum of the numbers in the "odd" position to the sum of the numbers in the "even" position multiplied by 2. The second number in the final sum is called the "check digit" and is the last number in the sequence.

For example, take the following MT3614511. The letter M represents the practitioner as a mid-level prescriber. The letter T represents the first letter of the last name Tanner. The numbers are randomly generated, and the final check digit is the number 1. The formula is as follows:
- Odd position: 3 + 1 + 5 = 9
- Even position: 6 + 4 + 1 = 11 × 2 = 22
- 22 + 9 = 31 "1" is the seventh or check digit

Be sure to understand this formula as it will be tested on the MPJE! Even though it is not used in practice much, it is still a valuable tool if a pharmacist suspects fraudulent activities.

Pharmacies, not pharmacists, get assigned a DEA registration number by filling out a DEA form 224 if they buy and sell controlled substances. The pharmacy must also comply with distributor and record keeping requirements. This also includes transfer of ownership or change of address; a new DEA registration must be completed before the change happens to note the changes. If the there is a transfer of a pharmacy business to another registrant, then the DEA needs to be notified at least 14 days before the transfer to make the following updates:

- The name, address, and registration number of the registrant transferring the pharmacy
- The name, address, and registration number of the registrant receiving the pharmacy
- Whether the pharmacy will continue at the current location with the current business owner or moved to another location
- The date when the controlled substances will be transferred to the person acquiring the pharmacy

On the day the controlled substances are transferred, a complete inventory must be taken, and a copy of the inventory must be included in the records of for both parties involved in the transfer of the pharmacy. If the registrant that is gaining the pharmacy owns another pharmacy licensed in the same state as the one he's acquiring, they will still need to apply for a new DEA number before the date of transfer.

PRACTIONERS

Even though practitioners may acquire a DEA registration, it's important to note that they are still limited in their scope of practice. An order for controlled substances that seems to be a valid prescription but is not issued in the usual course of professional treatment, or for investigational research, is not a valid prescription within the meaning and intent of the CSA. If a pharmacist suspects fraudulent prescribing but still dispenses the medication, he or she is subject to criminal and possibly civil actions. Practitioners are not allowed to get a supply of controlled substances for general dispensing to their patients and are limited to their scope of practice. For example, dentists can only prescribe for the treatment of the oral cavity area; you shouldn't expect a prescription of Ambien or Lyrica from them.

Mid-level practitioners (MLPs) are registered and authorized by the DEA and the state in which they practice dispensing, administering, and prescribing controlled substances in the course of professional practice. Examples of MLPs are nurse practitioners, nurse midwives, nurse anesthetists, clinical nurse specialists, physician assistants, and optometrists. They may serve in ambulance services, animal shelters, and nursing homes. MLPs can also get an individual DEA registration for controlled substance privileges. Also, some individual practitioners such as residents, staff physicians, and mid-level practitioners can be an employee of a hospital or facility and authorize the practitioner to dispense using the hospital's DEA registration number. Usually these institutions also have an internal code that is included in the end of the DEA registration number such as- GB1111119-W19. There's also a current list of internal codes that should be kept in the hospital or institution, and a pharmacist can call to verify the prescriber.

PRESCRIPTION BASICS

Prescriptions must be written in ink, typewritten or print, and information can only be entered by the prescribers or their agent. The only piece of information on the prescription that needs to be in the prescriber's own handwriting is their signature. Prescriptions are allowed to be transmitted orally by telephone or facsimile for Schedules III to V. The name of the person that a pharmacist or pharmacy intern has spoken to must be written down on a pharmacy pad and written into hard copy within 7 days.

In case of an emergency, a pharmacist may dispense a Schedule II medication when receiving the orally transmitted authorization of a prescribing practitioner, provided that the quantity prescribed and dispensed is limited to the amount adequate to treat the patient during the emergency period. The prescribing practitioner then must provide a written prescription for the emergency quantity prescribed to be delivered or postmarked to the dispensing pharmacist within 7 days after authorizing an emergency oral prescription. The prescription must also have written on its face "Authorization for Emergency Dispensing."

Upon receipt of the written prescription, the dispensing pharmacist must attach the prescription to the oral one. If the prescribing practitioner fails to deliver a written prescription within 7 days, the pharmacist needs to notify DEA or else will face criminal charges. Pharmacists and prescribers are co-liable for prescriptions written in error or with obvious problems. This is called corresponding responsibility.
A prescription for a controlled substance must be issued in good faith and for a legitimate medical purpose by a practitioner in the usual course of his or her professional practice. For example, a pharmacist receives a prescription order of antibiotics for the prescriber's daughter, if the prescriber is a veterinarian, this is obviously out of their scope of practice; however, if the prescriber is a medical family practice practitioner, then it may be allowable to fill the prescription.

A prescription is considered complete when the following information is included on its face:
- Date of issue

- Name and address of practitioner
- Controlled substance registration number
- Name of patient
- Address of patient
- Name, strength, dose, and quantity of controlled substances
- Directions for use and any cautionary statements required
- Number of times to be refilled
- Signature of prescriber

Prescriptions can be filed in a pharmacy in three different ways:
1. Three separate files for:
   - C-II
   - C-III through C-V
   - Non-controlled substances
2. §Two separate files for:
   - C-II
   - C-III through C-V and non-controlled substances
3. §Two separate files for:
   - C-II through C-V
   - Non-controlled substances

Note:
- §A red "C" must be stamped on the face of the prescription at least 1-inch-high in the lower right corner.
    - If a pharmacy utilizes a computer software for prescription that permits identification by prescription number and retrieving of the original documents by prescriber's name, patient's name, the name of the drug dispensed, and the date filled, this requirement is applicable.

The transfer of existing, filled prescriptions is allowed under federal law for prescription drugs in Schedules III through V. The transfer rule only applies with state pharmacy law. Individual states may have more stringent requirements.

METHADONE

Prescriptions for methadone are valid provided that the drug is used as an analgesic. They are not valid through the typical retail pharmacy distribution channels for the purposes of detoxification or maintenance therapy for drug addiction. The only exception is when it was written by a physician for an addicted patient, then you are allowed a single-day quantity for three consecutive days for the purpose of admitting that addicted person to a licensed treatment program.

UNITED STATES POSTAL REGULATIONS

United States postal regulations allow the mailing of any filled prescription containing a narcotic of any quantity or federal schedule to patients. If not, we would not be able to do mail order prescriptions! When mailing controlled substances, two rules must be followed:

1. The inner container must be marked, sealed, and labeled with the name and address of the practitioner, or the name and address of the pharmacy or other person dispensing the prescription and the prescription number.
2. The outside container must be plain with no markings of any kind that would indicate the contents contained within.

PRESCRIPTION LABELING

The prescription label must be on the container and have the following information:
- Pharmacy name, address, and telephone number
- Assigned serial number
- Date of initial dispensing
- Name of patient
- Name of prescriber
- Directions for use and any cautionary statements
- Federal controlled substances warning label or "transfer label" for a Schedule II, III, and IV controlled substance

A controlled substance warning label, also known as the federal transfer label, must on the prescription containers of any drug listed in Schedules II to IV. The label reads as follows:
- "CAUTION: Federal law prohibits the transfer of this drug to any person other than the patient for whom it was prescribed."

Expiration dates listed on a manufacturer's stock container are set based on appropriate stability data that would support some amount of shelf life. Many states though require some form of expiration dating on prescription labels. Most use the Standards as described by the United States Pharmacopoeia (USP). Unless otherwise specified in the individual monograph, the beyond-use date (expiration date) should not be any later than the expiration date on the manufacturer's container, or one year from the date from when the drug is dispensed, whichever is earlier. USP also specifies that the expiration date for insulin products is 24 months from their date of manufacture. Expiration dates on OTC drug products are exempt from expiration dating if they are stable for at least 3 years, have no dosing limitations, and are safe and suitable for frequent and prolonged use (i.e. toothpaste, medicated shampoo).

SAFETY CLOSURES AND CONTAINERS

It's important read the Poison Prevention Packaging Act of 1970 that specifies child-resistant closures must be used on prescription containers unless the prescription is for an exempt drug (i.e., sublingual nitroglycerin, cholestyramine powder, unit dose or effervescent potassium supplements, erythromycin ethylsuccinate preparations, oral contraceptives packaged in mnemonic packages). Patients can authorize easy-to-open packaging and even issue a "blanket waiver" for prescription containers so that all of them are easy-to-open. A physician cannot issue a "blanket waiver" for dispensing in an easy-to-open packaging; the order must be on each prescription.

PHARMACY REQUIREMENTS

Every pharmacy must be registered with the DEA and receive a certificate of registration to distribute or dispense controlled substances. Each pharmacy has its own DEA registration number. These certificates of registration must be renewed every 3 years. Every pharmacy registrant must keep and maintain an accurate record of each controlled substance received. Dated invoices for controlled substances in Schedules III, IV, and V constitute complete records for these drugs. Copy 3 of DEA Form 222 constitutes complete record for the receipt of Schedule II controlled substances. The DEA requires every registrant who changes his or her business address to notify them and receive their approval before moving. Registrants may keep records at a location other than the registered location by notifying the nearest DEA office. Unless this request is denied, registrants may transfer records 14 days after notification. All records must be kept for a period of 2 years.

INVENTORY REQUIREMENTS

When first opening up a new pharmacy store or first having a controlled substance in stock, an initial inventory must be taken even if there is zero stock. The initial inventory must contain the following:
- Name
- Address
- DEA number of the registrant
- The date and time of the inventory
- The signature of the person taking the inventory
- The name of the medication, dosage form, dosage, and quantity on hand.

Then, once every 2 years, a biennial inventory must be taken of all federally controlled substances (C-II through C-V) after the date on which the original inventory was taken. This biennial inventory can be done on any date within the 2-year period. An exact count of C-II drugs must be done while only an estimation is need for C-III, C-IV or C-V drugs, unless the container holds more than a 1000 units then an exact count must be done.

COMPUTERIZED PRESCRIPTION PROCESSING SYSTEMS

Federal law permits record keeping to be done through a computerized prescription processing system. A pharmacy can use a system for the storage and retrieval of prescription information. It should still be able to supply immediate retrieval of information by either an electronic display or hard copy printout for prescriptions currently being filled. The computerized prescription processing system must still have the following:
- Date of issuance
- Original prescription number
- Name and address of patient
- Physician's name and DEA number
- Name, strength, dosage form, and quantity of control
- Total number of refills authorized by the physician

The system must keep records for at least two years from the date of inventory or records for inspection by the Drug Enforcement Agency (DEA) based off Section 1304.04 Maintenance of records and inventories. Please note this is based off federal law, the state law may be more specific.

DRUG ENFORCEMENT ADMINISTRATION (DEA) FORMS

FORM 222
Use this form to order Schedule I and II drugs to stock a pharmacy. Pharmacists who want to borrow or transfer (from registrant to registrant) Schedule II controlled substances from other pharmacies need to use a DEA Form 222. The form is in triplicate and can be signed by the registrant or any person who has written authorization. Each form contains ten lines to write the C-II medication to be ordered. One line on the order form should be used to describe one item ordered, if two lines are used for the same item, they count as only one line. These forms must be submitted to the supplier error free- if there is any error it will be rejected. Therefore, voiding a line on the order form because of an error is not permitted and the entire form should be voided.

When complete, the person ordering the medication must separate the third copy of the form and retain it in the pharmacy. Once receiving the drugs, the person who ordered them, or any other authorized person, must fill out the last two columns of the store's copy with quantity and date. The first copy goes to the supplier and second copy to DEA.
- Copy 1 is brown (supplier)
- Copy 2 is Green (DEA)
- Copy 3 is Blue (Pharmacy)

After a pharmacy places an order, it keeps copy 3 (blue) while copy 1 and 2 are mailed to the supplier to get the drugs requested. The supplier fills the order and keeps copy 1 and 2. Copy 2 (green) is then mailed to the DEA. If the supplier can't fill the order, they can send it to another supplier. However, each form must be signed and dated by a person with power of attorney from the registrant. Once the pharmacy receives the order, it completes copy 3 to ensure the order was received and accurate. These records must be maintained for at least four (4) years.

FORM 106
Loss of controlled substances (federally scheduled II to V) must be reported to the DEA using this form. If the pharmacy is involved in a robbery or significant shortage of controlled substances is caught, after reporting to the local police department, a DEA Form 106 should be filled out in triplicate. Two copies must be sent to the DEA as soon as possible; one copy must be kept on file by the pharmacy. If a pharmacist knowingly fails to report theft within 24 hours of discovery, they could be charged criminal charges and fined.

FORM 41
Use this form for the destruction of controlled substances. The DEA should be contacted for instructions when destroying outdated, damaged, or otherwise unusable controlled substances. Breakage, damage, or spillage of recoverable or destruction of controlled substances must be on DEA form 41, and the drug disposed of through a reverse distributor. However, any spillage or damage of non-recoverable drugs must be documented in inventory records. Two individuals who witnessed the breakage must sign the inventory records.

FORM 224
Use this if filing for a new retail pharmacy, hospital/clinic, practitioner, teaching institution, or mid-level practitioner.

FORM 224a
Use this to renew for facilities listed in form 224.

FORM 224b
Use this as an affidavit for chain renewal operating under a single registration.

FORM 225
Use this if filing a new application for a manufacturer, distributor, analytical laboratory, or importer/exporter.

FORM 363
Use this if filing a new application for narcotic treatment programs such as methadone maintenance program.

FORM 510
Use this if filing a new application for domestic chemical businesses such as precursors for controlled substances.

MISCELLANEOUS

Patient package inserts (PPIs) are required by FDA regulation to be provided to the patient when dispensing certain drugs. Patient package inserts must be given to the patient on the initial dispensing and on refills if so requested. All of the following are drugs that must be dispensed with a PPI:
- Isoproterenol inhalation products
- Oral contraceptives
- Estrogen/progestogen containing drug products
- Intrauterine devices
- Pregestational drug products
- Accutane R

SCHEDULE LISTED CHEMICAL PRODUCT (SLCPS)

These are products used in the production of methamphetamine. Drugs commonly used are ephedrine, pseudoephedrine, and phenylpropanolamine. It's important that sellers must self-certify through the DEA's website at www.deadiversion.usdoj.gov and under their "Required Training and Self-Certification" as this is required for retail pharmacies or any regulated seller of scheduled listed chemical products. Portions of this self-certification are that regulated sellers are confirming that employees have been trained, and these records of training must be maintained. Sale limits need to be enforced, and products stored behind the counter or in a locked cabinet as well as a written or electronic logbook must be maintained at all times.

Drugs listed as "List 1 Chemicals" are drugs involved in the manufacture of a controlled substance such as: Ephedrine, Pseudoephedrine, Ergonovine, Iodine, Safrole, Piperidine.

Drugs listed as "List 2 Chemicals" are solvents used in the manufacture of a controlled substance such as: Acetone, HCl, K/NA-Permanganate.

REFERENCES
1. Poison Prevention Packaging: A Guide for Healthcare Professionals. Revised 2005. US Consumer Product Safety Commission (CPSC) Accessed on November 25th, 2018 at: *https://www.cpsc.gov//PageFiles/113945/384.pdf*.

2. Title 21 United States Code (USC) Controlled Substances Act. 2012 Edition. Accessed on November 26th, 2018 at: *http://www.deadiversion.usdoj.gov/21cfr/21usc/*.

3. Drug Enforcement Administration (DEA). Accessed on November 26th, 2018 at: *http://www.dea.gov/druginfo/ds.shtml*.

POISON PREVENTION PACKAGING

Background
- The US Consumer Product Safety Commission (CPSC) enforces the Poison Prevention Packaging Act of 1970 (PPPA) which requires child-resistant packaging on many products, including prescription drugs. This is to prevent children from unnecessary and dangerous ingestion of medications.

PPPA Exemptions
- Hint: It is important to know the list of products that are EXEMPT from the PPPA standards!
    - Sublingual nitroglycerin
    - Sublingual and chewable isosorbide dinitrate in dosage strengths of 10 mg or less
    - Erythromycin ethylsuccinate granules (for oral suspension) and oral suspensions in packages containing not more than 8 grams or the equivalent of erythromycin.
    - Erythromycin ethylsuccinate tablets in packages containing no more than the equivalent of 16 grams erythromycin.
    - Anhydrous cholestyramine in powder form
    - Potassium supplements in unit dose forms (including effervescent tablets, vials of liquid potassium, and powdered potassium) containing not more than 50 mEq per unit dose.
    - Sodium fluoride dosage forms containing no more than 264 mg of sodium fluoride per package.
    - Betamethasone tablets in packages containing no more than 12.6 mg betamethasone.
    - Mebendazole tablets in packages containing no more than 600 mg of the drug.
    - Methylprednisolone tablets in packages containing not more than 84 mg of the drug.
    - Colestipol powder in packages containing not more than 5 grams of the drug.
    - Pancrelipase tablets, capsules, or powders
    - Oral contraceptives in memory-aid dispenser packages
    - Prednisone tablets in packages containing no more than 105 mg of the drug.
    - Conjugated estrogen tablets in packages containing no more than 32 mg of the drug.
    - Norethindrone acetate tablets in packages containing no more than 50 mg of the drug.
    - Medroxyprogesterone acetate tablets
    - Sucrase preparations in a solution of glycerol and water
    - Hormone Replacement Therapy products

Specific Labelling Requirements

o Certain drug products require specific labeling of the following:

Drug Product	Specific Label
Mineral Oil*	Caution: To be taken only at bedtime. Do not use at any other time or administer to infants, except upon the advice of a physician.
Wintergreen oil (methyl salicylate)	Any drug containing more than 5% wintergreen oil may be dangerous if used other than directed. Keep out of reach of children.
FD&C Yellow No. 5 (tartrazine)	May cause allergic reactions.
Sodium Phosphates	Must not contain more than 90 ml per OTC container.
Aspartame	Phenylketonurics: Contains phenylalanine ___ mg per ____ (dosage unit).
Isoproterenol inhalation preparations	Do not exceed dose prescribed. Contact physician if difficulty in breathing.
Sulfites	Prescription drugs containing sulfites must include an allergy warning on the label.
Ipecac Syrup	Warning: Keep out of reach of children. Do not use in unconscious persons. In red letters in a box: For emergency use to cause vomiting in poisoning. Before using, call the physician, the Poison Control Center, or hospital emergency room immediately for advice". Usual dosage: 1 tablespoon (15 mL) in persons over 1 year of age May only be sold in 1 oz (30 mL) containers.
Potassium Salt for oral ingestion	Warning of nonspecific small bowel lesions consisting of stenosis (with or without ulceration) associated with enteric-coated thiazides with potassium salts
OTC Nonsteroidal Anti-inflammatory Drugs (NSAIDs)	"NSAID" must be on label. Warning of stomach bleeding.
OTC Acetaminophen (APAP)	"Acetaminophen" must be on label. Warning of liver toxicity. Do not use with other products containing APAP. Talk to a doctor or pharmacist before taking it with warfarin.
Alcohol Warning	Products containing NSAIDs or APAP must have a warning that people who have 3 or more drinks per day must consult with a doctor beforehand.
Salicylates (i.e. aspirin)	Warning of Reye's Syndrome in children. OTC pediatric aspirin (1 ¼ grain size) cannot be sold in containers of more than 36 tablets.

Acetophenetidin (Phenacetin)-containing products	Warning: This medication may damage the kidneys when used in large amounts or for a long period of time.

REFERENCES:

1. Poison Prevention Packaging: A Guide for Healthcare Professionals. Revised 2005, CPSC 384. US. Consumer Product Safety Commission, Washington, D.C. 20207. Accessible at: https://www.cpsc.gov/s3fs-public/384.pdf

2. Title 21 United States Code (USC) Controlled Substances Act. 2012 Edition. Accessible at: *http://www.deadiversion.usdoj.gov/21cfr/21usc/*.

3. Drug Enforcement Administration (DEA). Accessible at: *http://www.dea.gov/druginfo/ds.shtml*.

4. Code of Federal Regulations Title 21: Food and Drugs, Part 201- Labeling, accessible at: https://www.ecfr.gov/cgi-bin/text-idx?SID=5310e9cd99b942b3d62521ee7e54cb19&mc=true&node=pt21.4.201&rgn=div5#se21.4.201_120

HEALTH INSURANCE PORTABILITY AND ACCOUNTABILITY ACT (HIPAA)

HIPAA (Health Insurance Portability and Accountability Act of 1996) is the United States legislation that provides data privacy and security provisions for safeguarding personal health information. Most likely you have gone through an annual HIPAA required training module or course from your pharmacy school, workplace, or other work that involves patient care and personal health information (PHI). HIPAA has two main purposes:

1. To provide continuous health insurance coverage for workers who lose or change their job, and to reduce the administrative burdens and cost of healthcare by standardizing the electronic transmission of administrative and financial transactions.

2. Combating abuse, fraud and waste in health insurance and healthcare delivery and improving access to long-term care services and health insurance.

The HIPAA Privacy Rule
From the Health and Human Services (HHS) website, it states the HIPAA Privacy Rule establishes national standards to protect individuals' medical records and other personal health information and applies to health plans, health care clearinghouses, and those health care providers that conduct certain health care transactions electronically. The Rule requires appropriate safeguards to protect the privacy of personal health information and sets limits and conditions on the uses and disclosures that may be made of such information without patient authorization. The Rule also gives patient's rights over their health information, including rights to examine and obtain a copy of their health records, and to request corrections.

Personal health information (PHI) can be pharmacy prescription records, computer records, prescription container labels, other pharmacy records identifying the patient and even oral communication about patients' prescriptions and health care treatment.

Information is protected through technical and physical safeguards to ensure no disclosures are made, and if a disclosure must be made the minimum necessary rule is applied where the least amount of information needed to provide the disclosure is given.

Note that this differs with state laws which may be stricter.

Who must follow HIPAA?
Entities that must follow the HIPAA regulations are called "covered entities." Covered entities include the following:
- Health Plans, including health insurance companies, company health plans, and certain government programs that pay for health care, such as Medicare and Medicaid.
- Health Care Providers—those that conduct certain business electronically, such as electronically billing your health insurance—including doctors, clinics, hospitals, psychologists, chiropractors, nursing homes, pharmacies, and dentists.
- Health Care Clearinghouses—entities that process nonstandard health information they receive from another entity into a standard (i.e., standard electronic format or data content), or vice versa.

- Contractors, subcontractors, and other outside persons and companies that are not employees of a covered entity will need to have access to your health information when providing services to the covered entity.
- Companies that help your doctors get paid for providing health care, including billing companies and companies that process your health care claims
- Companies that help administer health plans
- People like outside lawyers, accountants, and IT specialists
- Companies that store or destroy medical records

Who is NOT required to follow HIPAA?

Examples of organizations that do not have to follow the Privacy and Security Rules include the following:
- Life insurers
- Employers
- Workers compensation carriers
- Most schools and school districts
- Many state agencies like child protective service agencies
- Most law enforcement agencies
- Many municipal offices

What rights do patients have with their health information?

Health insurers and providers who are covered entities must comply with a patient's right for the following:
- Ask to see and get a copy of your health records
- Have corrections added to your health information
- Receive a notice that tells you how your health information may be used and shared
- Decide if you want to give your permission before your health information can be used or shared for certain purposes, such as for marketing
- Get a report on when and why your health information was shared for certain purposes
- If you believe your rights are being denied or your health information isn't being protected, you can file a complaint with your provider or health insurer and/or file a complaint with HHS

Who can access and receive protected health information?

Allowable disclosures are when it's necessary to provide patient health care services such as dispensing prescriptions, patient treatment, billing, and managing the patient. The Privacy Rule sets rules and limits on who can look at and receive patient health information. Patient health care information can be shared in the following ways:

- For your treatment and care coordination
- To pay doctors and hospitals for your health care and to help run their businesses
- With your family, relatives, friends, or others you identify who are involved with your health care or your health care bills, unless you object. HIPAA allows health care providers (such as pharmacists) to give prescription drugs, medical supplies, and other health care items to a designated family member, friend, or other identified individual
- To make sure doctors give good care and nursing homes are clean and safe
- To protect the public's health, such as by reporting when the flu is in your area
- To make required reports to the police, such as reporting gunshot wounds or reports to law enforcement

Your health information **cannot** be used or shared without your written permission unless this law allows it. For example, without your authorization, your provider generally cannot:

- Give your information to your employer
- Use or share your information for marketing or advertising purposes or sell your information

REFERENCES:
1. U.S. Department of Health & Human Services (HHS). Health Information Privacy. www.hhs.gov.

Federal Pharmacy Law Exam

Objectives
- This is a 120-question exam that mimics the Federal pharmacy portion of the MPJE exam. We have focused on more questions from federal law as recent graduates have stated the exam focuses heavily on this portion.
- Use these questions as a supplement to test your self-study learning and go back to review questions missed. There will be material covered in the questions not covered in the text above so use the questions as a supplement for further learning.
- Ensure to time yourself at 1 hour and 45 minutes to complete the questions in one sitting.
- Answers can be reviewed after the federal pharmacy law exam section.
- If you do not get above a 75% score, it's prudent to review the laws discussed in the previous chapters

GOOD LUCK!

1. Within what period of time of two documented attempts of detoxification does an 18-year-old become eligible for narcotic maintenance treatment?
    A. 1 month
    B. 3 months
    C. 6 months
    D. 12 months
    E. 18 months

2. Which act, or amendment granted the FDA the authority to inspect factories?
    A. Pure Food and Drug Act
    B. Food, Drug, and Cosmetic Act
    C. Durham-Humphrey
    D. Food, Drug and Insecticide Administration
    E. FDA

3. Which of the following acts or amendments was the first to regulate the transportation of adulterated or misbranded drugs in interstate commerce?
    A. Pure Food and Drug Act
    B. Food, Drug and Cosmetic Act
    C. Food, Drug and Insecticide Administration
    D. Drug Abuse Control
    E. Drug Importation Act

4. Which of the following must be ordered using a DEA Form 222?
    I. Secobarbital Suppository
    II. Pentobarbital Injection
    III. Amobarbital Capsule

    A. I only
    B. III only
    C. I & II only
    D. II & III only
    E. I, II, & III

5. Which of the following items must be ordered from a wholesaler on DEA order Form 222?
    I. Morphine Sulfate, extended release tablet 100 mg
    II. Meperidine HCL, injection 50 mg/mL
    III. Diazepam tablet 5 mg

    A. I only
    B. III only
    C. I & II only
    D. II & III only
    E. I, II, & III

6. Which of the following products is classified as Schedule III controlled substance?
   I. A product containing 90 mg of codeine per dose
   II. A product containing 15 mg of hydrocodone per dose
   III. A product that contains 3 mg of diphenoxylate and 25 mcg of atropine sulfate per dose

   A. I only
   B. III only
   C. I & II only
   D. II & III only
   E. I, II, & III

7. All of the following would be considered as incidences of misbranding EXCEPT:
   A. The active drug is not identified on the label
   B. The original bottle of 40 contains only 35 tablets
   C. The names of inactive ingredients are not on the label
   D. The level of the drug in the product is 10% V/V but the label states 15% V/V
   E. The pharmacist dispenses a drug without the prescription

8. Partial refilling of which of the following prescriptions of controlled substances may be granted upon request of the patient?
   I. Valium
   II. Concerta
   III. Alfenta

   A. I only
   B. III only
   C. I & II only
   D. II & III only
   E. I, II, & III

9. The formulary of a pharmacy providing services under MMA (Medicare Modernization Act) may be limited to which of the following?
   A. The top 200 drugs
   B. Generic drugs
   C. At least one drug from each of all therapeutic categories developed by the USP
   D. Top 100 drugs
   E. Single-sourced drugs

10. Which portion of the following federal counseling regulations is (are) a requirement for each individual state?
    I. Prospective review
    II. Meta-analysis review
    III. Retrospective review

    A. I only
    B. III only
    C. I & II only

D. II & III only
E. I, II, & III

11. When a controlled substance inventory is conducted, which of the following must be included?
   I. Drugs returned by a customer
   II. Drugs ordered by a customer but not yet paid for
   III. All controlled substances dispensed over the past month

   A. I only
   B. III only
   C. I & II only
   D. II & III only
   E. I, II, & III

12. An individual is eligible for Medicare Plan D enrollment on May 8th, 2017. Which of the following is the exact period he can enroll in the Part D Plan without a penalty?
   A. February 1st to August 31st
   B. May 1st to May 31st
   C. May 1st to August 31st
   D. January 1st to December 1st
   E. May 8th to November 31st

13. Drug products of the same strength and same dosage form may be interchangeable if they are in which of the following classes? (Select ALL that apply)
   A. A
   B. BC
   C. B
   D. BS
   E. AB

14. If the following DEA number is authentic MS242651_ Which of the following is true about the letter S and the last missing digit?
   A. S is the first letter of the practitioner's last name; 1 is the missing digit
   B. S is the practitioner's code; 1 is the missing digit
   C. S is the first letter of the practitioner's last name; 0 is the missing digit
   D. S is the first letter of the practitioner's first name; 1 is the missing digit
   E. S is the first letter of the practitioner's first name; 0 is the missing digit

15. Which one of the following is NOT true about the Pure Food and Drug Act? (Select ALL that apply)
   A. This law was passed because of the mistaken use of diethylene glycol that lead to death
   B. The law prohibits the commerce of foods, drugs and cosmetics to be adulterated or misbranded
   C. This law was passed by the congress in 1938
   D. The law failed to protect the public
   E. This law was passed by the congress in 1906

16. Which drug is correctly assigned to its schedule?
    A. Schedule III - 1.5 g of codeine/100 mL
    B. Schedule III - 350 mg of ethylmorphine/100 mL
    C. Schedule IV - 300 mg of ethylmorphine/100 mL
    D. Schedule IV - 150 mg of dihydrocodeine/100 mL
    E. Schedule III - 350 mg of dihydrocodeine/100 mL

17. Health professionals self-prescribing is acceptable:
    I. In most states
    II. Nationwide
    III. It is not acceptable at all

    A. I only
    B. III only
    C. I & II only
    D. II & III only
    E. I, II, & III

18. Examples of drugs that can be exempted from child-resistant packaging requirements are:
    I. No drugs are exempted
    II. Acetaminophen effervescent tablets with 20% of the drug
    III. Aspirin effervescent tablets containing 15% of the drug

    A. I only
    B. III only
    C. I & II only
    D. II & III only
    E. I, II, & III

19. A pharmacy should limit interstate distribution of compounding prescription products to not more than _____% of the total prescriptions filled by the pharmacy.
    A. 2
    B. 5
    C. 10
    D. 15
    E. 20

20. Under which of the following conditions may practitioners of "Traditional Chinese Medicine" sell ephedra containing products?
    A. The level of ephedra is less than 2 mg per dose
    B. Only a 5-day supply of the product is sold
    C. The label does not indicate that the product is a dietary supplement
    D. A prescription is issued for the product
    E. Sales are illegal

21. How should sales of drug products covered by the Combat Methamphetamine Epidemic Act be recorded?
    A. Electronic tracking
    B. Doctor's prescription
    C. Bound logbook
    D. Photocopy of purchaser's ID
    E. No record is required

22. The DEA registration form 363 is required from which of the following entities?
    A. Narcotic Treatment Programs
    B. Researchers
    C. Pharmacies
    D. Medical center
    E. Manufacturers

23. What is the main purpose of the Phase 3 clinical trial for a new drug?
    A. To evaluate the drug's safety on animals
    B. To determine adverse effects and dosage
    C. To determine the drug's effectiveness versus the effectiveness of the gold standard
    D. To determine whether the drug can be safely given to humans
    E. To assess the marketability of the drug

24. What is the term for a pharmaceutical agent that has been developed specifically to treat a rare medical condition?
    A. Orphan drug
    B. Targeted drug
    C. Type 3 drug
    D. Type N drug
    E. Subsidized drug

25. What is the correct order for the 3 segments of the NDC code?
    A. Package Segment, Labeler Code, Product Segment
    B. Product Segment, Labeler Code, Package Segment
    C. Labeler Code, Package Segment, Product Segment
    D. Package Segment, Product Segment, Labeler Code
    E. Labeler Code, Product Segment, Package Segment

26. A drug is found to be under-strength, although it is not used to treat a life-threatening disease. What type of recall will be required?
    A. Class I
    B. Class II
    C. Class III
    D. Class IV
    E. No recall is required

27. Which profession or status is student loan forbearance offered based off federal regulations?
    A. Medical Residency
    B. Pharmacy Residency
    C. Dental Residency
    D. A, B, C
    E. A, C

28. For a drug to be considered Pharmaceutically Equivalent, all of the following must be true EXCEPT:
    A. Identical amounts of the same active ingredient
    B. Identical strength or concentration
    C. Same route of administration
    D. Same excipients
    E. Same dosage form

29. Which of the following would NOT be a privacy violation under HIPPA?
    I. Leaving an extensive message regarding a script with the patient's spouse
    II. Allowing a pharmaceutical sales rep to review the script files of only the patients who use the firm's products
    III. Mailing a script reminder to a patient in a sealed envelope

    A. I only
    B. III only
    C. I & II only
    D. II & III only
    E. I, II, & III

30. There is positive evidence that a new drug could create a risk to the human fetus based on investigational studies. However, the potential benefits of the drug may still justify use of the drug in pregnant women despite these possible risks. What pregnancy category would this drug be classified in?
    A. Category A
    B. Category B
    C. Category C
    D. Category D
    E. Category X

31. Heroin would be classified as which type of controlled substance?
    A. I
    B. II
    C. III
    D. IV
    E. V

32. Which of these would be classified as Schedule III controlled substances?
    I. Anabolic Steroids
    II. Marinol
    III. MS Contin

    A. I only
    B. III only
    C. I & II only
    D. II & III only
    E. I, II, & III

33. Schedule III, IV, and V controlled substance prescriptions may be transmitted to a community pharmacy by which of the following means?
    I. Written
    II. Oral
    III. Fax
    IV. Electronic

    A. I, II, III & IV
    B. I, II & III only
    C. I & II only
    D. I, III & IV only
    E. I only

34. A community pharmacist dispenses a partial supply of a C-II controlled substance. Within what period of time must the pharmacist dispense the balance, otherwise the balance may not be dispensed?
    A. 24 hours
    B. 48 hours
    C. 72 hours
    D. 7 days
    E. 14 days

35. A new community pharmacy must register itself with the DEA before it can order and dispense controlled substances. What form does such pharmacy use to initially register with DEA?
    A. DEA Form 41
    B. DEA Form 106
    C. DEA Form 222
    D. DEA Form 224
    E. No form will need to be filed

36. What form does a permitted pharmacy complete in order to destroy damaged, outdated or otherwise unwanted controlled substances?
    A. DEA Form 41
    B. DEA Form 106
    C. DEA Form 222
    D. DEA Form 224
    E. No form will need to be completed

37. Someone broke into your pharmacy, but no medications were stolen. What form do you need to file when you discover that no CS drugs have been stolen?
    A. DEA Form 41
    B. DEA Form 106
    C. DEA Form 222
    D. DEA Form 224
    E. No form will need to be filed

38. Which about controlled substance medications is correct? Select all that apply.
    A. Partial refilling of CIII-V RXs is not permitted
    B. Pharmacies placing emergency kits containing CS medications in LTCFs are responsible for the proper control & accountability of such kits within the facility
    C. RXs for CIII-V drugs filled by central fill pharmacies for community pharmacies cannot be refilled
    D. Any community pharmacy that accepts electronic RXs written for CS medications must register as an online pharmacy
    E. Physicians are legally permitted to prescribe methadone (CII) for pain

39. A DEA registrant plans to transfer its business to another registrant. Within what period of time must DEA be notified?
    A. 5 days before the transfer
    B. 7 days before the transfer
    C. 10 days before the transfer
    D. 14 days before the transfer
    E. 30 days before the transfer

40. Which schedule of controlled substance medications must a community pharmacy keep in a locked cabinet?
    A. Schedule I only
    B. Schedule II only
    C. Schedule I & Schedule II drugs only
    D. Schedule II – Schedule V drugs
    E. None of the above, as federal law does not require controlled substances to be kept in locked cabinets

41. How can controlled substances prescription records at a community pharmacy without an electronic order processing system be stored?
    I. 2 Files: One file for all controlled substances & one file for all non-controlled drugs
    II. 3 Files: One file for all Schedule II controlled substances, one file for Schedule III-V controlled substances, & one file for all non-controlled drugs
    III. 2 Files: One file for all Schedule II controlled substances & one file for all other drugs (non-controlled & Schedule III-V)

    A. I only
    B. II only
    C. III only
    D. II & III only
    E. I, II & III

42. Which of the following about inventory records of controlled substances is incorrect? Select all that apply.
    A. A pharmacy has complied with the CSA if it inventories a newly-scheduled or rescheduled drug within 30 days of the change
    B. Inventories for controlled substances must be completed biennially
    C. Exact counts must be made only in those instances where the container holds 1,000 or more tablets/capsules
    D. Inventory records of CII drugs must be kept separate from the inventory records of CIII-V drugs
    E. Record must be made of whether the inventory was conducted at the beginning or close of business

43. Copy 3 of DEA Form 222 stays in the custody of which entity?
    A. Supplier of the drug
    B. Pharmacy
    C. DEA
    D. Wholesale distributor
    E. Recipient of the drug

44. In states where nurse practitioners may prescribe controlled substances as mid-level practitioners. What letter will that number begin with?
    A. A
    B. B
    C. M
    D. N
    E. P

45. Facsimiles may serve as original prescriptions for Schedule II's for which of the following? Select all that apply.
    A. Any Schedule II substance for a hospice patient
    B. Schedule II narcotic substances compounded by a pharmacy for direct IV administration to a patient undergoing home infusion
    C. Any Schedule II medication for a patient residing in a long-term care facility
    D. Any Schedule II medication for patients of a community pharmacy
    E. Any Schedule II medication for patients of a community pharmacy in emergency situations

46. The Rx label for drugs in Schedule(s)_____ must contain the following warning: "CAUTION: Federal law prohibits the transfer of this drug to any person other than the patient for whom it was prescribed".
    A. I & II only
    B. II only
    C. II & III only
    D. II, III & IV only
    E. II, III, IV, & V only

47. A pharmacist may partially dispense prescriptions for Schedule II controlled substances for an individual residing in a LTCF who has been diagnosed with a terminal illness. How many days are the prescriptions valid for unless terminated earlier by discontinuance of the medication?

A. 7
B. 30
C. 60
D. 180
E. 365

48. On January 1, 2018, a pharmacist partially dispenses Synalgos-DC® with codeine. What is/was the last date the balance to be filled?
    A. January 4, 2018
    B. January 8, 2018
    C. June 30, 2018
    D. December 31, 2018
    E. None of the above because a pharmacist, under federal law, cannot partially dispense drugs in this CSA Schedule

49. Which is correct about the over-the-counter sales of CV meds? Select all that apply.
    A. Not more than 240 ml. (8 fluid ounces) of any substance containing opium may be distributed at retail to the same purchaser in any given 48-hour period without a valid RX
    B. All purchasers must provide a valid photo ID, regardless of whether or not the pharmacist knows him/her
    C. The purchaser must be at least 21 years' old
    D. A student pharmacist under the direct supervision of a pharmacist is legally authorized to distribute such drugs
    E. A pharmacy technician may ring up the sale for such drugs after the pharmacist has fulfilled all legal/professional responsibilities

50. How can a community pharmacy transmit controlled-substance prescription information to a central fill pharmacy?
    I. A pharmacist in the community pharmacy may phone in a prescription for a controlled substance in Schedules II-V, provided that the oral order is given only to a pharmacist at the central fill pharmacy
    II. A prescription for a controlled substance in Schedules II-V can be transmitted electronically by the community pharmacy to the central fill pharmacy
    III. A facsimile of a prescription for a controlled substance in Schedules II-V may be provided by the community pharmacy to the central fill pharmacy

    A. I only
    B. II only
    C. III only
    D. II & III only
    E. I, II & III

51. Dr. Brown is a practitioner & not registered as an opioid treatment program. Which is correct?
    A. Dr. Brown is strictly prohibited from prescribing methadone to her patient for this indication because she is not registered as an OTP
    B. Dr. Brown is permitted to administer up to a day's supply of the drug for this indication for up to 72 hours
    C. Dr. Brown is strictly prohibited from administering the drug to her patient for this indication, for any length of time, because she is not registered as an OTP

D. A & B only
E. A & C only

52. A pharmacy registered as a dispenser doesn't need to register as a distributor as long as it does not exceed what percent of controlled substances dispensed by the pharmacy in a calendar year?
    A. 5
    B. 10
    C. 20
    D. 25
    E. 50

53. Abuse of a what class of controlled substance medications may lead to moderate or low physical dependence or high psychological dependence?
    A. Schedule I
    B. Schedule II
    C. Schedule III
    D. Schedule IV
    E. Schedule V

54. For how long is a pharmacy's DEA registration effective?
    A. 6 months
    B. 1 year
    C. 2 years
    D. 3 years
    E. 5 years

55. Which statement about ordering &/or transferring Schedule II medications is correct?
    I. A pharmacy may transfer a bottle of a CII medication to another pharmacy, provided that the pharmacy transferring the drug properly executes a DEA form 222
    II. A pharmacy may purchase a bottle of a CII medication from a wholesale distributor, provided that the distributor properly executes a DEA form 222
    III. A pharmacy may order a bottle of a CII medication electronically, provided that the pharmacy signs an order form using a DEA-issued digital signature

    A. III only
    B. I & II only
    C. I & III only
    D. II only
    E. I, II & III

56. Which if the following is required under the Methamphetamine Production Prevention Act of 2008?
    A. Seller must require all purchasers of PSE to sign the sales logbook, either manually or electronically
    B. Seller must maintain each entry in the sales logbook for a minimum of 5 years
    C. All purchasers of PSE must present government issued photographic identification
    D. If the seller uses a bound paper sales logbook, he/she must affix a printed sticker next to the signature line that displays product name, quantity, name of purchaser, date & address, or a unique identification that can be linked to that information
    E. All of the above are required under MAPA

57. The drug products regulated by the federal Combat Methamphetamine Epidemic Act of 2005 are restricted to sale of what quantity (per patient) in one day?
    A. 1.2g
    B. 2.4g
    C. 3.6g
    D. 4.8g
    E. 6.0g

58. Which statement regarding multiple Schedule II prescriptions written on the same day for the same drug & patient is correct?
    A. Each RX must be dated on the day the prescription is to be dispensed.
    B. The prescriber must specifically indicate on each RX the earliest date on which each RX may be dispensed.
    C. The total quantity prescribed cannot exceed a 90-day supply.
    D. All of the above
    E. A & C only

59. Which statement about refill transfers of Schedules III through V controlled substances is correct?
    A. Transfers can only be done once if the pharmacies do not share a real-time online database
    B. All refills may be transferred electronically if the pharmacies share a real-time online database
    C. Transferring pharmacist must write "VOID" on the face of the transferred RX
    D. Transfer must occur between two pharmacists
    E. All of the above

60. If a pharmacy opts to print out a daily controlled substances refill record, how long must this record be maintained by the pharmacy?
    A. 6 months
    B. 1 year
    C. 2 years
    D. 3 years
    E. 5 years

61. What information must a controlled substance prescription contain?
    I. Patient name and address
    II. Practitioner's name, address, and DEA number
    III. Drug name and strength
    IV. Directions for use
    V. Date of issue

    A. I, II, III, IV & V
    B. I & II only
    C. I, II & IV only
    D. I, II & V only
    E. I, II, IV & V only

62. Which of the following is true about Risk Evaluation & Mitigation Strategies (REMS)?
    I. REMS are not required for generic products

II. REMS only be required during the drug pre-approval process
III. REMS can be required for a single drug or a class of drugs

A. I only
B. II only
C. III only
D. I & III only
E. I, II & III

63. How can drug products be switched from prescription status to OTC status?
    I. Manufacturer submits a supplemental NDA
    II. Petition for reclassification is filed
    III. Via the OTC Review Process

    A. I only
    B. II only
    C. III only
    D. II & III only
    E. I, II & III

64. What is the name of the voluntary system for healthcare professionals to report ADRs to FDA?
    A. MEDMARX
    B. STEPS
    C. MEDWATCH
    D. VAERS
    E. CLIA

65. Which of the following recalls is implemented in instances when a product is not likely to cause adverse health consequences?
    A. Class I
    B. Class II
    C. Class III
    D. Class IV
    E. Class V

66. Big Pharma, Inc. wants to change the salt of its existing blockbuster medication from acetate to carbonate. Through which mechanism is Big Pharma likely to proceed in order to gain FDA approval for this change?
    A. Full NDA
    B. 505(b)(2)
    C. ANDA
    D. IND
    E. Any of the above mechanisms are appropriate

67. From what potential violation of the FDCA does the IND provision provide an exemption?
    A. Adulteration
    B. Compounding
    C. Introduction into interstate commerce of an unapproved new drug

D. Misbranding
E. Current Good Manufacturing Practices

68. Mrs. Pill is a patient for whom child-resistant medication vial closures are inappropriate. Under the Poison Prevention Packaging Act, who may make a blanket request that all medications be dispensed in non-child resistant closures?
    A. The prescriber only
    B. The patient only
    C. The pharmacist only
    D. Either the prescriber or the patient only
    E. Either the prescriber or the pharmacist only

69. Two products are listed in the Orange Book. One product is rated as AB and the other is rated as AA. What can be concluded based on the Orange book about the equivalence of the two products?
    A. They are therapeutically equivalent
    B. They are bioequivalent
    C. They are rated as bioequivalent
    D. They are not rated as therapeutically equivalent
    E. They are not therapeutically equivalent

70. Which of the following levothyroxine 0.025 mg products are rated as equivalent to one another?
    A. Levothyroxine Sodium (Mylan) & Levothroid (Lloyd)
    B. Unithroid (Stevens J) & Levothroid (Lloyd)
    C. Synthroid (Abbott) & Levothroid (Lloyd)
    D. All of the above
    E. A & B only

71. In the package insert, there is a section that describes any situation in which the drug should not be used because the risk of use clearly outweighs the benefit. What is that section called?
    A. Warnings
    B. Precautions
    C. Prohibitions
    D. Contraindications
    E. Limitations

72. The federal agency that regulates the advertising of OTC drugs is:
    A. The Centers for Medicare and Medicaid Services (CMS)
    B. The Food and Drug administration (FDA)
    C. The Federal Trade Commission (FTC)
    D. The Drug Enforcement Agency (DEA)
    E. Center for Drug Evaluation and Research (CDER)

73. Prescription drug products containing estrogen must be dispensed with what?
    A. Package insert
    B. Patient package insert
    C. Medication guide
    D. REMS
    E. Pamphlet about the importance of routinely taking the drug written by the dispensing pharmacy

74. The term "label" refers to which of the following when it is accompanying an article of drug and is not upon the immediate container of drug?
    A. Written matter only
    B. Written or printed matter only
    C. Printed or graphic matter only
    D. Written or graphic matter only
    E. None of the above

75. Tamper-evident packaging refers to which of the following?
    A. Packaging that contains an indicator or barrier that if missing can reasonably be expected to alert the consumer to the possibility that tampering has occurred
    B. A permanent barrier to the product that only the consumer can remove after purchase
    C. A permanent barrier that the store removes before the consumer purchases
    D. An alarm that notifies the retailer that a product has been tampered with
    E. A statement on the outside of the package that alerts the consumer to the possibility of tampering

76. Which of the following drug(s) is/are exempt from poison prevention packaging? Select all that apply.
    A. Estrogen-containing oral contraceptives in memory-aid packaging
    B. Sublingual nitroglycerin
    C. Combination colestipol products
    D. Anhydrous cholestyramine in any form
    E. Bottles of prednisone in any size & strength

77. Which of the following laws required drug manufacturers to prove to FDA the effectiveness of their products before marketing them?
    A. Durham-Humphrey Amendment of 1951
    B. Kefauver-Harris Drug Amendments of 1962
    C. Drug Price Competition and Patent Term Restoration Act of 1984
    D. Food and Drug Administration Modernization Act of 1997
    E. Food and Drug Administration Amendments Act (FDAAA) of 2007

78. A generic manufacturer wishes to obtain approval of a product believed to be bioequivalent to the FDA-approved innovator product. Through what mechanism will the generic manufacturer most frequently obtain this approval?
    A. Supplemental NDA
    B. Abbreviated NDA
    C. Additional NDA
    D. Bioequivalency NDA
    E. Full NDA

79. Which of the following is a/are requirement(s) of the Compounding Quality Act law?
    A. Compounded medications must be for an identified individual patient on receipt of a valid RX.
    B. Compounding in advance of an RX is allowed, but in "limited quantities," based on historical RX orders.
    C. Drugs removed or withdrawn from the market because they are unsafe or not effective may not be used in compounding.

D. Generally, a compounded drug may not be "essentially a copy" of an FDA-approved drug, unless the alteration to that copied product produces a significant difference for the patient.
E. All of the above

80. According to the Health Insurance Portability and Accountability Act (HIPAA), under which situation should the pharmacist generally provide only the "minimum necessary" information about a particular patient? Select all that apply.
    A. When responding to a prescriber's request to discuss the treatment of the patient
    B. When advising the patient about the use of her medications
    C. When communicating with a PBM about potential coverage for a drug a physician has prescribed for the patient
    D. When speaking with a software vendor about a glitch in the patient's electronic medical record
    E. When meeting with the pharmacy's attorneys about an RX that was filled incorrectly, causing injury to the patient

81. Which device requires FDA pre-market approval?
    A. Replacement heart valve
    B. Crutch
    C. Liquid bandage
    D. Tongue depressor
    E. Oxygen mask

82. A drug is misbranded if:
    A. Its labeling is false or misleading.
    B. It is manufactured by a drug company not registered with the FDA.
    C. Its manufacturer fails to comply with a REMS requirement.
    D. It is a compounded drug, & the advertising or promotion of it is false or misleading.
    E. All of the above

83. A manufacturer of a nutritional shake decides to add calcium to its product. Which of the following statements can the manufacturer make in the product's labeling and still have it considered a dietary supplement and not a drug?
    A. "Treats osteoporosis"
    B. "You'll feel great"
    C. "Cures the common cold"
    D. "Prevents colorectal cancer"
    E. "Mitigates the incidence of obesity"

84. The *primary* purpose of a Phase 2 clinical trial is to determine:
    A. Safety
    B. Efficacy
    C. Toxicity
    D. Compatibility with other drugs
    E. Cost

85. How many refills may a practitioner authorize on a Schedule II controlled substance prescription?
    A. 0
    B. 1

C. 2
D. 5
E. 12

86. What does federal law say about e-prescribing controlled substances?
    A. Partial fills of e-prescriptions for Schedule II controlled substances are NOT allowed
    B. An office manager can act as a proxy and electronically sign e-prescriptions for a prescriber
    C. E-prescriptions must be maintained electronically for five years
    D. Refills are not allowed for Schedule III controlled substance e-prescriptions
    E. E-prescriptions must be maintained electronically for two years

87. Which is an acceptable Schedule II prescription according to federal law?
    A. A faxed prescription for fentanyl patch 100 mg, one every 3 days, #10 for a patient in hospice
    B. A written script for morphine 10 mg, one every 8 hours PRN pain, #60 with 1 refill
    C. A written prescription filled out and signed by a registered nurse for morphine 60 mg, one daily, #30
    D. A phoned in prescription for oxycodone 20 mg, one BID, #60 to be delivered to a homebound patient
    E. A faxed prescription for fentanyl patch 100 mg, one every 3 days, #5

88. What does federal law mandate for multiple prescriptions for Schedule II controlled substances?
    A. There is a limit of 3 prescriptions that can be written on the same day for the same Schedule II controlled substance for a single patient
    B. The date on the prescription should be the same day that they are written and cannot be post-dated
    C. They can total no more than a 90-day supply
    D. They can total no more than a 120-day supply
    E. They must all be filled on the same day they are dropped off at the pharmacy

89. What could you share with a colleague regarding partial fills of Schedule II controlled substances according to federal law?
    A. You are not required to notify the prescriber if you fill the remaining quantity on a partially filled prescription within 7 days
    B. They're allowed only for patients in long-term care facilities
    C. You don't need to document the amount dispensed when you are planning on dispensing the remainder within 72 hours
    D. If you do not dispense the remaining quantity within 72 hours, it will be voided
    E. If you do not dispense the remaining quantity within 24 hours, it will be voided

90. What is a requirement for filling prescriptions for methadone or buprenorphine according to federal law?
    A. A valid prescription for buprenorphine for treating pain requires a valid DEA number only
    B. Naloxone can only be dispensed by a retail pharmacy for the treatment of opioid dependence
    C. Prescribers must obtain a waiver to use buprenorphine for the treatment of pain
    D. Methadone can only be dispensed by a retail pharmacy for the treatment of opioid dependence
    E. When methadone is used for opioid dependence the prescription only needs to include a DEA number

91. Which is a federal rule regarding inventory requirements for Schedule II through V drugs?
    A. You need to get an exact count of the number of units of each Schedule III and IV drug in your facility
    B. A full inventory of Schedule II through V drugs must be performed at least every year
    C. Inventory forms can be kept outside the pharmacy as long as they are readily retrievable
    D. A drug changing from Schedule III to II can be inventoried per its new schedule when the next inventory is due
    E. A full inventory of Schedule II through V drugs must be performed at least every six months

92. According to FEDERAL law, which is an acceptable form of ID for an adult over 18 years old purchasing a pseudoephedrine product without a prescription?
    A. Social Security card
    B. Birth certificate
    C. U.S. military card
    D. Credit card
    E. ATM Debit card

93. What is a quantity limit imposed by the CMEA?
    A. You cannot sell more than 3.6 g per day of pseudoephedrine HCl to a customer
    B. You cannot sell a customer more than 9 g of pseudoephedrine base per day
    C. You can sell a patient any amount of pseudoephedrine liquid since it is extremely dilute
    D. Non-liquid forms of pseudoephedrine must be sold in blister packs or unit-dose packaging
    E. You cannot sell a customer more than 7.5 g of pseudoephedrine base per day

94. What information can you share with a new employee about DEA Form 222?
    A. It's the form to use when ordering Schedule III controlled substances
    B. If an erasure is made while filling out the form, it will not be accepted by the supplier
    C. Any person employed by the pharmacy can sign Form 222
    D. Your wholesaler must provide the exact package size you specify on Form 222
    E. Your supplier must provide the exact package size you specify on Form 222

95. What should you do in order to comply with DEA 106 procedures?
    A. You must notify the DEA of any theft of controlled substances within one business day of discovery
    B. Your pharmacy is responsible for notifying the DEA of the loss of controlled substances if your receipt from your distributor doesn't match what you received from them
    C. A significant loss is when you lose more than 40% of the total amount of any single controlled substance
    D. A significant loss is when you lose more than 20% of the total amount of any single controlled substance
    E. You need to complete DEA Form 106 right away when you discover missing controlled substances

96. What can you tell a colleague about exclusivity rights?
    A. They give the brand-name drug company property rights to the new drug
    B. Pediatric exclusivity adds an extra 6 months to the life of a patent
    C. Orphan drug exclusivity gives 5-years market exclusivity
    D. Pediatric exclusivity adds an extra 12 months to the life of a patent
    E. They give the brand-name drug manufacturer marketing rights for an unlimited time

97. What does the first manufacturer to successfully bring a generic drug to market gain?
    A. Nothing more than other manufacturers
    B. Significant market share
    C. 30-day generic exclusivity
    D. 180-day generic drug exclusivity
    E. 240-day generic drug exclusivity

98. In order to be approved for marketing, a generic drug must meet ALL of which criteria?
    A. The same rate and extent of absorption
    B. The same strength or concentration, route of administration, and dosage form
    C. The same rate and extent of absorption AND the same strength, route of administration, and dosage form
    D. The same strength, route of administration, and dosage form, AND inactive ingredients
    E. None

99. How much variability in drug levels does FDA allow between brand name products and their generic counterparts?
    A. The same as the variability between different batches of the brand-name drug
    B. 12.5%
    C. 25%
    D. 45%
    E. 23%

100. Which is an accurate description of the Orange Book coding system?
    A. The first letter of the Orange Book code determines the dosage form of the drug
    B. AB2 codes identify drugs that are not FDA-approved
    C. Drug products designated with a "T" code are therapeutically equivalent
    D. BD codes represent drug products that are not therapeutic equivalents
    E. DB codes represent drug products that are not therapeutic equivalents

101. Which is an accurate description of biosimilars?
    A. Biosimilars are true generics to a parent biological product
    B. It is possible for biosimilar products to also be classified as interchangeable
    C. Biosimilar products are listed in FDA's Orange Book
    D. Biosimilar products are listed in FDA's Green Book
    E. Differences in clinically inactive components are not allowable in biosimilar products

102. When can FDA require REMS for a specific drug?
    A. At any time, pre- or post-approval
    B. Only prior to marketing
    C. Only after marketing
    D. Only after marketing based on post-marketing surveillance
    E. If there is a large number of minor side effects

103. Which of the following is an Element to Assure Safe Use (ETASU)?
    A. A Dear Healthcare Provider Letter
    B. A REMS advertisement in a major journal
    C. A MedGuide

D. A Patient Registry
E. A Drug Guide

104. Which of the following is a part of the long-acting and extended-release opioid REMS?
    A. A mandatory education program for pharmacists
    B. A volunteer education program for prescribers
    C. An implementation system
    D. A volunteer education program for pharmacists
    E. A mandatory education program for prescribers

105. What is required by federal law when logging methamphetamine precursor sales?
    A. You must make sure that the patient name matches their identification
    B. You always have to enter the patient's name and address
    C. You must keep the logbook for at least 7 years
    D. You have to keep a hardcopy logbook
    E. You must keep the logbook for at least 10 years

106. Which is an accurate limit on precursor sales imposed by the CMEA?
    A. You cannot sell more than 3.6 g of pseudoephedrine sulfate to a customer per day
    B. You cannot sell more than 9 g of pseudoephedrine sulfate to a customer in a 90-day period
    C. You cannot sell more than 146 tablets of pseudoephedrine HCL 30 mg in a single day to the same customer
    D. Non-liquid dosage forms of methamphetamine precursors can be sold as loose capsules or tablets
    E. You cannot sell more than 9 g of pseudoephedrine chloride to a customer in a 90-day period

107. Which transaction can be completed based on federal precursor drug sales limits?
    A. 830 mL of pseudoephedrine HCl 30 mg/5 mL syrup per customer per day
    B. 30 tablets of pseudoephedrine HCl 120 mg per customer per day
    C. 155 tablets of pseudoephedrine sulfate 60 mg per customer per day
    D. 90 tablets of pseudoephedrine sulfate 240 mg to a customer in 30 days
    E. 120 tablets of pseudoephedrine sulfate 240 mg to a customer in 30 days

108. What can happen if CMEA rules are violated?
    A. Financial penalties for failing to comply with CMEA requirements can be up to $500
    B. Imprisonment up to 1 year if the violation is committed unknowingly
    C. You can be imprisoned for up to 10 years for knowingly violating CMEA
    D. Your pharmacy may no longer be able to sell precursor drugs
    E. Imprisonment up to 2 years if the violation is committed unknowingly

109. What is important to know about the Drug Quality and Security Act?
    A. Large scale compounding ("outsourcing") is regulated by the FDA
    B. All compounding is regulated by the FDA
    C. Only sterile compounding is regulated by the FDA
    D. Only non-sterile compounding is regulated by the FDA
    E. Small scale compounding ("insourcing") is regulated by the FDA

110. Why can't you fill a prescription for Effexor XR capsules with venlafaxine extended-release tablets?
    A. The tablets are less effective than capsules

B. The tablets are not as safe as the capsules
C. The tablets are dosed differently than the capsules
D. The tablets are not AB-rated to the capsules
E. The capsules are less effective than tablets

111. What is important to know about the DEA requirements for suspected theft of controlled substances?
    A. You only need to report this if more than five tablets are stolen
    B. You have to report this in writing to the DEA within one business day
    C. DEA Form 106 must be submitted the very same day of discovery
    D. You have to complete a DEA Form 106 EVEN IF the investigation reveals no actual loss or theft
    E. You only need to report this if more than ten tablets are stolen

112. What's important for a pharmacist to know to prevent misbranding and adulteration?
    A. Dispensing a drug stored at room temperature when it's supposed to be refrigerated is considered adulteration
    B. You can re-use returned medications as long as it's been less than 24 hours since you dispensed them
    C. Manufacturers are responsible for providing MedGuides, not pharmacists
    D. Dispensing a light-sensitive drug in a light-resistant container is considered misbranding
    E. Dispensing a scent-sensitive drug in a scent-resistant container is considered misbranding

113. If receiving multiple schedule II prescriptions, what is the maximum day limit for the prescriptions?
    A. 30 days
    B. 60 days
    C. 90 days
    D. 120 days
    E. 160 days

114. The DEA registration form 363 is required from which of the following entities?
    A. Manufacturers
    B. Medical center
    C. Pharmacies
    D. Researchers
    E. Narcotic Treatment Programs

115. Whenever a prescription department of any community pharmacy establishment is closed, who is permitted to enter or remain in the prescription department?
    I. A pharmacy intern
    II. A pharmacy owner
    III. A pharmacist

    A. I only
    B. III only
    C. I, II, and III
    D. II and III
    E. None of the above

116. Sally is upset that her pain medications are not working. She would like to return her controlled substance prescription medication to the pharmacy. What can you do?
    A. Accept the return of unused or unwanted controlled substance medication as long as you are DEA authorized
    B. Give to your pharmacy owner and fill out DEA form 363
    C. Instruct Sally to dispose of her medications with DEA approval
    D. Only return if Sally's medication has a known recall
    E. If you made a dispensing error, you must accept Sally's medication return and refund her money

117. Which of the following references is/are useful for the safe handling of antineoplastic and hazardous drugs?
    I. OSHA Technical Manual—Section VI
    II. NIOSH Alert
    III. MSDSs

    A. I only
    B. I and II only
    C. II and III only
    D. All
    E. None of the above

118. Which of the following is/are TRUE ABOUT preparing allergen extracts as compounded sterile preparations?
    I. All allergen extracts as CSPs shall contain appropriate substances in effective concentrations to prevent the growth of microorganisms.
    II. Before beginning compounding activities, personnel perform a thorough hand-cleansing procedure by removing debris from under fingernails using a nail cleaner under running warm water followed by vigorous hand and arm washing to the elbows for at least 30 seconds with either non-antimicrobial or antimicrobial soap and water.
    III. Compounding personnel don hair covers, facial hair covers, gowns, and face masks.

    A. I only
    B. I and II only
    C. II and III only
    D. All
    E. None of the above

119. Section 503B of the Federal Food, Drug, and Cosmetic Act addresses which of the following?
    A. Traditional Compounders
    B. Outsourcing Facilities
    C. Compounding pharmacies
    D. Compounding nuclear pharmacies
    E. None of the above

120. Which of the following information is/are TRUE ABOUT PPE (Personal Protective Equipment) while reconstituting, preparing or admixing hazardous drugs?
   I. Make sure that gloves are labelled as chemotherapy [ASTM 2005] gloves
   II. Use double gloving for all activities involving hazardous drugs
   III. Use disposable gowns made of polyethylene-non-coated polypropylene

   A. I only
   B. I and II only
   C. II and III only
   D. All
   E. None of the above

Answers to Federal Pharmacy Law Exam

1. **D**
    Please view 42 CFR 8.12 - Federal opioid treatment standards. Maintenance treatment for persons under age 18. A person under 18 years of age is required to have had two documented unsuccessful attempts at short-term medical withdrawal (detoxification) or drug-free treatment within a 12-month period to be eligible for methadone maintenance treatment.

2. **B**
    The Federal Food, Drug, and Cosmetic (FDC) Act of 1938 is passed by Congress, containing new provisions:
    - Extending control to cosmetics and therapeutic devices.
    - Requiring new drugs to be shown safe before marketing-starting a new system of drug regulation.
    - Eliminating the Shirley Amendment requirement to prove intent to defraud in drug misbranding cases.
    - Providing that safe tolerances be set for unavoidable poisonous substances.
    - Authorizing standards of identity, quality, and fill-of-container for foods.
    - <u>Authorizing factory inspections</u>.
    - Adding the remedy of court injunctions to the previous penalties of seizures and prosecutions.

3. **A**
    The key to this question is the word "first". The original Pure Food and Drugs Act (by Dr. Wiley) is passed by Congress on June 30, 1906 and signed by President Theodore Roosevelt. It prohibits interstate commerce in misbranded and adulterated foods, drinks and drugs.

4. **D**
    View *http://www.deadiversion.usdoj.gov/schedules/*. Substances in this schedule have a high potential for abuse which may lead to severe psychological or physical dependence.
    - While secobarbital capsule is C-II, secobarbital suppository is C-III (Remember that multiple DEA Schedules exist based on differences in the route, form, or strength of the substances).
    - Examples of Schedule II narcotics include hydromorphone (Dilaudid®), methadone (Dolophine®), meperidine (Demerol®), oxycodone (OxyContin®, Percocet®), and fentanyl (Sublimaze®, Duragesic®). Other Schedule II narcotics include morphine, opium, codeine, and hydrocodone.
    - Examples of Schedule II narcotic stimulants include amphetamine (Dexedrine®, Adderall®), methamphetamine (Desoxyn®), and methylphenidate (Ritalin®).
    - Other Schedule II substances include: amobarbital, glutethimide, and pentobarbital.

5. **C**
    Morphine and meperidine are schedule II drugs. Diazepam is a schedule IV drug. Only schedule I & II drugs need a DEA form 222 to order.

6. **A**
    For choice I., "Not more than 1.8 grams of codeine per 100 milliliters or not more than 90 milligrams per dosage unit, with an equal or greater quantity of an isoquinoline alkaloid of opium."

For choice II., "Not more than 300 milligrams of hydrocodone per 100 milliliters or not more than 15 milligrams per dosage unit, with a fourfold or greater quantity of an isoquinoline alkaloid of opium." "Not more than 300 milligrams of hydrocodone per 100 milliliters or not more than 15 milligrams per dosage unit, with recognized therapeutic amounts of one or more active ingredients that are not controlled substances." Note: Hydrocodone has been reclassified as a C-II drug, a drug that contains any amount of hydrocodone will most likely be considered as C-II.
For Choice III., "Not more than 2.5 milligrams of diphenoxylate and not less than 25 micrograms of atropine sulfate per dosage unit."

7. **D**
   Adulteration is reducing the purity of a drug/product by adding a foreign or inferior substance to it or even removing a valuable ingredient. So, this could be a difference in strength, quality, or purity from what it was supposed to be or contains harmful or dirty/decomposed substances. Examples include making a drug in a place that results in adulteration, container system (bottle) could cause adulteration (if bottle is opened), strength/quality differs from claim on label, etc.
   Misbranding- Presence or absence of information on label of a product which is false, deceptive or misleading. Examples of this would be filling for Crestor but putting Lipitor in the bottle. Lots of examples of this pertains to the label itself (false claims of where product came from or where it was made, size of type is not accordance to standards, wrong name of drug, lack of directions or warnings, MedGuide wasn't provided when it was supposed to, etc).
   A. is considered misbranding
   B. is considered misbranding
   This is considered misbranding since the bottle is labelled to have 40 but actually contains 35
   C. is considered misbranding
   D. is considered adulterated. This is considered adulterated as the actual ingredient is inferior to what it is supposed to be
   E. is considered misbranding, view **21 U.S. Code § 353**

8. **A**
   View Title 21 CFR. PART 1306 — PRESCRIPTIONS. CONTROLLED SUBSTANCES LISTED IN SCHEDULE II. Section 1306.13 Partial filling of prescriptions for exceptions in specific cases.
   Prescriptions for schedule II-controlled substances cannot be refilled unless noted above in C21 Section 1306.13. A new prescription must be issued. Prescriptions for schedules III and IV controlled substances may be refilled up to five times in six months. Prescriptions for schedule V controlled substances may be refilled as authorized by the practitioner.
   Concerta and Alfenta are schedule II substances; Valium is a schedule IV substance. List of scheduled medications:
   http://www.deadiversion.usdoj.gov/schedules/orangebook/c_cs_alpha.pdf

9. **C**
   Part D sponsors that use a classification system that is consistent with the United States Pharmacopeia (USP), will qualify for a safe harbor, meaning that Centers for Medicare and Medicaid (CMS) will approve their formulary classification system.

Medicare drug plans cover both generic and brand-name drugs. Each plan has a list of drugs it covers, called a formulary. This list must always meet Medicare's minimum requirements (for example, plans are required to include at least 2 drug options in each drug category), but it is not required to include all prescription drugs. Medicare may allow plans to change their formularies during the year.

Two examples are: 1. If a new generic version of a covered brand-name drug becomes available, or 2. If new FDA or clinical information shows a drug to be unsafe.

Health plans cannot discontinue or reduce the coverage of a drug you are currently taking. If a formulary change is made that affects you, the plan must let you know at least 60 days before the change takes place. View: https://www.cms.gov/Medicare/Prescription-Drug-Coverage/PrescriptionDrugCovContra/downloads/chapter6.pdf

10. **B**

    Drug utilization review (DUR) is an authorized, structured, ongoing review of prescribing, dispensing and use of medication. DUR entails a drug review against criteria that results in changes to drug therapy when these criteria are not met. It involves a comprehensive review of patients' prescription and medication data before, during and after dispensing to ensure appropriate medication decision-making and positive patient outcomes. As a quality assurance measure, DUR programs provide corrective action, prescriber feedback and further evaluations. Types of DUR:
    - Prospective - evaluation of a patient's drug therapy before medication is dispensed
    - Concurrent - ongoing monitoring of drug therapy during the course of treatment
    - Retrospective - review of drug therapy after the patient has received the medication

11. **C**

    View Title 21 CFR §1304.11 Inventory requirements- extract below
    General requirements. Each inventory shall contain a complete and accurate record of **all controlled substances on hand on the date the inventory is taken**, and shall be maintained in written, typewritten, or printed form at the registered location. An inventory taken by use of an oral recording device must be promptly transcribed. **Controlled substances shall be deemed to be "on hand" if they are in the possession of or under the control of the registrant, including substances returned by a customer, ordered by a customer but not yet invoiced**, stored in a warehouse on behalf of the registrant, and substances in the possession of employees of the registrant and intended for distribution as complimentary samples. Section can be viewed here: https://www.deadiversion.usdoj.gov/21cfr/cfr/1304/1304_11.htm

12. **A**

    You can enroll in Medicare Part D coverage during your Initial Enrollment Period (IEP) for Part D, which is the period that you first become eligible for Medicare Part D. For most people, the IEP begins three months before you turn 65 years of age, includes the month you turn 65, and ends three months after. Thus, in this question three months before May is February and three months after is August.

    If you enroll in Medicare Part D during your Initial Enrollment Period, your Medicare Part D coverage will begin on the first day of the following month that you apply for the plan. If you enroll in one of the three months prior to turning 65 years of age, your Medicare Part D coverage begins on the first day of the month that you turn 65.

If you do not enroll during your Initial Enrollment Period for Part D, you can enroll into prescription drug coverage during the Annual Election Period (AEP), which occurs from October 15 to December 7 of every year. During this time, you have the chance to make changes to your current Medicare prescription drug coverage for the following year, including:
- Enrolling into a Medicare Prescription Drug Plan.
- Switching from one Medicare Prescription Drug Plan to another Prescription Drug Plan.
- Switching from a Medicare Advantage plan that does not include drug coverage to a Medicare Advantage plan that does, and vice versa.
- Dropping your Medicare prescription drug coverage entirely.

View: https://www.ehealthmedicare.com/medicare-part-d-prescription/enrollment/

13. **A, E**

The FDA considers drug products pharmaceutical equivalents if they contain the same active ingredient(s), are of the same dosage form and route of administration and are identical in strength or concentration. Bioequivalent products are products with comparable bioavailability (rate and extent of absorption) when studied under similar experimental conditions.

Drug products must demonstrate pharmaceutical equivalence and bioequivalence to be considered A-rated (therapeutic equivalents). The primary reference for therapeutic equivalence is the FDA's Approved Drug Products with Therapeutic Equivalence Evaluations, commonly known as The Orange Book. It's available as a searchable database: http://www.fda.gov/cder/ob/default.htm.

The Orange Book rates each generic with a code. This "code" has two letters and it usually begins with an "A" or a "B" (e.g., **A**B-rated, **B**N-rated, etc.). The <u>first</u> letter "A" designates products that have demonstrated therapeutic equivalence. The <u>first</u> letter "B" indicates those that have **not**. The <u>second</u> letter in the Orange Book rating code can give additional information about the product, such as its dosage form. For example, the <u>second</u> letter "A" indicates an oral dosage form, "N" indicates a product for aerosolization, "P" means a parenteral or injectable product, and "T" stands for topical. Products that have been studied and proven to be bioequivalent are AB-rated, which is the most common code you will see. In some states, only products given an "A" rating (e.g., AB-rated, AT-rated, AP-rated, etc.) in the Orange Book can be substituted. View this link for more info: http://www.fda.gov/Drugs/InformationOnDrugs/ucm537866.htm

14. **A**

A valid DEA number consists of:
- 2 letters, 6 numbers, & 1 check digit
- The first letter is a code identifying the type of registrant
- The second letter is the first letter of the registrant's last name, or "9" for registrants using a business address instead of name

A sum of the seven digits helps validate the DEA number:
- Add together the first, third and fifth digits
- Add together the second, fourth and sixth digits and multiply the sum by 2
  - Add both of these values together as the check sum
- The rightmost digit of the check sum (the digit in the ones place) is used as the check digit in the DEA number

Common first letter types:
- A – Deprecated (used by some older entities)
- B – Hospital/Clinic
- C – Practitioner
- D – Teaching Institution
- E – Manufacturer
- F – Distributor

15. **A, B, C**
The pure food and drug act was enacted in 1906 (not 1938), thus C is incorrect. Its main purpose was to ban foreign and interstate traffic in adulterated or mislabeled food and drug products and required that active ingredients be placed on the label of a drug's packaging and that drugs could not fall below purity levels established by the USP or the National Formulary. B is incorrect as it includes "cosmetics" but this act was limited to food and drugs. Choice A is incorrect as the diethylene glycol (or sulfanilamide) deaths led to the passing of the 1938 Food, Drug, and Cosmetic Act as the 1906 act failed to protect the public so it was largely replaced by the 1938 act.

16. **A**
View Title 21 CFR Part 1308 Schedules, https://www.deadiversion.usdoj.gov/21cfr/cfr/1308/1308_13.htm
C-III controlled substance: "Not more than 1.8 grams of codeine per 100 milliliters or not more than 90 milligrams per dosage unit, with an equal or greater quantity of an isoquinoline alkaloid of opium"

17. **A**
Laws governing physicians differ significantly from state to state. On a federal level there is no guidance and most states do not have a defined law regarding self-prescribing.

18. **B**
View the Poison Prevention Packaging guidance from 2010- https://www.cpsc.gov/s3fs-public/384.pdf
There are two exceptions to child-resistant packaging from the guidance above-
1. Effervescent tablets or granules containing not more than 15 percent acetaminophen or aspirin, provided the dry tablet or granules have an oral LD50 of 5 grams or more per kilogram of body weight.
2. Unfavored acetaminophen or aspirin- containing preparations in powder form (other than those intended for Pediatric use) that are packaged in unit doses providing not more than 13 grains of acetaminophen or 15.4 grains of aspirin per unit dose.

19. **B**
Under the Pharmacy Compounding of Human Drug Products Under Section 503A of the Federal Food, Drug, and Cosmetic Act it limits interstate distribution at a baseline of 5%. View: http://www.fda.gov/downloads/Drugs/GuidanceComplianceRegulatoryInformation/Guidances/UCM469119.pdf

20. **C**

According to Section III B of the final rule, the FDA ban applies only to "dietary supplements containing ephedrine alkaloids, including, but not limited to, those from the botanical species *ephedra sinica* Stapf, *ephedra equisetina* Bunge, *ephedra intermedia* var. tibetica Stapf, *ephedra distachya* L., *sida cordifolia* L. and *pinellia terneta* (Thunb.) Makino or their extracts." However, "conventional food products" that contain ephedrine alkaloids are exempted, as are "OTC (over-the-counter) or prescription drugs that contain ephedrine alkaloids."

Section IIIB also includes a caveat for the use of ephedra as it applies to "traditional Asian medicine". This final rule does not affect the use of ephedra preparations in traditional Asian medicine. This rule applies only to products regulated as dietary supplements.

21. **C**
    Logbook Provisions
    View: https://www.deadiversion.usdoj.gov/meth/cma2005_general_info.pdf
    Please note, as Oregon has classified these substances as prescription only, there is no logbook for them kept in Oregon pharmacies. Under Oregon law, the best answer for this question would be B, as a doctors' prescription provides the record for the pharmacy of the sales of these products.

22. **A**
    - DEA Form 224a – Retail Pharmacy, Hospital/Clinic, Practitioner, Teaching Institution, or Mid-Level Practitioner
    - DEA Form 225a – Manufacturer, Distributor, Researcher, Analytical Laboratory, Importer, Exporter
    - DEA Form 363a – Narcotic Treatment Programs
    - DEA Form 510a – Domestic Chemical

    View: https://www.deadiversion.usdoj.gov/drugreg/

23. **C**
    Phase 1
    Patients: 20 to 100 healthy volunteers or people with the disease/condition.
    Length of Study: Several months
    Purpose: Safety and dosage
    Approximately 70% of drugs move to the next phase

    Phase 2
    Patients: Up to several hundred people with the disease/condition.
    Length of Study: Several months to 2 years
    Purpose: Efficacy and side effects
    Approximately 33% of drugs move to the next phase

    Phase 3
    Patients: 300 to 3,000 volunteers who have the disease or condition
    Length of Study: 1 to 4 years
    Purpose: Efficacy and monitoring of adverse reactions
    Approximately 25-30% of drugs move to the next phase

    Phase 4
    Patients: Several thousand volunteers who have the disease/condition
    Purpose: Safety and efficacy

Purpose of phase III trials: Efficacy and monitoring of adverse reactions
View: http://www.fda.gov/ForPatients/Approvals/Drugs/ucm405622.htm

24. **A**
An orphan drug is defined in the 1984 amendments of the U.S. Orphan Drug Act (ODA) as a drug intended to treat a condition affecting fewer than 200,000 persons in the United States (rare medical condition), or which will not be profitable within 7 years following approval by the FDA
http://www.fda.gov/downloads/drugs/developmentapprovalprocess/smallbusinessassistance/ucm311928.pdf

25. **E**
The 3 segments of the NDC identify the labeler, the product, and the commercial package size. The first set of numbers in the NDC identifies the labeler (manufacturer, repackager, or distributer). The second set of numbers is the product code, which identifies the specific strength, dosage form (i.e., capsule, tablet, liquid) and formulation of a drug for a specific manufacturer. Finally, the third set is the package code, which identifies package sizes and types. The labeler code is assigned by the FDA, while the product and package code are assigned by the labeler.
View: https://www.drugs.com/ndc.html

26. **B**
Class I - A reasonable probability exists that use of the product will cause or lead to serious adverse health events or death. An example of a product that could fall into this category is a label mix-up on a lifesaving drug.
Class II - The probability exists that use of the product will cause adverse health events that are temporary or medically reversible. One example is a drug that is understrength but that is not used to treat life-threatening situations.
Class III - The use of this product will probably not cause an adverse health event. Examples might be a container defect, off taste, or color in a liquid.
View: http://www.careerstep.com/blog/pharmacy-technician-news/drug-recalls

27. **E**
Federal regulations no longer require lenders to place student loans into forbearance for a pharmacy residency or fellowship. The new regulation states that only medical and dental residencies or internship programs qualify for mandatory loan forbearance. Mandatory forbearances may be granted for no more than 12 months at a time. If you continue to meet the eligibility requirements for the forbearance when your current forbearance period expires, you may request another mandatory forbearance. View: http://studentaid.ed.gov/repay-loans/deferment-forbearance

28. **D**
Pharmaceutical Equivalents. Drug products are considered pharmaceutical equivalents if they contain the same active ingredient(s), are of the same dosage form, route of administration and are identical in strength or concentration (e.g., chlordiazepoxide hydrochloride, 5mg capsules).

Pharmaceutically equivalent drug products are formulated to contain the same amount of active ingredient in the same dosage form and to meet the same or compendial or other applicable standards (i.e., strength, quality, purity, and identity), but they may differ in characteristics such as shape, scoring configuration, release mechanisms, packaging, **excipients** (including colors, flavors, preservatives), expiration time, and, within certain limits, labelling. View: http://www.fda.gov/ohrms/dockets/ac/05/briefing/2005-4137B1_07_Nomenclature.pdf

29. **B**

    The HIPAA guidelines don't tell you how to send your mail or what you have to do. It just must be done in a manner to protect confidentiality and make sure it securely gets to the person it was intended to get to.

    HIPAA violations come in two broad categories: negligent and intentional. Negligent violations can be as simple as faxing documents containing PHI to the wrong number in error, forgetting to log out of the electronic patient record, or in this case identifying a possible security flaw but not doing anything about it.

    Remember a violation does not have to be reported by someone to count. Just knowing there is a vulnerability of PHI being seen by someone else can get you in trouble. Also, if you identify and document your changes in your risk assessment it will show you are proactive about security when you do get audited.

    View: http://mor-of.net/1604_CWirght_SimpleSeal_Envelopes_HIPAA.html

30. **D**

Category	Risk
Category A	The safest drugs to take during pregnancy. No known adverse reactions.
Category B	No risks have been found in humans.
Category C	Not enough research has been done to determine if these drugs are safe.
Category D	Adverse reactions have been found in humans.
Category X	Should never be used by a pregnant woman.

    Note that FDA came out with new labeling requirements and the A, B, C, D, and X categories are replaced with the new format (below). Drugs approved after June 2015 will need to follow this format:

    Pregnancy (includes Labor and Delivery):
    - Pregnancy Exposure Registry
    - Risk Summary
    - Clinical Considerations
    - Data

    Lactation (includes Nursing Mothers)
    - Risk Summary
    - Clinical Considerations
    - Data

    Females and Males of Reproductive Potential
    - Pregnancy Testing

- Contraception
- Infertility

View: https://www.drugs.com/pregnancy-categories.html

31. **A**

    Schedule I drugs, substances, or chemicals are defined as drugs with no currently accepted medical use and a high potential for abuse. Some examples of Schedule I drugs are: heroin, lysergic acid diethylamide (LSD), marijuana (cannabis), 3,4-methylenedioxymethamphetamine (ecstasy), methaqualone, and peyote
    View: https://www.dea.gov/druginfo/ds.shtml

32. **C**

    Schedule III drugs, substances, or chemicals are defined as drugs with a moderate to low potential for physical and psychological dependence. Schedule III drugs abuse potential is less than Schedule I and Schedule II drugs but more than Schedule IV. Some examples of Schedule III drugs are: Products containing less than 90 milligrams of codeine per dosage unit (Tylenol with codeine), Marinol (dronabinol), ketamine, anabolic steroids, testosterone
    View: https://www.dea.gov/druginfo/ds.shtml

33. **A**

    A prescription for controlled substances in Schedules III, IV and V issued by a practitioner may be communicated either orally, in writing or by facsimile to the pharmacist and may be refilled if so authorized on the prescription. DEA published in the Federal Register an interim final rule that would allow electronic transmissions of prescriptions of controlled substances (CII-CV).
    This rule gives prescribers the option of e-prescribing CS, permits pharmacies to receive, dispense & archive electronic RXs, reduces paperwork for DEA registrants, & potentially reduces RX forgeries. DEA believes this rule could reduce the number of RX errors caused by illegible handwriting, as well as the number of misunderstood orally ordered RXs.
    http://www.deadiversion.usdoj.gov/ecomm/e_rx/thirdparty.htm

34. **C**

    21 USC § 1306.13 Partial filling of prescriptions. (a) The partial filling of a prescription for a controlled substance listed in Schedule II is permissible, if the pharmacist is unable to supply the full quantity called for in a written or emergency oral prescription and he makes a notation of the quantity supplied on the face of the written prescription (or written record of the emergency oral prescription).
    The remaining portion of the prescription may be filled within 72 hours of the first partial filling; however, if the remaining portion is not or cannot be filled within the 72-hour period, the pharmacist shall so notify the prescribing individual practitioner. No further quantity may be supplied beyond 72 hours without a new prescription
    http://www.deadiversion.usdoj.gov/21cfr/cfr/1306/1306_13.htm

35. **D**

    DEA Form 224 - Retail Pharmacy, Hospital/Clinic, Practitioner, Teaching Institution, or Mid-Level Practitioner
    DEA Form 225 – Manufacturer, Distributor, Researcher, Analytical Laboratory, Importer, Exporter.
    DEA Form 363 – Narcotic Treatment Programs
    DEA Form 510 – Domestic Chemical

http://www.deadiversion.usdoj.gov/online_forms_apps.html

36. **A**
   §1307.21 Procedure for disposing of controlled substances.
   http://www.gpo.gov/fdsys/pkg/CFR-2011-title21-vol9/pdf/CFR-2011-title21-vol9-part1307.pdf

37. **E**
   http://www.deadiversion.usdoj.gov/pubs/manuals/pharm2/pharm_manual.htm

38. **B & E**
   A pharmacist may partially dispense a prescription for schedules III-V controlled substances provided that each partial filling is recorded in the same manner as a refilling, the total quantity dispensed in all partial fillings does not exceed the total quantity prescribed, and no dispensing occurs beyond six months from the date on which the prescription was issued.
   LTCFs do not need to register with DEA to house emergency kits containing CS so long as there are safeguards in place to minimize access to the drugs, and only limited amounts are provided. Records of placement of kits in DEA must be maintained & available for inspection.
   http://www.deadiversion.usdoj.gov/pubs/manuals/pharm2/pharm_manual.pdf

39. **D**
   Transfer of Business: A pharmacy registrant that transfers its business operations to another pharmacy registrant must submit in person or by registered or certified mail, return receipt requested, to the Special Agent in Charge in his/her area, at least <u>14 days</u> in advance of the date of the proposed transfer (unless the Special Agent in Charge waives this time limitation in individual instances), the following information:
   - The name, address, registration number, and authorized business activity of the registrant discontinuing the business (registrant-transferor);
   - The name, address, registration number, and authorized business activity of the person acquiring the business (registrant-transferee);
   - Whether the business activities will be continued at the location registered by the person discontinuing business, or moved to another location (if the latter, the address of the new location should be listed); and

   http://www.deadiversion.usdoj.gov/pubs/manuals/pharm2/pharm_manual.pdf

40. **E**

	Schedule II	Schedules III & IV	Schedule V
Registration	Required	Required	Required
Receiving Records	DEA Form 222	Invoices, readily retrievable	Invoices, readily retrievable
Prescriptions	Written or electronic prescriptions	Written, electronic, oral, or fax	Written, electronic, oral, or fax
Refills	No	No more than 5 within 6 months	As authorized when prescription is issued or if renewed by a practitioner

Maintenance of Prescriptions	Separate file	Separate file or readily retrievable	Separate file or readily retrievable
Distribution Between Registrants	DEA Form 222	Invoices	Invoices
Security	Locked cabinet or dispersed among non-controlled pharmaceuticals	Locked cabinet or dispersed among non-controlled pharmaceuticals	Locked cabinet or dispersed among non-controlled pharmaceuticals
Theft or Significant Loss	Report to DEA and complete DEA Form 106	Report to DEA and complete DEA Form 106	Report to DEA and complete DEA Form 106

All records must be maintained for 2 years, unless state law requires a longer period.
- Written prescriptions include paper prescriptions and electronic prescriptions that meet DEA's requirements for such prescriptions.
- Emergency prescriptions require a signed follow-up prescription within seven days. Exceptions: A facsimile prescription serves as the original prescription when issued to residents of Long-Term Care Facilities, hospice patients, or patients with a diagnosed terminal illness, or for immediate administration
- The record of dispensing can also be a schedule V logbook, if state law allows.

http://www.deadiversion.usdoj.gov/pubs/manuals/pharm2/pharm_manual.pdf

41. **E**

    View 20 CFR 1304.04, Maintenance of records and inventories, Section(h):
    - "red ink in the lower right corner with the letter "C" ... and *filed either in the prescription file for controlled substances listed in Schedules I and II or in the usual consecutively numbered prescription file for non-controlled substances*. However, if a pharmacy employs a computer application for prescriptions that permits identification by prescription number and retrieval of original documents by prescriber name, patient's name, drug dispensed, and date filled, then the requirement to mark the hard copy prescription with a red "C" is waived.

    http://www.deadiversion.usdoj.gov/21cfr/cfr/1304/1304_04.htm

42. **A & C**

    The registrant is required to take a <u>biennial inventory</u> (every two years) of all controlled substances on hand. The biennial inventory may be taken on any date which is within two years of the previous inventory date. There is no requirement to submit a copy of the inventory to DEA.

    [Pharmacies must make a] count of the substance - if the substance is listed in CII, an exact count or measure of the contents or if the substance is listed in C III-V, an estimated count or measure of the contents, unless the container holds <u>more than</u> 1,000 tablets or capsules in which case, an exact count of the contents is required.
    When a drug not previously listed as a controlled substance is scheduled or a drug is rescheduled, the drug must be inventoried <u>as of the effective date of scheduling or change in scheduling</u>.

The CSA also requires that all inventory records be maintained at the registered location in a readily retrievable manner for at least two years for copying and inspection. In addition, the inventory records of schedule II-controlled substances must be kept separate from all other controlled substances.
http://www.deadiversion.usdoj.gov/pubs/manuals/pharm2/pharm_manual.pdf

43. **E**
Only Schedule I & II controlled substances are ordered with a DEA Form-222. An Official Order Form is required for each distribution, purchase or transfer of a Schedule II controlled substance.

DEA Form 222 is in triplicate. The pharmacy (or recipient of the CII medications) keeps copy 3, and then sends copies 1 & 2 to the supplier. Once the supplier ships the medication to the pharmacy, it keeps copy 1 and forwards copy 2 to the DEA.
When ordering Schedule II substances, the pharmacist is responsible for filling in the number of packages, the size of the package and the name of the item.

Each Official Order Form must be signed and dated by a person authorized to sign a registration application. When the items are received, the pharmacist must document on the purchaser's copy (copy 3) the actual number of packages received, and the date received.
http://ecfr.gpoaccess.gov/cgi/t/text/text-idx?c=ecfr&rgn=div6&view=text&node=21:9.0.1.1.6.2&idno=21

44. **C**
DEA is announcing that, effective immediately, DOD personal service contractors will be issued a new DEA registration number that begins with the letter "G". This new first character will be in addition to the current first characters A, B, F of the DEA registration for practitioners. The G series DEA registration number will be listed in the database provided to NTIS and available on the DEA website validation query system.
Registrant type (first letter of DEA Number):
- A/B/F/G – Hospital/Clinic/Practitioner/Teaching Institution/Pharmacy
- M – Mid-Level Practitioner (NP/PA/OD/ET, etc.)
- P/R – Manufacturer/Distributor/Researcher/Analytical Lab/Importer/Exporter/Reverse Distributor/Narcotic Treatment Program

http://www.deadiversion.usdoj.gov/drugreg/

Mid-level practitioners (MLP) are registered and authorized by the DEA and the state in which they practice to dispense, administer and prescribe controlled substances in the course of professional practice. Examples of MLPs include, but are not limited to, health care providers such as: Nurse practitioners, nurse midwives, nurse anesthetists, clinical nurse specialists, physician assistants, & optometrists
http://www.deadiversion.usdoj.gov/pubs/manuals/pharm2/pharm_manual.pdf

45. **B & C**
View CFR Title 21, Sec. 1306.11 Requirement of prescription.
http://www.accessdata.fda.gov/scripts/cdrh/cfdocs/cfcfr/CFRSearch.cfm?CFRPart=1305&showFR=1
http://www.deadiversion.usdoj.gov/pubs/manuals/pharm2/pharm_manual.pdf

46. **D**

    View CFR, Sec. 290.5-
    The label of any drug listed as a "controlled substance" in schedule II, III, or IV of the Federal Controlled Substances Act shall, when dispensed to or for a patient, contain the following warning: "Caution: Federal law prohibits the transfer of this drug to any person other than the patient for whom it was prescribed."
    http://www.accessdata.fda.gov/scripts/cdrh/cfdocs/cfcfr/CFRSearch.cfm?CFRPart=290&showFR=1

47. **C**

    An exception to the partial fill rule (i.e. balance must be filled within 72 hours) has been made for patients in Long Term Care Facilities (LTCF) and patients who have been diagnosed with a terminal illness.

    A prescription for a schedule II-controlled substance written for a patient in a [LTCF] or for a patient with a medical diagnosis documenting a terminal illness, may be filled in partial quantities to include individual dosage units... Both the pharmacist and the prescribing practitioner have a corresponding responsibility to assure that the controlled substance is for a terminally ill patient.
    http://www.deadiversion.usdoj.gov/pubs/manuals/pharm2/pharm_manual.pdf

48. **C**

    Synalgos-DC is listed as a Schedule III drug –
    http://www.deadiversion.usdoj.gov/schedules/orangebook/e_cs_sched.pdf
    The pharmacist may partially dispense a prescription for a Schedule III-V controlled substance if the pharmacist notes the quantity dispensed and initials the back of the prescription order. The partial dispensing may not exceed the total amount authorized in the prescription order. The dispensing of all partially-filled prescriptions and all refills must be within the six-month limit (for CIII & CIV drugs).
    http://www.deadiversion.usdoj.gov/pubs/manuals/pharm2/pharm_manual.pdf

49. **A & E**

    In states where limited quantities of Schedule V preparations may be sold over-the-counter, the pharmacist is responsible for making sure that such sales comply with state law.
    http://www.deadiversion.usdoj.gov/pubs/manuals/pharm2/pharm_manual.pdf

    Note that in Oregon law, there are no over-the-counter CV medications. All medications must be obtained using a valid prescription. Photo identification is not required before dispensing these substances, and a student pharmacist may dispense and counsel on the substance if the final verification was completed by a pharmacist. Therefore, under Oregon law the best answer would be D only.

50. **D**

    A central fill pharmacy will not be permitted to prepare prescriptions provided directly by the patient or individual practitioner or to mail or otherwise deliver a filled prescription directly to a patient or individual practitioner. Community pharmacies are permitted to transmit prescription information to a central fill pharmacy in two ways.

First, a facsimile of a prescription for a controlled substance in Schedule II-V may be provided by the community pharmacy to the central fill pharmacy. The community pharmacy must maintain the original hard copy of the prescription and the central fill pharmacy must maintain the facsimile of the prescription.
http://www.deadiversion.usdoj.gov/pubs/manuals/pharm2/pharm_manual.pdf

51. **D**

    A practitioner who wants to use Schedule II narcotic drugs for maintenance and/or detoxification must obtain separate registration from DEA as a narcotic treatment program pursuant to the Narcotic Addict Treatment Act of 1974.

    An **exception** to the registration requirement, known as the **"three-day rule"** (Title 21, Code of Federal Regulations, Part 1306.07(b)), allows a practitioner who is not separately registered as a narcotic treatment program, to administer (but not prescribe) narcotic drugs to a patient for the purpose of relieving acute withdrawal symptoms while arranging for the patient's referral for treatment, under the following conditions:
    - Not more than one day's medication may be administered or given to a patient at one time;
    - This treatment may not be carried out for more than 72 hours and;
    - This 72-hour period cannot be renewed or extended.

    http://www.deadiversion.usdoj.gov/drugreg/faq.htm

52. **A**

    A pharmacy registered to dispense controlled substances may distribute such substances (without being registered as a distributor) to another pharmacy or to a registered practitioner for the purpose of general dispensing by the practitioner to patients, provided that the following conditions are met:
    - The pharmacy or practitioner that will receive the controlled substances is registered under the CSA to dispense controlled substances;
    - The distribution is recorded by the distributing practitioner and the receipt is recorded by the receiving practitioner
    - If the pharmacy distributes a schedule II-controlled substance, it must document the transfer on an official order form (DEA Form 222) or the electronic equivalent
    - "Five Percent Rule" - total number of dosage units of all controlled substances distributed by a pharmacy may not exceed five percent of all controlled substances dispensed by the pharmacy during a calendar year. If at any time the controlled substances distributed exceed five percent, the pharmacy is required to register as a distributor.

    http://www.deadiversion.usdoj.gov/pubs/manuals/pharm2/pharm_manual.pdf

53. **C**

    View 21 USC § 812 (a):
    Note that the schedules of controlled substances are based on the potential for abuse, the recognition of a medical use, and the possibility of physical or psychological dependence.
    http://www.deadiversion.usdoj.gov/21cfr/21usc/812.htm

54. **D**

    Under the CSA, only certain parties are permitted to possess controlled substances legally. These parties must be registered with the DEA, or they must be exempt from registration.
    http://www.deadiversion.usdoj.gov/21cfr/21usc/822.htm

Note: A pharmacy registration must be renewed every three years utilizing DEA Form 224a
http://www.deadiversion.usdoj.gov/pubs/manuals/pharm2/pharm_manual.pdf

55. **A**

    To order controlled substances in schedules III through V, no special-order form is required. However, to order controlled substances in Schedules I or II, a special-order form (DEA form 222) must be used. Note that in transferring schedule II-controlled substances from one registrant to another, it is necessary to use <u>DEA form 222</u>. For example, if one pharmacy is temporarily out of a schedule II-controlled substance, and another pharmacy agrees to transfer to that pharmacy one bottle of 100 tablets to "help out in a pinch," the receiving pharmacy must send its DEA form 222 to the dispersing pharmacy. When the time comes to return the favor, the same process is followed. Be mindful of the 5 percent rule!

    View 21 CFR § **1305.21** requirements for electronic orders.
    http://www.deadiversion.usdoj.gov/21cfr/cfr/1305/1305_21.htm

56. **E**

    The logbook must be maintained by the regulated seller for not fewer than two years after the date on which the entry is made (21 U.S.C. 830(e)(1)(A)(vi)).
    http://www.deadiversion.usdoj.gov/fed_regs/rules/2011/fr1201.htm

    <u>Please note, as Oregon has classified these substances as prescription only, there is no logbook for them kept in Oregon pharmacies. However, it is still good to be familiar with the Methamphetamine Production Prevention Act of 2005.</u>

57. **C**

    The Combat Methamphetamine Epidemic Act of 2005 created a new category of products called "scheduled listed chemical product (SLCP)." It includes any product that may be marketed or distributed lawfully in the United States under the Federal Food, Drug, and Cosmetic Act as a nonprescription drug that contains ephedrine, pseudoephedrine, or PPA (includes salts, optical isomers, and salts of optical isomers) (21 U.S.C. § 802(45)).
    http://www.deadiversion.usdoj.gov/pubs/manuals/pharm2/pharm_manual.pdf

    Please note, as Oregon has classified these substances as prescription only, there is no quantity restriction applicable to these substances under state law. Medication obtained via prescription are not subject to the restrictions listed in this law.

58. **D**

    The DEA does permit the issuance of multiple prescriptions on the same day, all dated on the date of <u>issuance</u>, with instructions to the pharmacist to dispense the medications at a future time.
    View 21 CFR § 1306.12 Refilling Prescriptions; Issuance of Multiple Prescriptions
    http://www.deadiversion.usdoj.gov/21cfr/cfr/1306/1306_12.htm

59. **E**

    View Section 1306.25 Transfer between pharmacies of prescription information for Schedules III, IV, and V controlled substances for refill purposes.

http://www.deadiversion.usdoj.gov/21cfr/cfr/1306/1306_25.htm

60. **C**
    Note: Federal law (2 years) vs. IL law (5 years) for recordkeeping of all controlled substance prescriptions, IL law is more stringent. Unless the MPJE specifically asks for federal law, you should always pick the more stringent law, which is 5 years.
    ***View 21 CFR § 1306.22* Refilling of prescriptions.**
    http://www.deadiversion.usdoj.gov/21cfr/cfr/1306/1306_22.htm

61. **A**
    A prescription is an order for medication which is dispensed to or for an ultimate user. A prescription is not an order for medication which is dispensed for immediate administration to the ultimate user (for example, an order to dispense a drug to an inpatient for immediate administration in a hospital is not a prescription).

    The practitioner is responsible for ensuring that the prescription conforms to all requirements of the law and regulations, both federal and state.
    http://www.deadiversion.usdoj.gov/pubs/manuals/pract/section5.htm

62. **C**
    REMS are required risk management plans that use risk minimization strategies beyond the professional labeling to ensure that the benefits of certain prescription drugs outweigh their risks.
    http://www.fda.gov/downloads/AboutFDA/Transparency/Basics/UCM328784.pdf

63. **E**
    Ways in which a drug may be switched to OTC from prescription:
    - The manufacturer may request the switch by submitting a supplemental application to its approved NDA (i.e. SNDA)
    - The manufacturer may petition the FDA
    - The drug may be switched through the OTC drug review process. Generally, applies to all manufacturers' products at the same time

    http://www.fda.gov/Drugs/DevelopmentApprovalProcess/SmallBusinessAssistance/ucm069917.htm

64. **C**
    MedWatch, the FDA's safety information and adverse event reporting program, plays a critical role in the agency's post-marketing surveillance--the process of following the safety profile of medical products after they've begun to be used by consumers.

    Through MedWatch, a <u>voluntary program</u>, health professionals report adverse reactions, product problems, and use errors related to drugs, biologics, medical devices, dietary supplements, cosmetics, and infant formulas.

65. **C**
    FDA classification of recalls.
    - A Class I recall applies when there is a reasonable probability that the product will cause serious adverse health consequences or death.

- A Class II recall applies when the product may cause temporary or medically reversible adverse health consequences, but the probability of serious adverse consequences is remote.
- A Class III recall applies when a product is not likely to cause adverse health consequences.

http://www.fda.gov/Safety/Recalls/ucm165546.htm

66. **B**

View 21 U.S. Code § 355 - New drugs at http://www.law.cornell.edu/uscode/text/21/355
http://www.fda.gov/downloads/Drugs/Guidances/ucm079345.pdf

67. **C**

Before a drug can be shown to be safe and effective, it is necessary to study the drug in clinical trials.

These trials occur throughout the country; thus, it is necessary to place the as yet unapproved new drug into interstate commerce so that the drug can be provided to those who will use it for clinical trials.

If there were no exemption from the FDCA provisions that prevent the introduction into interstate commerce of an unapproved new drug, then clinical trials could not occur. Thus, an exemption has been provided through the IND (Investigational New Drug) provisions of the Act.

68. **B**

A physician may request that a prescribed medication not be dispensed in child-resistant closures, & this request will be honored as long as it is made for each prescription to which it applies (i.e., no "blanket requests"). However, patients may request that all dispensed drugs not be placed in child-resistant containers.

http://www.cpsc.gov//PageFiles/113945/384.pdf

69. **C**

Orange Book – Terminology
Bioequivalence
- Products display comparable bioavailability

Pharmaceutical equivalents (PEs)
- Products that contain same active ingredients, identical in strength and same dosage form

Therapeutic equivalents (TEs)
- PEs that can be expected to have the same clinical effect and safety
-

http://www.fda.gov/Drugs/DevelopmentApprovalProcess/ucm079068.htm

70. **A**

Levothyroxine Sodium. Because there is multiple reference listed drugs of levothyroxine sodium tablets and some reference listed drugs' sponsors have conducted studies to establish their drugs' therapeutic equivalence to other reference listed drugs, FDA has determined that its usual practice of assigning two or three-character TE codes may be potentially confusing and inadequate for these drug products.

See http://www.fda.gov/Drugs/DevelopmentApprovalProcess/ucm079068.htm

71. **D**
View 21 CFR §201.57
http://www.accessdata.fda.gov/scripts/cdrh/cfdocs/cfCFR/CFRSearch.cfm?fr=201.57

72. **C**
Accurate and complete information is vital to the safe use of drugs. While drug companies have traditionally promoted their products directly to physicians, more and more they are advertising directly to consumers.
http://www.fda.gov/Drugs/ResourcesForYou/Consumers/ucm143462.htm

73. **B**
View 21 CFR§ 310.515 (a) Requirement for a patient package insert. FDA concludes that the safe and effective use of **drug products containing estrogens** requires that patients be fully informed of the benefits and risks involved in the use of these drugs.
http://www.accessdata.fda.gov/scripts/cdrh/cfdocs/cfcfr/CFRSearch.cfm?fr=310.515

74. **E**
View SEC. 201. [21 U.S.C. 321]
http://www.fda.gov/regulatoryinformation/legislation/federalfooddrugandcosmeticactfdcact/fdcactchaptersiandiishorttitleanddefinitions/ucm086297.htm

75. **A**
View 21 CFR § 211.132 (b)Requirements for tamper-evident package.
http://www.accessdata.fda.gov/scripts/cdrh/cfdocs/cfcfr/CFRSearch.cfm?fr=211.132

76. **A & B**
View 16 CFR 1700.14 - Substances requiring special packaging
http://www.gpo.gov/fdsys/pkg/CFR-2012-title16-vol2/pdf/CFR-2012-title16-vol2-sec1700-14.pdf

77. **B**
Durham-Humphrey Amendment of 1951
Kefauver-Harris Drug Amendments of 1962
http://www.fda.gov/aboutfda/whatwedo/history/milestones/ucm128305.htm

Drug Price Competition and Patent Term Restoration Act of 1984
http://thomas.loc.gov/cgi-bin/bdquery/z?d098:SN01538:@@@D&summ2=m&|TOM:/bss/d098query.html

Food and Drug Administration Modernization Act of 1997
http://www.fda.gov/RegulatoryInformation/Legislation/FederalFoodDrugandCosmeticActFDCAct/SignificantAmendmentstotheFDCAct/FDAMA/FullTextofFDAMAlaw/default.htm
Food and Drug Administration Amendments Act (FDAAA) of 2007
http://www.fda.gov/RegulatoryInformation/Legislation/FederalFoodDrugandCosmeticActFDCAct/SignificantAmendmentstotheFDCAct/FoodandDrugAdministrationAmendmentsActof2007/FullTextofFDAAALaw/default.htm

78. **B**

A new chemical entity that is developed by a sponsor and is approved as a new drug under an NDA is granted a period of exclusive marketing, and during that time no other manufacturer may market the chemical entity. Patent laws protect the new drug's exclusivity for a period of time, and under some circumstances, the FDCA provides additional non-patent exclusivity. After all applicable periods of exclusivity have expired, it is possible for another manufacturer to formulate the chemical entity into a product and market the product as a generic equivalent of the innovator product.

The most frequent way of getting to market as a generic equivalent is through an Abbreviated New Drug Application (ANDA). An ANDA relies on the safety and efficacy studies of the innovator product's NDA. Through an ANDA, a sponsor of a generic equivalent is required only to show bioequivalence with the innovator product. If such bioequivalence is shown, then the assumption is made that the bioequivalent product must be as safe and effective as the innovator product.

79. **E**
Applies only to human drugs. Section 503A of the FD&C Act from 1997
http://www.hpm.com/pdf/blog/Summary%20of%20HR3204%20-%20Compounding.pdf

Text of Compounding Quality Act
http://www.fda.gov/Drugs/GuidanceComplianceRegulatoryInformation/PharmacyCompounding/ucm376732.htm

80. **C-E**
View § 164.502 Uses and disclosures of protected health information: general rules.
https://www.law.cornell.edu/cfr/text/45/164.502
http://www.hhs.gov/ocr/privacy/hipaa/understanding/coveredentities/businessassociates.html

81. **A**
View 21 USC § 360c (a) Classes of devices.
http://www.gpo.gov/fdsys/pkg/USCODE-2010-title21/html/USCODE-2010-title21-chap9-subchapV-partA-sec360c.htm

Sec. 870.3925 **Replacement heart valve.**
http://www.accessdata.fda.gov/scripts/cdrh/cfdocs/cfcfr/CFRSearch.cfm?fr=870.3925

Sec. 890.3150 Crutch.
http://www.accessdata.fda.gov/scripts/cdrh/cfdocs/cfcfr/CFRSearch.cfm?fr=890.3150

Sec. 880.5090 Liquid bandage.
http://www.accessdata.fda.gov/scripts/cdrh/cfdocs/cfcfr/CFRSearch.cfm?fr=880.5090

Sec. 880.6230 Tongue depressor.
http://www.accessdata.fda.gov/scripts/cdrh/cfdocs/cfcfr/CFRSearch.cfm?fr=880.6230

Sec. 868.5580 Oxygen mask.
http://www.accessdata.fda.gov/scripts/cdrh/cfdocs/cfcfr/CFRSearch.cfm?fr=868.5580

82. **E**
    View 21 U.S. Code § 352 - Misbranded drugs and devices
    http://www.law.cornell.edu/uscode/text/21/352

83. **B**
    The labelling on dietary supplements may make structure/function claims but may not make therapeutic claims.
    View 21 USC § 343(r)(6)
    http://www.law.cornell.edu/uscode/text/21/343
    http://www.fda.gov/regulatoryinformation/legislation/federalfooddrugandcosmeticactfdcact/fdcactchaptersiandiishorttitleanddefinitions/ucm086297.htm

84. **B**
    Phase 2 studies begin if Phase 1 studies don't reveal unacceptable toxicity. While the emphasis in Phase 1 is on safety, the emphasis in Phase 2 is on **effectiveness**.
    http://www.fda.gov/Drugs/ResourcesForYou/Consumers/ucm143534.htm

85. **A**
    View 21 USC § 829
    http://www.deadiversion.usdoj.gov/21cfr/21usc/829.htm

86. **E.**
    View 75 FR 16236
    https://www.deadiversion.usdoj.gov/ecomm/e_rx/faq/faq.htm

87. **A.**
    Faxed prescriptions can only be done for patients in hospice or LTCF. No refills can be given for schedule II substances and a registered nurse cannot write for C-II prescriptions. Choice E does not specify what type of patient, and choice D is a phoned prescription for a homebound patient. You need a written prescription for choice D to be true.
    https://www.deadiversion.usdoj.gov/pubs/manuals/pharm2/pharm_content.htm

88. **B.**
    They can total no more than a 90-day supply.
    View: https://www.deadiversion.usdoj.gov/faq/mult_rx_faq.htm

89. **D.**
    View: https://www.deadiversion.usdoj.gov/21cfr/cfr/1306/1306_13.htm

90. **A.**
    From DEA website, "Practitioners wishing to prescribe and dispense FDA approved schedule II-controlled substances (i.e., methadone) for maintenance and detoxification treatment must obtain a separate DEA registration as a Narcotic Treatment Program via a DEA Form 363.
    If a practitioner wishes to prescribe or dispense schedules III, IV, or V controlled substances approved by the FDA for **addiction** treatment (i.e., Suboxone® or Subutex® drug products), the practitioner must request a waiver from CSAT which will then notify DEA of all waiver requests. These practitioners are referred to as DATA waived practitioners."

https://www.buppractice.com/node/12256
View: https://www.deadiversion.usdoj.gov/pubs/manuals/pharm2/pharm_content.htm

91. **C.**
"All required records concerning controlled substances must be maintained for at least two years for inspection and copying by duly authorized DEA officials. Records and inventories of schedule II-controlled substances must be maintained separately from all other records of the registrant. All records and inventories of schedules III, IV, and V controlled substances must be maintained either separately from all other records or in such a form that the information required is readily retrievable from the ordinary business records."
https://www.deadiversion.usdoj.gov/pubs/manuals/pharm2/pharm_manual.htm

92. **C.**
Buyers must:
Present a photo identification card issued by the State or the Federal Government or a document that is considered acceptable by the seller
Enter into the logbook their information such as name, address, date and time of sale, and signature

Please note, as Oregon has classified these substances as prescription only, there is no logbook for them kept in Oregon pharmacies. In addition, Oregon law does not require photo identification to be presented prior to dispensing a prescription for any substance.

93. **D.**
CMEA requires all non-liquid forms (including gel caps) to be in 2-unit blister packs (with exception when blister pack is not technically feasible, the product may be in unit dosage packets or pouches). The daily limit is 3.6 g per day of pseudoephedrine base, or mobile retail vendor (or mail-order) can't sell more than 7.5 g per 30 days. 120 mg of pseudoephedrine HCL is equivalent to 36 tablets, about 4.32 g per day of the salt form.

https://www.deadiversion.usdoj.gov/meth/cma2005.htm

Please note, as Oregon has classified these substances as prescription only, there is no limit to the quantity that may be dispensed.

94. **B.**
View https://www.deadiversion.usdoj.gov/faq/dea222.htm

95. **A.**
It is suggested that initial reports be required within one business day and that DEA Form 106 must be filed within 30 days.

https://www.deadiversion.usdoj.gov/fed_regs/rules/2005/fr0812.htm

96. **B.**
Orphan drug exclusivity adds 7-years not 5-years of market exclusivity.

https://www.fda.gov/downloads/drugs/developmentapprovalprocess/smallbusinessassistance/ucm447307.pdf

97. **D.**
View http://www.nejm.org/doi/full/10.1056/NEJMhle1002961#t=article

98. **C.**
View "What standards must generic medicines meet to receive FDA approval?"- https://www.fda.gov/drugs/resourcesforyou/consumers/questionsanswers/ucm100100.htm#q5

99. **A.**
Any generic drug modeled after a single, brand name drug must perform approximately the same in the body as the brand name drug. There will always be a slight, but not medically important, level of natural variability – just as there is for one batch of brand name drug compared to the next batch of brand name product.

https://www.fda.gov/drugs/resourcesforyou/consumers/buyingusingmedicinesafely/understandinggenericdrugs/ucm167991.htm

100. **D.**
The Orange Book Codes supply the FDA's therapeutic equivalence rating for applicable multi-source categories. Codes beginning with 'A' signify the product is deemed therapeutically equivalent to the reference product for the category. Codes beginning with 'B' indicate bio-equivalence has not been confirmed. 'EE' is assigned by RED BOOK Online to products that have been evaluated by the FDA but for which an equivalence rating is not available.

http://www.micromedexsolutions.com/micromedex2/4.36.0/WebHelp/RED_BOOK/Orange_Book_Codes.htm

101. **B.**
Biosimilars are listed in the Purple Book.

https://www.fda.gov/drugs/developmentapprovalprocess/howdrugsaredevelopedandapproved/approvalapplications/therapeuticbiologicapplications/biosimilars/

102. **A.**
A REMs may be required by the FDA as part of the approval of a new product, or for an approved product when new safety information arises. REMS is a safety strategy to manage a known or potential serious risk associated with a medicine and to enable patients to have continued access to such medicines by managing their safe use.

https://www.fda.gov/aboutfda/transparency/basics/ucm325201.htm

103. **D.**
Examples of ETASU are:
- Prescribers have specific training/experience or special certifications
- Pharmacies, practitioners or healthcare settings that dispense the drug be certified
- Drug be dispensed only in certain healthcare settings (e.g., infusion settings, hospitals)

- Drug be dispensed with evidence of safe-use conditions such as laboratory test results
- Each patient using the drug be subject to monitoring •Each patient using the drug be enrolled in a registry

    https://www.fda.gov/downloads/aboutfda/transparency/basics/ucm328784.pdf

104. **B.**

    An education program for prescribers and patients is emphasized but not required.

    http://er-la-opioidrems.com/IwgUI/rems/home.action

105. **A.**

    Purchaser must sign the logbook and enter his or her name, address, and date and time of sale not the seller.

    https://www.deadiversion.usdoj.gov/meth/cma2005.htm

    Please note, as Oregon has classified these substances as prescription only, there is no logbook for them kept in Oregon pharmacies. Prescription records must be kept in accordance with the state law for these substances.

106. **C.**

    The daily sales limit of ephedrine base, pseudoephedrine base, or phenylpropanolamine base is 3.6 grams per purchaser, regardless of number of transactions.

Ingredient	Number of Tablets [as base]
25 mg Ephedrine HCl	175
25 mg Ephedrine Sulfate	186
30 mg Pseudoephedrine HCl	146
60 mg Pseudoephedrine HCl	73
120 mg Pseudoephedrine HCl	36
30 mg Pseudoephedrine Sulfate	155
60 mg Pseudoephedrine Sulfate	77
120 mg Pseudoephedrine Sulfate	38
Phenylpropanolamine	The FDA issued a voluntary recall of this ingredient as being unsafe for human consumption. Veterinary use is by prescription only.

    View: https://www.deadiversion.usdoj.gov/meth/cma2005.html

    Please note, as Oregon has classified these substances as prescription only, there is no limit to the quantity that may be dispensed.

107. **B.**

    View question 106 explanation

Please note, as Oregon has classified these substances as prescription only, there is no limit to the quantity that may be dispensed.

108. **D.**
Usually pharmacies lose their right to sell precursor drugs for a period of time in addition to fines.

Here is a real-life example: http://www.pharmacytimes.com/news/pharmacy-pays-penalties-for-violating-controlled-substances-laws

109. **A.**
The DQSA was enacted primarily in response to an outbreak of fungal meningitis among patients who received products compounded at the New England Compounding Center. Title I of the DQSA amends Section 503A and clarifies federal authority of compounding and defines "traditional compounders." Title I also creates Section 503B of the FDCA, which addresses outsourcing facilities. The Food and Drug Administration Modernization Act (FDAMA) of 1997 created Section 503A of the FDCA and distinguished manufacturing from compounding activities that could be completed by pharmacies. The DQSA removes advertising and promotion clauses of the original Section 503A that were rendered unconstitutional.

https://www.fda.gov/drugs/guidancecomplianceregulatoryinformation/pharmacycompounding/ucm375804.htm

110. **D.**
Because generic drugs subject to a suitability petition cannot be AB rated, there is a reduced risk of a classic "switch" by pharmacists from Effexor XR to a generic tablet. There is a real risk, however, that managed care organizations may mandate that plan physicians prescribe the generic tablet.

https://www.fda.gov/ohrms/dockets/dailys/03/Sept03/090503/03p-0159-c000001-01-vol1.pdf

Please note that in Oregon, a pharmacist may use their professional judgement to substitute a therapeutically equivalent product, even if the products are not AB rated.

111. **B.**
Specifically, the commenter suggested that initial reports be required within one business day and that DEA Form 106 must be filed within 30 days.

https://www.deadiversion.usdoj.gov/fed_regs/rules/2005/fr0812.htm

112. **A.**
As choice A affects the drug contents inside as well as going against the label it is considered adulterated and misbranded.

https://www.fda.gov/cosmetics/guidanceregulation/lawsregulations/ucm074248.htm#Adulterated

113. **C.**
90-days

114. **E.**

https://www.deadiversion.usdoj.gov/drugreg/reg_apps/363/363_instruct.htm

115. **B.**

The pharmacy owner or "registrant" can enter the pharmacy.
https://www.deadiversion.usdoj.gov/pubs/manuals/pharm2/pharm_manual.htm

116. **A.**

In an effort to reduce drug exposure and abuse, the DEA has allowed the take back of unused, unwanted controlled substances.
https://ptcb.org/who-we-serve/pharmacy-technicians/cphts-state-regulatory-map/il#.WZivg62ZMdU

117. **B.**

NIOSH and OSHA provide guidance's to help promote the safe handling of antineoplastics.
https://www.cdc.gov/niosh/topics/antineoplastic/

118. **D.**

https://www.aaaai.org/about-aaaai/advocacy/Allergy-Extract-Compounding-Requirements-Updates

119. **B.**

Outsourcing facilities
https://www.fda.gov/downloads/Drugs/Guidances/UCM496288.pdf

120. **B.**

Currently, guidelines are only available for testing "chemotherapy gloves" [ASTM 2005] and information may not be available for other types of hazardous drugs. Wear two pairs of gloves when compounding, administering, and disposing of hazardous drugs.

https://www.cdc.gov/niosh/docs/wp-solutions/2009-106/pdfs/2009-106.pdf

Oregon Pharmacy Law Review

Photo by Umit Aslan on Unsplash

OREGON PHARMACY LAW REVIEW

ABBREVIATIONS

ACPE: American Council on Pharmaceutical Education
BOP: Board of Pharmacy
BPS: Board of Pharmaceutical Specialties
DOB: Date of Birth
EPT: Expedited Partner Therapy
FDA: Food and Drug Administration
MDV multi dose vial
NHA: National Healthcareer Association
OAR 855: Oregon Administrative Rules Chapter 855

ORS 333: Oregon Revised Statute Chapter 333
ORS 475: Oregon Revised Statute Chapter 475
ORS 689: Oregon Revised Statute Chapter 689
P&P: Policy and Procedure
PIL: Product Identification Label
PTCB: Pharmacy Technician Certification Board
SDV: single dose vial
X DEA: DEA of practitioner that has obtained a DATA waiver, and whose DEA number therefore starts with X.

The review of Oregon Law will loosely follow the three main sections tested by the MPJE as outlined in the NABP Candidate Application bulletin[1] of the following:

Part 1: Pharmacy Practice
~83% of MPJE
> Reviews pharmacy personnel, prescription processing for both controlled and non-controlled substances, expanded practice for pharmacists, providers, laws regarding specific pharmacy practice areas, and record keeping.

Part 2: Licenses, Registrations, and Operations
~15% of MPJE
> Reviews licensing requirements for individuals, registration requirements for businesses, CE requirements, equipment requirements, and disciplinary actions for both licensees and registrants

Part 3: General Regulations
~2% of MPJE
> There is minimal state related material in this section, as the bulletin[1] indicates this section is primarily federal law, such as the Food, Drug, and Cosmetic Act, Poison Prevention Packaging act, etc. However, a review of information related to the Board of Pharmacy and other applicable Oregon state regulatory bodies is listed here for lack of a better place to include it.

As this review is an interpretation of the law and does not cover every law listed, only the information that our guide reviewers who recently passed the Oregon MPJE exam felt was most important is included. It is recommended that you read through the entirety of the Oregon state law (and federal law) in addition to using this review in your studies. An incomplete list of state law documents you should review is as follows:

- Oregon Revised Statute Chapter 475 and Chapter 689
- Oregon Administrative Rules Chapter 855
- Oregon Board of Pharmacy (BOP) Newsletters and FAQ's (Specifically the Compliance FAQ)

To aid in your comprehensive review, the applicable Oregon laws are referenced throughout this guide as ORS 475, ORS 689, and OAR 855. The Oregon BOP has a number of FAQ documents that you can access on their website (https://www.oregon.gov/pharmacy/pages/laws_rules.aspx). These documents will also be referenced throughout the guide.

OREGON PHARMACY LAW PART 1: INSIDE THE PHARMACY

PERSONNEL

Do pharmacy personnel have to wear a name badge?
Pharmacy personnel, including pharmacists, interns and technicians, must be able to be clearly identified by the public. This includes the person's name and position.
OAR 855.025.0025, OAR 855.031.0020

[handwritten: ALL WEAR BADGES]

PHARMACIST IN CHARGE (PIC)
OAR 855.019.0300

Is a pharmacy required to have a PIC?
Yes, each pharmacy must have one PIC that is regularly employed.

What is the PIC responsible for?
In general, the PIC is responsible for the day-to-day operations of the pharmacy. More specifically:

PIC is responsible for completing the following themselves:	
Initial Annual Self-Inspection form	Within 15 days of becoming PIC
Reporting PIC change	Within 15 days of occurrence
Quarterly Compliance Audit	Only applies if PIC of >1 pharmacy, complete for EACH location on Quarterly PIC Compliance Audit Form
Plan of Correction after board inspection	Within 30 days of receiving notice from board
Maintain possession of keys to pharmacy, authorize other pharmacists to have keys	Non-pharmacy personnel cannot have access to "prescription area" when pharmacist is not present.
Responsible for all policies and procedures	Responsible for their existence and ensuring they are followed
PIC is responsible for making sure the following tasks below are completed, but they may be completed by other pharmacy personnel:	
Inventory of ALL controlled substances, upon initial PIC change and then annually	Complete initial inventory within 15 days before or after effective date of change in PIC. Must be dated and signed by NEW PIC. Then complete annually.
Verify licensure of all pharmacy personnel	At least annually, upon initial employment, and any other time it is deemed necessary.
Annual Self-Inspection Form	Annually by February 1st, must be signed and dated by PIC.
Reconciliation of Schedule II Controlled drugs	Complete quarterly, unless in hospital setting. Hospital pharmacies must complete monthly reconciliation.

[handwritten annotations in margins: 15 DAYS; 30 DAYS; FOR EACH PHARMACY; 15 DAYS THEN ANNUALLY; ANNUALLY; SELF INSPECT FEB 1; Q 3 MTS HOSPITALS Q MTH]

[handwritten at bottom: CII RECONCILIATION = QUARTERLY (HOSP = MONTHLY)]

[handwritten at bottom: INVENTORY ALL CONTROLS = ANNUALLY]

	Appropriate training of all pharmacy staff	Training must include reviewing the PIC Self-Inspection Report, and all training must be documented.
	Implement quality assurance plan for pharmacy	A quality assurance plan must provide the pharmacy with a process to assess and improve on the services the pharmacy provides. Depending on the activities of the pharmacy, this may include the quality of products being compounded. The quality assurance plan for a pharmacy must go beyond a policy and procedure document; **assessments and improvement measures must be documented.**
FOR 3 YEARS	Filing and maintaining all records	See section on Records and Reviews. All records must be kept for 3 years.

PIC is also required to ensure the pharmacy is in compliance with state and federal laws and rules, including those for controlled substance (CS) records and inventories. HOWEVER, Oregon rules state this is responsibility of ALL LICENSED pharmacy personnel (so other pharmacists and licensed technicians are included!)

How many pharmacies can a pharmacist be PIC of at one time? #2
A pharmacist may be the PIC of two pharmacies at one time. In order to be PIC of more than two pharmacies, a pharmacist must obtain written approval from the BOP. Two, unless prior written approval by the board.

Are there any exceptions to this?
Yes. If you are the PIC of a nuclear pharmacy, you can only be PIC of ONE pharmacy. ONLY #1 NUCLEAR
OAR 855.042.0015

PHARMACISTS
OAR 855.019.0200

What is a pharmacist responsible for in the pharmacy?
- Following federal, and state laws and rules
- Supervising non-pharmacist personnel, and making sure they work within their scope of duties
- Securing the pharmacy from theft and diversion of medications
- Maintaining records and inventories according to the law
- Preventing non-pharmacist personnel from accessing the pharmacy when it is closed

What tasks can only a pharmacist perform?
- Receiving or transferring an oral prescription
- Drug Utilization Review (DUR)
- Laboratory monitoring (includes ordering and interpretation)
- Final verification
- Counseling
- Any other type of medication review, including drug regimen reviews, medication therapy management, and practice under collaborative drug therapy management agreement

PHARMACY INTERNS
OAR 855.031, OAR 855.019.0200

When is a pharmacy student allowed to practice as an intern? *SRI (FIRST YEAR)*
Once licensed as an intern, a student is allowed to participate in a School-based Rotational Internship (SRI) such as a school rotation but may not practice in a Traditional Pharmacy-practice Internship (TPI) such as a job employment until completing their first year of pharmacy school. The intern in a SRI is only allowed to perform technician duties until they successfully complete their first year of pharmacy school.

Can an intern perform any function that a pharmacist performs? *NOT FINAL VERIFICATION*
Yes, with the only exception being the final verification of a prescription. Note that the intern must only perform duties after successfully completing coursework related to those duties. *FIRST*

What are the intern supervision requirements?
An intern can only perform the functions of a pharmacist while being directly supervised by a pharmacist.

How is supervision defined by the BOP?
The BOP considers supervision to be when a pharmacist is in the same working area as the intern.
OAR 855.006.0005

How many interns may be supervised by a pharmacist at any one time?
See tablet under personnel ratios, but in general:
1 Pharmacist may supervise 1 Traditional Pharmacy Intern and
1 Pharmacist may supervise 2 School-based Rotational Interns at any one time.

TECHNICIANS
OAR 855.25

	There are three categories of technicians as follows:	
Technician *(2 YR)*	Has not completed training program, is at least 18 and has a high school diploma or GED.	One time licensure by BOP that expires within two years.
Certified technician	Has completed training program (PTCB or NHA)	Licensed by BOP, license is renewable
Certified technician checker *(HOSP ONLY)*	Certified technician in hospital who has completed the technician checker validation process	Certified by facility

How soon must a technician obtain certification, after obtaining their initial license?
A technician must take a certification exam either within 2 years or by the 2nd June 30th, whichever comes first, of registering as a technician with the board. For example, if a technician becomes licensed on March 15, 2019, they have until June 30th, 2020 to obtain their certified technician license.

Can a technician license be renewed?
No

Can a certified technician license be renewed?
Yes

What can a technician do?
Enter patient information into computer. Technicians CAN enter medical information, as long as nothing entered requires professional judgment.
Initiate or accept oral or electronic REFILL authorizations from practitioner or agent (must be NO changes!) *w/ No CHANGES*
Pack, pour, or place prescription medication in a container
Reconstitute medications
Label prescriptions
Prepack and label multi-dose and unit-dose medications *(FINAL REVIEW)*
Cart fills (For hospital patients)
Checking nursing units for sanitation and out of date meds (problems must be verified with pharmacist)
Bulk compounding and preparation of parenteral medications
Note that all technician duties must have a final review by a pharmacist. OAR 855.025.0040

Can a technician override computer warnings?
No. This is in regard to DUR alerts (allergy interactions, drug interactions, etc.). ONLY a pharmacist can override computer alerts/warnings.[6]

Can a technician accept a new prescription transmitted orally?
No! This includes a refill medication that has new directions or a new strength!

Can a technician request refills from a provider's office?
Yes, a technician can initiate a refill request from a provider.

Can a technician reconcile CII perpetual inventory? = (LOOK FOR PROBS)
Yes.[6] → PROBS TO RPh

What is a perpetual inventory?
A perpetual inventory refers to the process of tracking the exact quantity of on hand medication with each prescription filled. For example, if a pharmacies inventory states they have 300 Percocet tablets in stock, and a prescription is filled for 30 tablets, a perpetual inventory system would immediately show that 30 tablets were taken out of the pharmacy stock and that there are 270 tablets remaining. A perpetual inventory may be kept electronically or on paper.

Can a technician resolve discrepancies found in a CII perpetual inventory reconciliation?
No.[6] Only a pharmacist can.

Can a technician make IV's?
Yes, under the supervision of a pharmacist.
ORS 689.225

Technician Checkers
The technician checker validation program (TCVP) applies to a hospital only.
OAR 855.041.5055

Facility requirements to use TCVP → (HOSP "CHECKER" TECH)

Hospital Pharmacy

Policy and Procedure (P&P) document includes a list of High risk medications that the technician CANNOT check

Approval from the "appropriate committee" in the hospital

Drug distribution system has **one additional check** after tech check before the patient receives the medication (i.e. Nurse checks medication)

BOP approval

What can a certified technician checker check?

Cart fills (unit of use medications)

ADC batch replacements (i.e. Pyxis)

Kits designed for use in non-emergency situations
OAR 855.041.5160

Is special training required to become a checking technician?

Yes. Technicians must have **at least one year of experience** and complete the Technician Checking Validation Program (TCVP) to become authorized.
OAR 855.041.5130

After initial training and validation, how often must quality checks be done on a TCVP technician?

Monthly, then if pass every 3 months then quarterly, then if pass every 4 months (i.e. 1 year) then every 6 months.
OAR 855.041.5140

How many mistakes can a TCVP make during quality checks?

None. If the technician makes just 1 mistake, they must repeat the quality check. If the technician makes ANOTHER mistake, the technician must be retrained.
OAR 855.041.5140

1 MISTAKE → REPEAT CHECK
2 MISTAKES → RETRAIN

What if there are no problems for the technician to find during the quality checks?

This should never happen. The pharmacist should put in mistakes for the technician checker to find.
OAR 855.041.5140

CLERKS

What are clerks allowed to do?[2]

Send and receive orders to replenish stock, unpack and price drugs, place drugs on pharmacy shelves

Inventory counts

Pull outdates from pharmacy stock

Housekeeping and bookkeeping

File prescriptions and other general recordkeeping

Cashier duties

Provide price quotes or answer other non-professional telephone inquires

Deliver medications already released by pharmacist

Enter NON MEDICAL information into patient chart such as patient demographics and billing information. Note that allergies and medical conditions, even when not related to the script are considered medical information and cannot be entered by clerks
Accept prescription and hand to other staff for processing (but CANNOT accept oral or electronic refill authorizations)
Accept refill requests BY RX # ONLY
IF TRAINED inform patient of change in manufacturer ONLY

What are clerks NOT allowed to do?
Clerks are not allowed to do anything that assists in the practice of pharmacy. Besides the obvious activities involving the filling of a prescription, clerks cannot pull medication from the shelf to fill a prescription, count, reconstitute, pack, or pour medications, or put a prescription label on anything, because all that is included in the practice of pharmacy. Think about it this way- clerks cannot do anything that could influence a prescription.[2]

PERSONNEL RATIOS

What is the pharmacist to technician (or certified technician) ratio?
There is none.

What is the pharmacist to intern ratio?
It depends on the type of intern- see table below. In general, 1 Pharmacist to 1 TPI, and 1 Pharmacist to 2 SRIs.
OAR 855.031.0026

TPI Traditional Pharmacy-practice Internship	SRI School-based Rotational Internship
This is employment work, NO academic credit	This is the school rotation, NO employment
Pharmacists may only supervise **ONE TPI** at a time, unless the other interns are not completing intern activities (i.e. Performing technician duties only)	Pharmacist may supervise **TWO SRIs** at a time but may obtain authorization from BOP to supervise more.
Precepting pharmacist must be licensed as preceptor.	Precepting pharmacist must be licensed as preceptor.

Do the ratios still apply for immunization clinics?
No. A pharmacist may supervise **two** immunizing interns at a time during immunization clinics.

Do the ratios still apply during Public Health outreach programs or health fairs?
No, as long as no direct patient care activities are being done. The pharmacist may supervise up to **TEN INTERNS** at a time but must get approval from the school before doing so.

Can pharmacist preceptors accept students on SRI's from different schools?
Yes, however preceptors must notify the school if they are precepting students from more than one school at the same time.

PROVIDERS

Who has prescriptive authority in Oregon?[4]

Specialty	Abbreviation	Prescriptive authority?	Limits
Chiropractor	DC/ DCM	No	N/A
✓ Dentist	DDM/DDS	Yes	For dental practice only, CII's ok
Dental Hygienist ✓ NO CII	RDH	Yes	Limited to Fluoride, fluoride varnish, antibiotic solutions for mouth and other non-systemic antibiotic agents
✓ Expanded practice dental hygienist NO CII	RDH	Yes	In addition to medications allowed for dental hygienists above, can prescribe proton pump inhibitors, antibiotics, and NSAIDs
Midwife	CNM	No	"May independently purchase and administer limited formulary"
✓ Naturopathic Physician (LIMITED FORMULARY)	ND	Yes	Limited to formulary, (see ORS 689.145) CII's ok, Expedited Partner Therapy (EPT) Ok
✓ Nurse Practitioner	NP	Yes	No restrictions, CII's ok
✓ Optometrist LIMITED CII	OD	Yes	Restricted to formulary regulated by board of optometry. CII's limited to hydrocodone combination products
✓ Physician Assistant	PA	Yes	Restricted only by practice agreement, CII's ok
✓ Podiatrist	DPM	Yes	Podiatry practice only, CII's ok
✓ Veterinarian	DVM	Yes	For animal treatment only, CII's ok

Do providers with prescriptive authority need a DEA?
Any provider who writes for controlled substances must have a valid DEA number.

How do I check that a DEA number is valid?
See federal law section.

Can midlevel practitioners prescribe buprenorphine products for substance abuse?
Yes, but they must have obtained a DATA waiver and will therefore have a DEA number that begins with an X (X DEA)

A midlevel provider writes a prescription for buprenorphine. The midlevel does NOT have an X DEA number, but the patient's diagnosis is pain, not substance abuse. Is this ok?
Yes. The X DEA is only needed when buprenorphine products are prescribed for substance abuse. When buprenorphine is prescribed for pain, the practitioner does NOT need the X DEA.

Are there any medications a naturopathic physician CANNOT prescribe?
Yes, most notably:
- Barbiturates (except for phenobarbital)
- Systemic oncology agents (with many exceptions, including tamoxifen, megesterol, methotrexate, anastrazole, tretinoin)

- General anesthetics
- Oxytocic's and mifepristone when used as abortifacient

For a complete list, you can look at the naturopathic physician formulary in OAR 850.060.0223 and .0226.

Can a pharmacy sell medication to a providers' office for office use?
Yes.

To obtain medication, can a provider give you a script that says, "for office use only"?
No.[6]

Then how does a provider obtain medication for office use?
Through the use of an invoice for all non-controlled and CIII-V substances, and a DEA 222 form for CII medications.

Can a provider dispense samples to a patient?
Yes

Do samples have to be labeled?
Yes! Samples dispensed by a provider have almost the same labeling requirements as the pharmacy. They must contain the following: Practitioner name, address and phone number, patient name, medication name, strength, quantity, directions, expiration date, and ancillary information for safety.
OAR 855.043.0435

At what point would a provider have to register with the board as a Dispensing Practitioner Drug Outlet?
If the provider was dispensing MORE than a 72 hour supply of medication or dispensing medication refills to a patient they need to register as a DPDO with the OR BOP. UNLESS the provider is ONLY dispensing approved samples, homeopathic remedies, medications related to a medication assistance program, or the sample is only more than a 72 hour supply because they are in unit-of-use packaging (i.e. creams).
OAR 85.042.0510, OAR 855.042.0505

If a provider dies or retires, are the prescriptions still valid?
No, because there is no longer a valid patient-provider relationship. At this point you use professional judgment and follow procedures on emergency prescriptions when reviewing these prescriptions.[6]

Can I fill a prescription from an internet-based provider?
No. The BOP does not consider internet-based providers to meet the requirements for an appropriate patient-provider relationship.
OAR 855.019.0210

Can I fill a prescription from an out-of-state provider?
Yes, as long as the provider is practicing within their scope of practice in that state, and the patient had a valid relationship with the provider.
ORS 689.525

Can I fill a prescription from a provider in Canada?
No.[6]

Can I fill a prescription that a provider writes for a family member?
Yes! The BOP allows providers to write prescriptions for their family members, but if, in your professional judgment, the prescriber is not practicing appropriately, notify the appropriate board.

[handwritten note: ONLY IF FISHY]

THE PRESCRIPTION PROCESS

What must be on a prescription for it to be valid?
There is no place in Oregon state or federal law that states exactly what must be on a non-controlled prescription for it to be valid. It is clear, however, that you must be able to identify the patient, the medication, dosage form, and strength requested, the quantity authorized, and the provider authorizing the prescription. You will also need directions for taking the medication, however the provider is allowed to state "take as directed". Guidance on controlled substance prescriptions is listed below in the controlled substance section.
OAR 855.041.1105

Is a prescription written based on a questionnaire or internet based relationship valid?
No.
OAR 855.0190210

When does a prescription expire?	
ORS 475.185, OAR 855.041.1125, OAR 855.041.4005	
CII	NO expiration date
CIII-IV	5 refills or 6 months from date of issue whichever is 1st
Non-controls	1 year
EPT prescriptions	30 days

Can a hard copy prescription be written on anything?
It depends. While there is guidance in the law on what makes a prescription tamper-resistant, the only time tamper-resistant prescriptions are required currently by the state is when the hard-copy prescription is for a Medicaid patient.
OAR 855.006.0015, https://www.oregon.gov/pharmacy/Imports/News/Tamper_Resistant_Rx3-28-08.pdf

What features make a prescription tamper resistant?
Tamper resistant prescriptions must have at least one feature that prevents either copying, erasing a prescription, or the ability to use a counterfeit prescription. Some examples of features that would meet these requirements would be heat sensitive or coin reactive ink or watermarks.

By what methods can an electronic prescription be transmitted?
OAR 855.006.0015

As long as provider name and contact information are on the prescription, and the prescription was encrypted when it was sent, prescriptions can be sent as the following:

Fax -> Fax
Computer -> Computer

Fax -> Computer
Computer -> Fax

Can a patient bring in a faxed prescription?
No. Faxed and electronically submitted prescriptions must come directly from the practitioner's office to the pharmacy. A prescription faxed to a patient is not considered valid.
ORS 475.188

What must I write down when I take an oral prescription?
OAR 855.019.0210

Date
Practitioner information: full name of practitioner AND name of person calling prescription in. Also, an address and DEA if for controlled substance ORAL
Patient information: name
Medication Information: name, strength, form, directions, quantity and refills
Pharmacist information: signature, initials, or electronic ID

Can a providers' agent call in a CIII-CV prescription?
Yes.

What do I have to document when a prescription is transferred into or out of my pharmacy?
OAR 855.041.1105

The name of the pharmacist transferring and receiving the prescription
Patient information: Name
Practitioner information: FULL name, along with address and DEA if medication is a controlled substance
Medication information: name, strength, dose form, directions for use, quantity prescribed AND quantity dispensed (if different than prescribed)
Prescription information: Date prescription was last filled and refills authorized

How many times can a prescription be transferred?
Non-controlled substances can be transferred as many times as possible within the quantity allowed on the prescription. Controlled substances can only be transferred once, unless the pharmacies share a common, real-time database.
OAR 855.041.2115

What must I document when I accept additional refills from a provider or a providers' agent?
Date of authorization
Name of prescriber AND prescribers' agent, if the agent was involved
Documentation of authorization

What does PRN refills mean? → FILL UNTIL 365 DAYS PASS
You can fill medication for 1 year from date of issue if the prescription is for a legend medication. For CIII-V substances you can refill up to 5 refills or 6 months
OAR 855.041.1125

Can refills be combined into one fill?
Yes, unless the prescription is for a controlled substance or psychotherapeutic substance.
OAR 855.041.1120

~~Do I~~ have to notify the provider if refills are combined into one fill?
Yes.
OAR 855.041.1120

Are auto-refill programs allowed?
Yes.
OAR 855.041.1120

What is an auto-refill program?
An auto-refill program is a program your pharmacy has in place to automatically refill a prescription when it is due to be refilled.

Can ~~I automatically~~ enter a patient's medication into an auto-refill program?
No. Each prescription must be individually enrolled in an auto-refill program.

Are there any medications that cannot be a part of the auto-refill program?
Yes, controlled substances cannot be enrolled in an auto-refill program.

Can a patient's medication stay in an auto-refill program forever?
Sure. As long as the patient picks up the medication every time. If the patient does not pick up the medication or if the medication can't be delivered to the patient it MUST be removed from the auto-refill program. Patients can also request that their medication be removed from the auto-refill program.

What am I legally required to evaluate a prescription for?
You are required to complete a therapeutic review and a legal review of the prescription, which the law defines as follows:
OAR 855.006.005

Therapeutic review	Legal review
Is this the right medication?	Is the prescription valid; has it been altered or forged, and does it meet all federal and state requirements?
Is this medication ok to take with the patient's other medications?	Was this medication prescribed for legitimate medical purpose?
Is the prescription safe? Look at dosing and frequency.	Pharmacist Judgment

When am I allowed to substitute a generic equivalent on a prescription?
You can substitute medication that, in your professional opinion, is therapeutically equivalent to the prescribed medication in terms of generic name, strength, quantity, dose, and dosage form.
ORS 689.515

NOT IF ↑ $$$

How does a provider indicate they do not want a substituted product?
By writing "Dispended As Written" (DAW), "No substitution", "brand necessary", or anything similar on the prescription, or telling you with an oral prescription.   *ANY NOTE, OR EVEN ORALLY*
OAR 855.041.1105

Do I have to substitute a medication with an AB rating in the orange book?

No. Oregon allows you to substitute a medication that in your professional judgment is therapeutically equivalent.

Can I substitute a liquid when the prescriber orders a tablet? Or vice versa?
For this type of substitution, you need to reach the provider. If this is not possible, you can make this substitution as long as the substituted liquid/tablet is equivalent to the prescribed medication, and the prescribed medication does not use any unique delivery system. EMERGENCY → YES
OAR 689.515

Can a pharmacist substitute a medication that costs more than the originally prescribed medication?
No. You can only substitute when the medication you will dispense will cost the same or less than the originally prescribed medication.
ORS 689.515

What about substitutions on prescriptions for biologic substances?
ORS 689.522, OAR 855.014.1105

You can substitute a biologic under the following conditions:
Biosimilar is considered interchangeable with prescribed biologic by the FDA (Listed in the Purple Book)
Prescriber did not note DAW on prescription
The patient is told about the substitution
The practitioner is notified or has access to a system that shows the product dispensed. This notification must occur within 3 BUSINESS days

If there are no FDA approved biosimilars that can be substituted for a biologic, and the prescription is therefore dispensed for the exact product written, do I still need to notify the prescriber what was dispensed?
No.

If the prescription was originally dispensed for a substituted biosimilar and the provider was notified at the initial fill, does the prescriber need to be notified again at each refill?
No. The provider only needs to be notified upon the initial fill and substitution.

What prescriptions require a drug utilization review (DUR)?
A drug utilization review must be completed for EVERY prescription, both NEW and REFILLED prescriptions.

What constitutes a DUR?
OAR 855.006.0005

A DUR involves a review of a patient's profile for:
Allergy to medication
Medication dose and frequency- is it appropriate?
Duplication of therapy (i.e. omeprazole and pantoprazole)
Drug-drug interactions
Interactions between medication and disease state (i.e. Kidney dysfunction and renally adjusted medication)
Potential misuse or abuse of medication
Utilization of the medication (watch for overuse or underuse)

What is required to be on the prescription label?
ORS 689.505, OAR 855.041.1130
- Pharmacy information: Name, address, telephone number
- Patient information: Name
- Medication information: Name (brand OR generic and manufacturer), strength, quantity, directions for use, physical description, expiration date, and cautionary statements for patient safety
- Prescriber information: Name
- Prescription information: prescription number, date, and "Caution: Federal law prohibits dispensing without prescription"

[handwritten note: JUST NAME]

Are there any exceptions to these items?
ORS 689.505
Yes!
- Name of patient- not required for EPT prescriptions
- Name of medication- provider can request that label does not include the medication name
- Directions- provider can state to take "as directed"
- Quantity- provider can request that label does not include the quantity, and quantity is not required on label for compounded medications
- Physical description: Not required on unit dose or unit-of-use medications (basically any medication that you are dispensing in the manufacturers original container, like an inhaler)

What is required to be on each unit dose container?
Medication Name, strength, manufacturer, lot number and expiration date
ORS 689.005

If a patient requests non-child resistant packaging, what do you have do document?
The patient has to sign a waiver to document that they want non-child resistant packaging.

What constitutes a med pack?
Medication packaged with two or more solid medications in the same container, labeled to indicate the day and time the medication should be taken.
OAR 855.041.1140

Can you dispense medications in a medpak?
Yes.

What is the beyond use date of medpak medications?
60 days or less.

Do medpaks meet the requirements of the Poison Prevention Packaging Act?
No. They are not automatically child resistant.

A patient requests her medications be placed in a medpak. Your med packs are not child resistant. Does she still have to sign a waiver?
Yes. If she does not sign a waiver you have to find a way to put the medpak in a child-resistant container.

What ID is a patient required to present in order to pick up a prescription?

There are no federal or state ID requirements to pick up a prescription, however a pharmacist may refuse to dispense a medication to anyone without "proper identification".
OAR 855.019.0210

Who can a medication be dispensed to?
The patient or the patient's agent.

Where can medication be delivered to a patient?
Patient's residence (primary or alternate), workplace, medical care facility, practitioner's office, or the patient's exact location. Note that a medication cannot be delivered to a provider's residence.[6]
OAR 855.041.1050

When do you have to counsel a patient?
Three scenarios: a new prescription, any change to an existing prescription (including directions and dose changes), and/or when the prescription is new to your pharmacy.
OAR 855.019.0230

Can a patient refuse counseling?
Yes.

Who can accept the refusal to be counseled?
ONLY a pharmacist. A technician cannot accept a refusal to be counseled.

If a patient refuses counseling, and you think it's important, can you deny dispensing the prescription?
Yes! Be careful regarding patient's rights, but you can technically deny dispensing if you think the patient's safety is at stake.

If a patient's agent is picking up the prescription, can you counsel them? Can they refuse counseling?
You treat a patient's agent the same as the patient. You DO counsel a patient's agent, and the patient's agent CAN refuse counseling.

What information MUST you tell the patient when you counsel them?
Oregon law requires you to tell the patient (or patient's agent) anything you deem important for their safety and to effectively use the medication.

Do you have to document counseling?
Yes. You must document that you counseled or that a patient refused. Counseling documentation must include more than just "counseled".

Do you have to counsel on medications that are being delivered to a patient (i.e. They are not coming into the pharmacy)?
No, but in these scenarios, you must include written information on how the patient can contact the pharmacist for counseling.

Once a medication leaves the pharmacy, when can it be returned?
OAR 855.041.1045

When the medication was dispensed in error, was defective, adulterated, misbranded, dispensed beyond its expiration date or subject to recall. In these instances, the medication must be disposed of. In these instances, it is ok to accept a controlled substance back as long as you document what was returned and what you provided the patient on the hardcopy prescription.[6]

When the pharmacist thinks the medication could cause the patient harm if it was not taken back. In this case it must also be disposed of.

If the medication was unable to be delivered to the patient

If you can verify the medication was kept and stored correctly and is in a tamper evident unit, you can accept the return AND re-dispense it afterwards (i.e. When it is returned from a long term care facility)

SPECIFIC PRESCRIPTION GUIDANCE

RESTRICTED SUBSTANCES

What non-prescription items are restricted for sale in Oregon and must be sold behind the pharmacy counter?
OAR 855.050.0035

Ammoniated Mercury Ointment 5%
Ammonia solution, USP 28%
Arsenic
Blue Ointment
Carbolic acid
Corrosive sublimate
Cyanides including hydrocyanic acid
Hydrochloric acid
Nitric Acid
Sulfa drugs
Sulphuric acid

Do substances sold behind the pharmacy counter need a label?
All of the substances listed above need a label that contains the pharmacy name and address and adequate warnings with the exception of Ammoniated mercury, sulfa drugs, or blue ointment, IF these items are sold in their original container.

Does the sale of the above substances need to be recorded in the Poison Register?
Yes, with the exception of Ammoniated mercury, sulfa drugs, and blue ointment.

Can I sell one of the above listed substances as a behind the counter item if the only products I have state RX Only?
No! Even if the product can be sold both behind the counter AND as a prescription product, the only time you can dispense one of the above products is when it does NOT have a prescription legend.

If a patient comes in with a script for one of the above substances, does the sale need to be recorded in the poison register?
No.

Are there any medications that OR BOP considers prescription medications that are not federally required to have a prescription?
Yes.

- Anything containing codeine or codeine salts
- Anything containing opium or paregoric
- Pseudoephedrine, ephedrine, and phenylpropanolamine

OAR 855.050.0070

Are there any other substances that are restricted for sale but do not have to be sold behind the pharmacy counter or be listed in the poison register?
Yes

- Dextromethorphan- sale is restricted to persons 18 years old or older
- Nitrous Oxide- sale is restricted to persons 18 years old or older

ORS 475.380 and .390

CONTROLLED SUBSTANCES
OAR 855.041.6600

Are there any substances that are considered controlled in OR that are not controlled federally?
Yes.

- Pseudoephedrine: schedule III
- Ephedrine: schedule III
- Phenylpropanolamine: schedule III

OAR 855.080.0023-0024, ORS 475.973

Marijuana

Marijuana is medically and recreationally legal in Oregon (OR). However, marijuana is still considered a schedule II controlled substance. How does that work?
Marijuana is not regulated by the OR BOP, it is instead regulated by the Oregon Department of Health and the Oregon Liquor Control Commission.[6]

The majority of regulations on controlled substances follow federal regulations, with the exceptions to specific substances listed above. Some additional, Oregon specific information is listed below.

Are there any additional items that must be on a CII prescription, beyond the general prescription requirements?
Yes. CII prescriptions must have the providers DEA number, the providers' address and the patients' address, and hardcopy prescriptions must have a hand-signature from the provider. It must also have the patient's FULL name.

Can I fill in the name if the provider writes only part of the patients' name? (i.e. A Smith)
Yes, you cannot change the name but you can fill in the missing information, (i.e. Update to Adam Smith), but only once you verify with the provider.

What information can I change on a CII prescription?[5]

Drug Strength	Yes, you can change.
Dosage Form	Yes, you can change this without the providers' authorization IF the provider is not reasonably available to confirm change AND as long as the drug does not have a unique delivery form.
Quantity	Yes, you can change.
Directions	Yes, you can change.
Date to fill	Yes, you can change! This is considered part of the directions
Patient Name	No, you cannot change. Unless provider only wrote first or last name you can only add the rest AFTER clarifying with the provider!
Drug	No, you cannot change, except for in case of a drug shortage
Provider Signature	No, you cannot change. Also note that hardcopy and faxed prescriptions must be HAND signed! No stamps! Also, the providers agent cannot sign for these medications!

[handwritten note on Patient Name row: "CLARIFY, NOT △"]

Aside from the patient's name, you can add and change all other patient related information on a prescription (i.e. Address, telephone, age), and you can add or change the prescriber's registration number WITHOUT confirming with the provider. All other changes allowed in the above table require the providers' authorization. Changes must ALWAYS be documented.

How long is a CII prescription valid?
Legally, it is good forever. However, you should use your professional judgment, and there must always be a patient-provider relationship for a prescription to be valid.

What is the quantity limit of a CII prescription?
There is no quantity limit

Can CII's be postdated?
No. If a provider wants a patient to pick up later, they must write "do not fill until" with a date, but the issue date of the prescription must still be the date it was written.

Can I process a CII prescription written by an out-of-state provider?
Yes, as long as the provider is practicing within their scope in that state.

Is a faxed CII prescription valid?
No.
ORS 475.185

[handwritten: NO FAXED CII's]

Are there any exceptions to this?
Yes. There are three instances when a faxed CII prescription is allowed: Home infusion, hospice care, and long-term or community based care.[4]

Are electronically submitted CII prescriptions valid?
Yes.
ORS 475.185

[handwritten: e script = yes]

Can a pharmacist accept a verbal order for a CII prescription?
No.
ORS 475.185

[handwritten: VERBAL = NO]

Are there any exceptions to this?
Yes. Verbal orders are allowed to provide an emergency supply for Home infusion, hospice, and long term care, care for terminally ill and for ambulatory care and community pharmacy. A signed hard copy prescription for the emergency supply must be obtained from the provider, postmarked within 7 days.[3]

Can I partial fill a CII prescription?
Yes.[6]

When do I have to provide the patient with the remaining quantity?
The remaining quantity must be DISPENSED within 72 hours.[6]

≤ 72° FOR CII COMPLETION FILL

What if the patient comes back after the 72 hour period?
The remaining quantity is voided, and you cannot provide the patient with any more of the medication without a new prescription. You will also need to contact the provider and notify them of the actual quantity that was dispensed to the patient.

Are there any other situations that allow a partial fill of a CII prescription?
Yes. Patients in an applicable care facility or diagnosed with a terminal illness. For these patients a CII script can be partially filled for 60 days from the date the prescription was written.[6]

What do I have to document when I partially fill a CII prescription in this situation?
Your initials, the date, quantity you dispensed AND the quantity remaining on the prescription. For example, if the prescription was initially for 120 tablets and you are providing 20 tablets today, you may write: "6/19/2019   Dispensed 20, 100 remaining   RPh initials"[5]

Are there any additional items that must be on a CIII-CV prescription, beyond the general prescription requirements?
Yes, the prescription must additionally contain the patient's full name and address, the providers address and DEA, and for hardcopy OR faxed prescriptions the providers hand-signature. Prescriptions sent electronically must be transmitted by the prescriber themselves.
OAR 855.019.0210

How long is a CIII-CV prescription valid?
Either for 6 months from the date written or for 5 refills, whichever comes first.
ORS 475.185

What is the quantity limit of a CIII-CV medication?
There is no quantity limit.

If there is no quantity limit, can I fill a prescription for a controlled substance that is written "Take one daily, quantity #365"?
Technically you CAN fill this prescription, even though it is more than a 6 months' supply of medication. However, you must always use your professional judgment in these cases!

A patient brings in a hardcopy prescription for lorazepam 1mg tablets, instructions to take 1.5 tablets daily as needed for anxiety, QTY 45, 5 refills. The patient has filled the prescription once, but instead of a refill the patient now wants a partial of 15. Does the partial count as one of the 5 refills?

No. The partial amount must be less than the full authorized amount (i.e. Less than 45). IF the patient were to request three partial quantities of 15 each, then you would use up 1 refill, as you have now provided the patient with a full 45 tablets.[6]

If a provider instructs a patient to return a controlled substance in exchange for another controlled substance, can you accept the returned medication?
No (unless in the case of an error or recall). The only thing you can do is watch the patient destroy the medication in front of you.

Can I accept a fax of a CIII-CV prescription?
Yes. Just remember that all faxed prescriptions must still meet the DEA system faxing requirements. i.e. A patient cannot fax in their own prescription, and a doctor cannot fax you a prescription from his home unless his home meets the system requirements.[3]
OAR 855.019.0210, ORS 475.185

Can the provider use a stamp on the faxed controlled substance prescriptions in place of his signature?
No! Prescriptions must have the ORIGINAL, MANUALLY SIGNED signature of the provider.
OAR 855.019.0210

Can a provider's agent fax a controlled substance prescription?
Yes. A providers' agent may fax a controlled substance prescription that has been hand signed by the provider.

To help clarify who can transmit what, please review the following table:

TRANSMISSION ROUTE	SCHEDULE II CS	SCHEDULE III-V CS
Verbal Rx	Prescriber only, limited cases	Agent or prescriber
Fax Rx	Prescriber only, limited cases	Agent or prescriber
Electronic Rx	Prescriber only	Prescriber only
Orally verify/change Rx	Prescriber only	Agent or prescriber
Signature on hard copy or fax	Prescriber only	Prescriber only

Can technicians accept refills of CIII-CVs?
No.

If you think a provider is inappropriately prescribing controlled substances, who do you contact?
The regulatory board that governs that provider.

Is there an age requirement to pick up controlled substances?
No.

Can you dispense a controlled substance to a patient without an ID?
Yes. Oregon does not require ID's for controlled substances; however, a pharmacist may refuse to dispense a medication to anyone without "proper identification".
OAR 855.019.0210

How many times can a controlled substance prescription be transferred?
Once, unless the pharmacies share an electronic database that functions in real-time.

Your inventory system allows you to pull up CIII-V scripts electronically, separated from non-controlled medications. If your pharmacy files CIII-V hard copies with prescriptions for legend medications, do the CIII-V hard copies still need a stamp?
No. If you can pull up CIII-V medications electronically separate from legend medications they do not need a stamp.[6]

Are syringes considered controlled substances?
No. Syringes are not considered controlled substances or paraphernalia.
ORS 475.525

Does a patient have to have a prescription to receive syringes?
No.

What is the quantity limit on syringes?
There is none. Syringes are not considered paraphernalia in OR, and it is legal to sell them without any limits on quantity.

Are there any restrictions on syringe sales?
Yes. Syringes cannot be sold to "minors" unless the minor has authorization from a practitioner. Otherwise syringes are not restricted, considered controlled substances, or considered paraphernalia.
ORS 475.744

Are providers required to check Oregon's Prescription Drug Monitoring Program (PDMP) before writing a controlled substance prescription?
No.

Are providers required to register with PDMP?
Yes.
ORS 333.023.0825

Are pharmacists required to check the PDMP before dispensing a controlled substance prescription?
No.

How soon to pharmacies have to submit information to the PDMP after filling a controlled substance prescription?
Information must be reported to the PDMP within 72 hours. Note that this ONLY applies for CII-CIV, so NOT CV!
ORS 333.023.0810

What is the pharmacy required to submit to the PDMP?
Patient information: FULL name, address, phone number, DOB, gender
Pharmacy information: DEA #
Prescriber information: Name, DEA #
Medication information: NDC, quantity, days' supply, refills authorized
Prescription Information: RX #, Date written and date dispensed, fill number

Can a patient request a report of their PDMP record?
Yes, but the request must be made to the Oregon Health Authority.

Do you have to tell the patient about the PDMP?
Yes. The patient is supposed to be notified of the monitoring program either before or when the medication is dispensed.
ORS 333.023.0815

Can law enforcement request a report of a patient's PDMP record?
Yes, they can, however the request must be made to and access granted by the Oregon Health Authority.
ORS 333.023.0820

EMERGENCY PRESCRIPTIONS

Can you provide a patient with an emergency refill when they are from an area that just suffered a natural disaster?
Yes, you can provide an emergency refill and/or an emergency new prescription.

Can you provide a patient with an emergency refill when additional refills are not currently authorized, and there is no natural disaster, state of emergency, etc.?
Yes, if you believe an additional refill is necessary and cannot reach the prescriber, and the medication is NOT a controlled substance

> **There are two different scenarios that may result in issuance of an "emergency prescription":**
> 1. Natural disaster, or declared state of emergency, either in your location or in the patient's place of residence   30 DAYS
> 2. Patient out of critical, chronic medication and provider cannot be reached   72°

Scenario 1: Natural disaster
OAR 855.007.0090
This scenario DOES NOT allow emergency prescriptions for controlled substances UNLESS the DEA grants permission via waiver or notification to the BOP.

30 DAYS, NO REFILLS

Emergency REFILL	Emergency NEW prescriptions
Refill of prescription from provider who has relationship with patient	Consult with provider who may not have relationship with patient
Must be essential therapy	Must be essential therapy
Dispense 30 day supply or less	Dispense minimum amount necessary until patient can be seen by healthcare provider
Notify patient refill is being given without provider authorization, and they need a provider to authorize additional refills	Notify patient that prescription being provided absent relationship but provider was consulted, and that any refills need authorization from provider.
Record indicates emergency prescription	Record indicates emergency prescription AND that therapy has been "initiated or modified"

Can you provide emergency refill for a controlled substance?
No! Unless the DEA has granted permission by providing the BOP with a waiver or other notification.

Scenario 2: Patient out of medication, provider cannot be reached
OAR 855.041.1120

Emergency Refill Requirements
Refill of prescription from provider who has relationship with patient
Must be essential therapy, but CANNOT be for a controlled substance
Dispense no more than 72 hour supply, or less if you think you can reach provider sooner
Notify the provider of the emergency supply

Can emergency rooms dispense medication to patients?
OAR 855.041.6400
Yes.

What duration of supply can the emergency room provide a patient?   ER = 48° OF MED
OAR 855.041.6410
No more than 48 hours' worth of medication, unless limited by package size (think: ointment tube, may last longer than 48 hours), or it is in the best interest of the patient to give the full course of medication.

How soon must a pharmacist review emergency room orders?
OAR 855.041.6410
Within 24 hours, although may be within 72 hours depending on pharmacy hours. Either way, orders should be reviewed the first day pharmacy is re-open.

EXPEDITED PARTNER THERAPY (EPT) Prescriptions
OAR 855.041.4005

TREATING SEX PARTNERS OF ORIGINAL PATIENT

Is an EPT prescription that states "EPT: Provide to all applicable partners" valid?
No! Need an individual prescription for EACH EPT dose given. (I.e. With either patient names or EPT Partner 1, 2, etc.)

What medications are included in EPT?[7]
DRIP DRIP   CLAP
EPT prescriptions are valid for the treatment of *Neisseria gonorrhea* and *Chlamydia trachomatis* only. No other STD treatments are currently included in Oregon's EPT program. This limits EPT prescriptions to azithromycin, and cefixime per OR EPT protocol.
SUPRAX

Are there any special notations that are required on an EPT prescription?
Yes, the provider must note that the prescription is for EPT, in those words or something similar.

When does an EPT prescription expire?   30 DAY EXP
After 30 days.

Can you refill EPT prescriptions?
No.

Who can pick up the EPT prescription?

EITHER the patient who obtained the prescription (they can pick up ALL EPT prescriptions) or the partner for whom the EPT dose is intended.
- ORIGINAL PT
- PARTNER PRESCRIBED FOR

When dispensing an EPT prescription, are there any special counseling requirements?
Yes. You must not only verbally counsel, but you must also provide written information with the prescription to each partner.
VERBAL INFO
+
WRITTEN INFO

Are there any special record-keeping requirements for EPT prescriptions?
Yes. Documentation must be attached to the EPT prescription and each partner prescription must be referenced.

HAZARDOUS MEDICATIONS
OAR 855.045.0250

Oregon law provides no state-specific guidance on hazardous medications, however any compounding involving hazardous medications are automatically considered at least medium risk.

DEATH WITH DIGNITY
ORS 127

What role does a pharmacist have in Oregon's Death with Dignity Act?
A pharmacist may be asked to fill a prescription that will be used in compliance with Oregon's Death with Dignity Act. The attending physician must inform the pharmacist of the prescription, deliver the prescription by hand or by mail, and the prescription may only be dispensed to the patient, the physician or an agent of the patient that is specifically identified.

NOT FAX
NOT e-SCRIPT

EXPANDED PRACTICE PHARMACY

Are there any statewide protocols for pharmacist prescribing in OR?
Yes. There is a statewide protocol for immunizations, travel health, and smoking cessation, although the protocol for smoking cessation has not been developed at this time. Further details on each of these can be found below.
OAR 855.019.0264
- IMMU
- TRAVEL HEALTH
- SMOKING

Do pharmacies or pharmacists have to obtain any special license to participate in the statewide protocols?
No, however the pharmacy must have a policy and procedure for each protocol it participates in and keep documentation of training required in the protocol.
OAR 855.019.0264
ORIGINATE + DOCUMENT
PROCEDURES AT PHARMACY LEVEL

Is there any other area in which pharmacists have prescriptive authority?
Yes. There is a statewide protocol for pharmacist prescribing of birth control, naloxone, and epinephrine. Further details on each of these can be found below.

Are pharmacists allowed to provide Medication Therapy Management services?
Yes.
OAR 855.019.0250

What are the objectives of medication therapy management (MTM)?
In MTM you are attempting to optimize a patient's therapeutic outcomes. To do this you may address adherence, appropriate use of the medication, adverse drug reactions, and outcomes.

Under MTM, can you independently change medication dosing, medication regimens, or switch the patient's medications?
No, but you recommend these things to the provider.

Are pharmacist collaborative practice agreements allowed in OR?
Yes, collaborative practice agreements are allowed.
OAR 855.019.0260

Are pharmacists allowed prescriptive authority under collaborative practice agreements?
No. While a pharmacist can make decisions on therapy within the scope of the practice agreement, the pharmacist is still writing a prescription under the providers name and authority.

What must be documented in a Collaborative Drug Therapy Management (CDTM) agreement?
Name of principal pharmacist and provider responsible for agreement
Name of all pharmacists that may practice under the agreement
Types of decisions that a pharmacist can make. With medication, must include specific medications, dosage, frequency, and route of administration.
Decision criteria and plan pharmacist must use when making decisions
When the pharmacist is required to contact the provider
Pharmacist training requirements
Quality assurance program that accompanies agreement (i.e. Reviews of pharmacist work)

How often must a CDTM agreement be reviewed?
At least every 2 years.

IMMUNIZATIONS
OAR 855.019.0270, 855.019.0280, ORS 689.645

What vaccines can a pharmacist administer?
There are no restrictions on the type of vaccines a pharmacist can administer, although only pharmacists with a Yellow Fever stamp may administer the Yellow Fever vaccine.[9]

Can an intern administer vaccines?
Only if they have had the appropriate training and are supervised by an appropriately trained pharmacist.

How old must a patient be for a pharmacist to vaccinate?
7 years.

When is a patient considered 7 years old?
On the day of their 7th birthday (i.e. patient's date of birth is March 1, 2020, on March 1, 2027 the patient will be considered 7 years old).

Are there any circumstances that would allow a pharmacist to vaccinate a patient younger than this?
Yes. You can vaccinate patients aged 3 years or older if the governor authorizes it due to an emergency situation.
OAR 855.007.0080

[handwritten: 3+ YEARS IF EMERGENCY BY GOVERNOR]

Can a pharmacist with CPR training give vaccines to pediatric patients?
ONLY if CPR training included training on pediatric CPR.

What reference do you need to have on hand if you give vaccines?
Centers for Disease Control and Prevention (CDC) "Epidemiology and Prevention of Vaccine-Preventable Diseases".

[handwritten: CDC VACCINE REFERENCE ON HAND]

Where do you report that a vaccine was given?
OHA Alert. Must report within 15 days.

Do you have to report that a vaccine was given to the primary care provider (PCP)?
No. You only need to report to the PCP if the patient had an adverse event.

If a patient has an adverse event, do you report it to anyone besides the PCP?
Yes! You need to enter it into the Vaccine Adverse Events Reporting System (VAERS).

What steps do you have to take before you give a patient a vaccine?
The patient must receive the VIS statement, have time to review it and ask any questions they have BEFORE you administer the vaccine.

If your practice site administers vaccines, do you have to have any specific policies and procedures on it?
Yes, you must have a policy and procedure that details how to handle used or contaminated equipment as well as a policy on vaccine administration in general.

What is a VFC vaccine? *[handwritten: → FREE VACCINATION TO POOR CHILDREN]*
VFC is 'vaccines for children', which some patients are eligible for. It is a designation for the source of the vaccine. *[handwritten: MUST BE RECOGNIZED PROVIDER]*

Can a pharmacist administer a VFC vaccine?
Yes, however you must be a recognized VFC provider.

Do you need to notate that the patient received a VFC vaccine somewhere?
Yes. You need to note if patient received a VFC vaccine in the administration record.

TRAVEL HEALTH

While Travel Health is an approved statewide protocol, the exact protocol has not yet been developed.

NALOXONE
ORS 689.681, 689.682, OAR 855.019.0450-0460

Does a pharmacist have to complete a training program to prescribe naloxone?
There are no specific training requirements in the law, but the pharmacist must have been educated on naloxone and opioid overdose.

Can you dispense supplies to be used with naloxone if you (the pharmacist) wrote the naloxone prescription?
Yes. You can dispense naloxone along with the supplies needed to use the medication.

Who can a pharmacist prescribe naloxone to?
To anyone who is seeking it. The law specifies this includes those completing overdose training.

Do you have to counsel on naloxone prescriptions?
Yes! Pharmacist prescribed naloxone is not exempt from counseling requirements

BIRTH CONTROL
ORS 689.689, OAR 855.019.0400-0435

Under what circumstances can a pharmacist prescribe birth control?
Patient is 18 years old or older OR *18+ OR PROOF OF RX*
Patient is less than 18 years old but has proof of previous prescription for patch or self-administered oral contraceptive *NOT SHOTS*
Patient has completed self-screening risk assessment tool within the last 12 months (if the patient is coming to you for the first time today, she needs to complete the assessment before you prescribe)
Pharmacist has completed mandatory training program and submitted training to the board
Pharmacist follows Oregon Standard Procedures Algorithm when prescribing
Pharmacist refers patient to primary care provider
Patient is provided with visit summary
If injectable, the medication is administered ASAP after prescription written *INJECTIONS ONSITE*

How often must the self-screening assessment questionnaire be completed?
Yearly

What must you do after providing a patient with birth control?
Provide the patient with a visit summary and recommend the patient contact their provider

- SUMMARY
- RECOMEND CONTACT PCP PROVIDER

Are there any restrictions on birth control prescribing by a pharmacist?
Yes:
- The patient must not be required to make an appointment
- The pharmacist cannot prescribe beyond three years of the patient's last clinical visit with a primary care provider.
- If the Standard Procedures Algorithm states the patient must be referred to the provider, the pharmacist cannot prescribe birth control!
- The pharmacist CANNOT prescribe for themselves or for members of their immediate family.

- WITHIN 12 MONTHS LAST ASSESMENT
- WITHIN 3 YRS LAST LAST CLINICAL VISIT
- NO SELVES
- NO FAMILY

EPINEPHERINE *EPIPEN*
OAR 855.041.2320

Who can obtain epinephrine without a script?
Anyone with a valid Authorization to Obtain Epinephrine certificate AND a Statement of Completion.

3 YEARS, 4 TIMES

How many epinephrine syringes can you dispense?
This is based on what is listed on authorization form. At any one time you can dispense ONE adult and ONE pediatric epinephrine package. The certificate can be used up to four times within a three-year period.

ONE PACKAGE EACH ADULT/CHILD, 4 TIMES IN 3 YEARS

How is epinephrine dispensing in this manner documented?
A pharmacist must write a script for the epinephrine and file it appropriately and should document on the Authorization certificate what was dispensed.

How long is an authorization to obtain epinephrine certificate valid?
3 years from date of issue. *(4 TIMES IN 3 YEARS)*

LAWS GOVERNING SPECIFIC PHARMACY PRACTICE AREAS

HOSPITAL PHARMACIES
(May be referred to as: Residential Drug Outlets, Institutional Pharmacy, Residential Pharmacy)

If an institution has more than one pharmacy, do they need multiple PIC's?
Yes. The institution will also need to designate a chief pharmacy officer (CPO) to oversee all pharmacy operations. The CPO may be the PIC of one of institution's pharmacies.
OAR 855.041.6150

CPO (PIC)
PIC   PIC   PIC

Can an institution have medication storage areas that are located outside of the pharmacy?
Yes. These are either called Remote Storage Areas or Secondary Drug Storage Areas. Secondary Drug Storage Areas may also be called drug rooms.
OAR 855.041.6050, ORS 689.005, ORS 689.605

How often must medication storage areas throughout the hospital be inspected?
At least every two months all areas in the institution that store medications must be inspected. In these inspections you must look for outdated medications, make sure emergency kits are in working order, and that required documentation is being completed. *DRUG ROOMS Q 2 MONTHS*
OAR 855.041.6200

An institutional pharmacy closes as 5pm. At 2AM the inpatient ward needs a medication that is not available from their med room. Can a non-pharmacist access the pharmacy to get the medication?
Yes. With prior approval and training, a nurse supervisor may obtain medication from the pharmacy. There must be a practitioner's order in the patient's chart BEFORE the medication is obtained, and removal of the medication must be documented.
OAR 855.041.6310

(1) ORDER IN CHART
(2) NURSE SUPERVISOR

What medications must be included in an emergency kit?
There is no specific medication list, rather the medications included must have been determined by the appropriate committee.

What is required to be on the label of an emergency kit?
OAR 855.041.6420

"For Emergency use" (or something similar)	① "EMERGENCY"
For EACH medication: Name, Strength, Quantity	② DRUG/QTY NAME/STRENGTH/QTY
Expiration date of kit	③ KIT EXP DATE

* TAMPER SEAL

Does an emergency kit have to be sealed?
Yes, and the seal must be tamper evident.

Who is responsible for an emergency kit (think: when emergency kit may be offsite)?
The providing pharmacy is responsible for the kit.
OAR 855.041.7060

What constitutes a valid medication order in an institutional setting?
Patient information: Name, location
Medication information: Name, strength
Administration information: Route, directions for use
Order information: Date and time, electronic or hand signature of provider
OAR 855.041.6500

Are verbal medication orders allowed in a hospital setting?
Yes, but they should not be used often, must be immediately reduced to writing and confirmed by reading the order back, and the prescriber must initial or sign the order as soon as possible.
OAR 855.041.6500

① REDUCE TO WRITING
② READ BACK
③ MD INITIALS ASAP

Under what circumstances is a DUR is NOT required before administration?
No pharmacist present, pharmacy is closed, and mediation being dispensed from cabinet
Medication is from an emergency kit (even if pharmacy is open)
Treatment of emergency needs with medication not in emergency kit.
OAR 855.041.6510

What must be on the label of a medication designated for inpatient use?
OAR 855.041.6270

Medication Name (brand or generic) and strength
Expiration date
Manufacturer and lot number (or pharmacy generated code)
Note: Patient information, route of administration and auxiliary labels are only required if medication is not packaged as unit dose or unit-of-use.

What must be on the label of an intravenous (IV) medication?
OAR 855.041.6270

Patient information: Name or identifier	– QTY
Medication information: Name, quantity and concentration of added medication	– CONCENTRATION
Administration information: Administration time, infusion rate	– ADMIN TIME

– WHO MADE
– WHO CHECKED
– WHAT PHARMACY
– RATE
– DATE/TIME MIXED

IV information: Date and time IV was mixed, expiration date, name/initials of person that made IV and verified IV, and a pharmacy identifier

Can a patient bring in their own medication to use while in the hospital?
OAR 855.041.6250

Yes, but it must:

Be Identifiable

Be in a labeled container

Be detrimental for the patient NOT to have it

...And the provider must write an order for it.

Are there any special inventory requirements for CII medications?
Yes. In an institutional setting, CII medications must be kept on a perpetual inventory that is reconciled monthly. *Q MONTH   (Q3 MONTH IF NOT HOSP)*

Are there any special storage requirements for controlled substances in this setting?
Controlled substances delivered to different units must be kept in separately locked compartments, and delivery receipts must be kept for controlled substances delivered as floor stock. CII medications in the pharmacy must be stored within a system that tracks each person that accesses the system when a pharmacist is not physically present.

Can controlled substances be kept in a robotic distribution system used in an institutional pharmacy?
Only CIII-V medications may be stocked. CII medications may not be stocked in a robotic distribution system. *CII NO ROBOT → NO ROBOTS*
OAR 855.041.6530

If a patient is sent home with medications, do you have to counsel them at discharge?
Yes. Proper counseling must be completed at discharge.
OAR 855.041.6270

A patient has been using an inhaler from the inpatient pharmacy while in the hospital. The patient is being discharged today and there are doses left in the inhaler. Can you give the patient the inhaler with the hospital labeling?
No. The label must comply with outpatient labeling requirements if the patient is going to take it home with them. *OUT PATIENTS MUST HAVE OUT PATIENT LABELING*
OAR 855.041.6270

PHARMACY OUTSOURCING: CENTRAL FILL AND REMOTE PROCESSING PHARMACIES

There are two ways to outsource the work in a pharmacy- through a **CENTRAL FILL PHARMACY**, which is essentially responsible for just filling the medication, and through a **REMOTE PROCESSING DRUG OUTLET (RPDO)**, which doesn't fill the medication but instead processes the prescription. A RPDO may complete DURs and interventions on the prescription and provide patient counseling.
OAR 855.041.3015, OAR 855.041.3110

What is required to legally use a central-fill pharmacy or RPDO?
Both pharmacies must have the same owner OR have a shared services agreement. Both pharmacies must be registered with the OR BOP, and have separate policies and procedures in place. Records of each pharmacy must be able to show who performed what function of prescription filling or processing.

What is a shared pharmacy service agreement? → CAN COMPOUND FOR OFFICE USE IF HAVE AGREEMENT
Agreement between two pharmacies or a pharmacy and provider office for a pharmacy to furnish dispensing, DUR, compounded products, or to make adjustments to claims or provide therapeutic interventions. The agreement must be approved by the BOP.
OAR 855.006.0005

Shared Pharmacy Service Agreements are important for pharmacies that provide compounded products to other pharmacies or providers offices. Through an approved shared pharmacy service agreement, a pharmacy can make these products for the other business WITHOUT registering as a manufacturer. In this situation the product can be provided for office use; it does NOT have to be pursuant to a patient-specific prescription.[6]

If a patient's medication is filled at a central fill pharmacy, which pharmacy's information should be on the prescription label?
The primary pharmacy (i.e. NOT the central fill pharmacy) information should appear on the prescription label.

Are central-fill pharmacies and remote processing drug outlets allowed to fill or process controlled substance prescriptions?
Yes.

A patients' medication is filled at a central-fill pharmacy and delivered to the primary pharmacy for pick up. If the patient does not pick up the medications, do they have to be returned to the central fill pharmacy?
Legally the medications are not required to be returned to the central fill pharmacy, they can be returned and added to the inventory at the primary pharmacy.

Does a central fill pharmacy have to use any specific carrier to transport medications back to the main pharmacy or to the patient?
No, as long as they follow all federal and state laws, the central fill pharmacy can use any carrier to transport medications. Note that the central fill pharmacy still has to put all medications in packaging that is tamper-evident and maintains proper storage conditions for the medication and is responsible for reporting any in-transit medication loss.
OAR 855.041.3035

CONSULTANT PHARMACY PRACTICE
OAR 855.019.0240

What services must a consultant pharmacist provide to the organization it serves?
You must provide anything that the facility requires from a pharmacist to be licensed, as well as what the facility requests from you. You are additionally responsible for providing the facility with policies and procedures for security and storage of medication, distribution of medication and guidance for documentation of medication administration.

COMPOUNDING PHARMACY
OAR 855.045

Does a pharmacy that makes non-sterile or sterile compounds have to comply with USP 795 or 797?
No, pharmacies are not required to adhere to the letter of the law of USP 795 or 797 but are required to adhere to the "spirit" of those guidelines.
OAR 855.045.0200

What are the classes of sterility for compounding?
OAR 855.045.0210, 0250

Category 1	**Nonsterile-** Simple	Mixing two or more commercial products, not considered compounding.
Category 2	**Nonsterile-** Complex	Compounding with bulk substances and/or calculations
Category 3	**Sterile-** Risk Level 1	Low risk: ISO Class 5, using 3 or less commercially made sterile products and 3 or less entries into any one container
Category 4	**Sterile-** Risk Level 2	Medium risk: Follows low risk requirements BUT either preparation will be used on multiple occasions or with multiple patients, complex mixing requiring more than a single-volume transfer, or compounding process has a long duration
Category 5	**Sterile-** Risk Level 3	High risk: use of non-sterile ingredients or devices before end sterilization, exposure to environment for at least 1 hour that does not meet ISO Class 5 (this includes for storage of products that do not have preservatives or sterile items used, or the compound itself before the end sterilization), personnel are not wearing appropriate attire (i.e. loves, gowns), water containing preparations that are stored for >6hrs.

What is the beyond-use date of compounds?
OAR 855.045.0250

These are the automatic beyond-use dates UNLESS the facility completes sterility testing.	
Category 3 (**Low** Risk)	48 hours at room temp, 14 days refrigerated, 45 days frozen
Category 4 (**Medium** Risk)	30 hours room temp, 9 days refrigerated, 45 days frozen
Category 5 (**High** Risk)	24 hours room temp, 3 days refrigerated, 45 days frozen

When can a compound be considered for "immediate use"?
OAR 855.045.0250

Use of aseptic manipulations
Use of only sterile products and NO hazardous medications
No more than three sterile ingredients/devices/components used
No direct contamination
Preparation made without interruption
Administration started within 1 hour of being made
ISO Class 5 or better is NOT required, and preparer is NOT required to wear gloves or gown for immediate use preparations.

Are there any special labeling requirements for sterile compounds?
Labels of sterile compounded products must include a beyond use date, rate of infusion, storage requirements, name, quantity and concentration of medication, primary solution, initials of verifying pharmacist.
OAR 855.045.0240

How often do the work surfaces and floors have to be cleaned in an ISO Class 7 or better environment?
Daily: Work surfaces, floors
Monthly: Shelves, walls, ceilings in ante and buffer rooms

NUCLEAR PHARMACIES
OAR 855.042

Is there any special wording that must be on a prescription for a radiopharmaceutical?
Yes. Review OAR 855.042.0015 for a list of what must be on the label of a radiopharmaceutical, but the label MUST say "Caution- Radioactive Material"

CHARITABLE PHARMACIES
ORS 689.772, OAR 855.044

What medications can a charitable pharmacy not DISTRIBUTE? OAR 855.044.0050	
Any medication the charitable pharmacy cannot accept (see list below)	
Compounds	
Refrigerated items	
Medications that require special registration	
Medications that have been repackaged, UNLESS it was repackaged for a LTC pharmacy. (I.e. Must be in original tamper evident container that shows the lot and expiration date of medication.)	
Medication that is adulterated or misbranded	
Medication that expires <9months from the date the drugs were donated	
What medications can a charitable pharmacy not ACCEPT? OAR 855.044.0030	
Controlled substances, including any package or container of medications that contains a controlled substance	
Any non-prescription medication	
FDA REMS programs drugs	
Drugs donated from another state	
Medication that does not have a product identification label (PIL), unless it is in the manufacturers original packaging	
Who can receive medications from a charitable pharmacy? ORS 689.778, OAR 855.044.0050	
Oregon resident	
Valid prescription	
Proof of underinsured or does not have adequate health insurance to get medication OR enrolled in program of public assistance	

Can you charge a fee for dispensing medications at a charitable pharmacy?
Yes! But it must not be more than 2.5 times the current Medicaid dispensing fee
ORS 689.772, OAR 855.044.0080

Specific pharmacy practice areas not covered in this review:
- Consulting Pharmacies (OAR 855.041.3300)
- Retail Drug Outlets for Home Dialysis Supplies (OAR 855.041.4025)
- Remote Dispensing and Remote Distribution Facilities (OAR 855.041.4100, OAR 855.041.4200)
- Long Term Care and Community Based Care facilities (OAR 855.041.7050)
- Home Health Care Agencies (OAR 855.041.8050)
- Supervising Physician Dispensing Outlets (OAR 855.043.0405)
- Dispensing Practitioner Drug Outlets (OAR 855.043.0505)
- Correctional Facilities (OAR 855.042.0600)
- Community Health Clinic Drug Outlet (OAR 855.042.0700)

[handwritten: 3 YEARS]

These practice areas are not covered because it is in our personal opinion that they comprise such a small portion of pharmacy that they are unlikely to be covered on the MPJE. We still recommend reading through these sections in the law so you have at least looked at them. Some general trends:

- There is a policy and procedure that must be written for EVERYTHING.
- EVERYTHING must be documented, and documents must be kept for three years.
- Counseling is ALWAYS required. When it seems like counseling is not possible, it is likely that you have to provide some kind of written counseling that provides a phone number where a pharmacist is accessible.
- If medications are dispensed to a patient, they must have appropriate labeling, even when they are dispensed from an outlet that is not a pharmacy, such as a Supervising Physician Dispensing Outlet. Appropriate labeling includes most everything that would be on a label of a prescription dispensed from a pharmacy. Note that any unit-of-use medications do not need to contain a description of the medication (or PIL).
- Medications and records must always be secured, which typically means limited or no access by a non-pharmacist when a pharmacist is not present, or limited access when the type of business does not employ a pharmacist. In addition, medications must be stored appropriately to prevent their degradation or adulteration. For example, it would likely be inappropriate to store medications on top of the break room refrigerator. They are not locked, they are being kept near food, and it is unlikely that the top of a refrigerator maintains an appropriate temperature to prevent adulteration of the medication.

LOSS AND THEFT

How quickly does a pharmacy have to report a theft or significant loss?
Must be reported within 1 business day.
OAR 855.019.0205

[handwritten: THEFT = 1 DAY]

Who is responsible for reporting the loss or theft?
The pharmacist.

Who do you report the loss or theft to?

[handwritten: CONTROLS → FORM 106 → DEA]

The DEA via form 106 if controlled substances are involved and must also send a copy of 106 to the BOP. If controlled substances are not involved, must report to BOP.
CFR 1301.74, OAR 855-019-0205

Who is responsible for reporting a loss that occurs or is discovered after a pharmacy takes custody of a shipment?
The pharmacist at the pharmacy that now has custody of the medication.

Who is responsible for reporting a loss that occurs in transit to the pharmacy?
The supplier is responsible for reporting to the DEA, and the supplier is responsible for reporting if the pharmacy refuses to take custody of a shipment due to a loss. This is not necessarily an Oregon law; however, this is required per federal regulations and is referenced in the Pharmacy Manual under Section V- Security requirements, under part D. 'Registrant's Responsibility for Identifying Significant Loss'.

Who is responsible for reporting a loss that occurs in transit to a patient when it comes from a central fill pharmacy?
The Central Fill pharmacy is responsible for reporting the loss.
OAR 855.041.3035

Who is responsible for reporting a loss when in transit from a central fill pharmacy to the retail pharmacy?
Although Oregon law does not define this, federal law does under 21 C.F.R. Section 1301.76(d) that states when a central fill pharmacy contracts with private, common or contract carriers to transport filled prescriptions to a retail pharmacy, the central fill pharmacy is responsible is responsible for reporting the in-transit loss and reporting the loss using DEA Form 106. To make this easier to understand, it should be logical that the loss should be reported by the central fill pharmacy as they are the ones supplying the medications. The retail pharmacy is not supplying the medications and also may not be notified vs. the central fill pharmacy that has shipped off. Think about how you go to the post office and ship off a letter to a relative. If the package gets lost, most likely the post office carrier will notify you or you can check if the package arrived to the receiver and if not can report the loss.

DESTRUCTION AND DISPOSAL

What drugs must be disposed?
Anything outdated, damaged, deteriorated, misbranded, or adulterated.
OAR 855-035-0023, 855-041-1025 855-043-0450

Do I have to keep mediations set for disposal somewhere specific?
No, but they must be physically separated from other medications.
OAR 855.041.1025

Can I accept medications back from a patient for disposal?
No, unless the medications were dispensed in error (i.e. Medication was already expired, or could cause patient harm- see above section on returning medications)

What if my pharmacy is registered with the DEA as an authorized collector?
If your pharmacy is registered with the DEA as an authorized collector, then you may accept both controlled and non-controlled substances for return
OAR 855.041.1046

Can I place a take-back receptacle or host a drug take-back program at my pharmacy?
Yes, however you must notify the BOP before hosting the program, and the receptacle must be placed in FRONT of the pharmacy counter. — OUTSIDE PHARMACY

Do I need any specific policies or procedures to accept returned medication?
Yes, you must have a policy for disposal of medications on file.

Can the pharmacy take an inventory of the medications being disposed in the receptacle?
No. Medications cannot be counted, sorted, or inventoried.

Since my pharmacy has this collection bin, can I put medications that the pharmacy needs to dispose into the receptacle?
No. No pharmacy stock can be placed in the collection receptacle.

If I am returning controlled substances, are there any forms I need to fill out?
Yes. You may send controlled substances back to a reverse distributor as long as you fill out an invoice for CIII-CV medications or a DEA 222 form for CII substances.

If I am disposing controlled substances, are there any forms I need to fill out?
Yes, you will need to fill out DEA form 41.

RECORDS

How long must a physical copy of a non-controlled prescription be kept?
120 days. Note that this is only applicable to non-controlled prescriptions that were presented to the pharmacy as a physical hard-copy, or when a hard-copy was created after receiving a verbal order from a provider. Prescriptions that are e-prescribed, for example, do not need to be printed to create a hard copy record!
OAR 855.041.1160

NON-C HARD COPIES KEPT FOR 120 DAYS → THEN AS e-scripts FOR 3 YEAR

But I need to keep records for 3 years. How do I store the prescription for the remaining time?
After 120 days, the prescription may be converted to an electronic format and stored electronically only for the remainder of the three year filing requirement.

OFF SITE AFTER 1 YR (3 DAY MAX RETRIEVAL TIME)

What about a controlled prescription?
FOREVER. Seriously though, you must keep the hard copy of all controlled prescriptions as long as you need to keep the files. For example, if you keep all prescription files for 3 years, you must keep the hardcopy prescription for 3 years. Again, as noted above, this is only applicable to prescriptions that were presented to your pharmacy as a physical hard-copy, or when a hard-copy was created after receiving a verbal order from a provider.
OAR 855.041.1160

HARDCOPIES 120 DAYS → e-file → 1 YR → OFF SITE → 3 YRS (3 DAYS TO RETRIEVE)

When can you move your prescription files offsite?
After 1 year.

How quickly must you retrieve the files if requested by an authorized agent?
3 business days.

DONE / FOREVER / CONTROLS

How often must you complete an inventory of your controlled substances?
While the DEA only requires a controlled substance inventory every 2 years, Oregon requires it yearly, and you must also reconcile CII's quarterly. If practicing in a hospital CII's must be on perpetual inventory and reconciled monthly.

Is there a certain way you must file prescriptions?
Oregon has no specific law on this, so follow the federal law which states that you can either
1. File CIIs separate from CIII-V separate from legend OR
2. File CII separate from all others, but any CIII-V must have a 1 inch high red stamp

For electronic filing, you do not have to keep separate files as long as you can electronic bring CII's up separately from CIII-V separately from legend medications

Are there certain ways you must file invoices?
Yes. Invoices, much like prescriptions must be separated. CII invoices must be separated from all other invoices. However, CIII-V invoices do not need to be kept separate from invoices for legend medications.

How long must pharmacy records be kept?
Oregon law requires essentially all records to be kept for 3 years, with the only exception being the Hormonal Contraception Self-Questionnaire, which you must keep for 5 years. Note that Medicare and Medicaid may have specific record-keeping requirements, however for exam purposes remember 3 years!

What records must be kept?
Every single record. Everything that is done in a pharmacy related and unrelated to a prescription (i.e. Temperature logs, training logs, intern logs) must be recorded and **kept for 3 years**. There is no comprehensive list of these things in this review because literally everything must be recorded and kept for three years.

There are a lot of details about what must be included in each type of record your pharmacy keeps. While it is our opinion you do not need to memorize all of the tables listed below, you may do that if you wish. We have summarized what I feel to be the most pertinent information under the next two tables: Regular Reviews and Dates and Deadlines. We do recommend doing your best to memorize this information.

Regular Reviews: When must certain items be reviewed by law?	
CII Med Inventory- hospital	Perpetual inventory, reconcile monthly
Hospital Drug Storage Areas	Every 2 months
CII Med Inventory- not hospital	Quarterly
Controlled Substances Inventory (CII-CV)- not hospital	Every 365 days
Review all Policies and Procedures	Annually
PIC Inspection	Annually by February 1st
Verification of employee licenses	Upon initial hire and then annually
Review of CDTM arrangement	Every 2 years

Dates and Deadlines: When to report to BOP, or agency specified	
Significant drug loss or theft	1 business day
Breach of access of PDMP	24 hours to the Oregon Health Authority
Temporary relocation of pharmacy due to disaster	3 working days
Adulteration of drugs due to disaster	3 working days
Retrieve off-site records	3 business days
Notify provider of substituted biological product (biosimilar) and manufacturer (1st fill only)	3 BUSINESS days
Obtain hardcopy for verbal CII	7 days
Breach of security	7 days
Report misdemeanor, felony charge, or conviction	10 days
Misconduct of license (NP, MD, etc.)	10 WORKING BUSINESS days to APPROPRIATE board, not necessarily BOP!
Termination or resignation of a "board licensee"	10 working days
Change in employment	15 days
Report immunizations given	15 days to OHA Alert, do NOT need to notify PCP
Change in PIC (resignation or new start)	15 days
Submit contraceptive training	15 days
Change in email or residential address	15 days
Change in pharmacy's name, ownership, or location	15 days
Closure of pharmacy	15 days
Removal of remote dispensing machine	15 days
Present to board after being served an order to stop doing things with controlled substances	Present to board within 30 days
Submit correction after board inspection	30 days
Arrest for misdemeanor (not convicted)	Report at license renewal

What items must be included in a patients record?
OAR 855.041.1165, 855.019.0220

- Patient's full name
- Address and phone number
- Gender and age or DOB
- Chronic diseases
- List of all drugs and devices patient receives from your pharmacy
- Allergies and adverse drug reactions
- Any other pharmacist comments or info needed to complete DUR (i.e. Pts weight)

DISEASES
ALLERGIES
DRUGS

What items must be included in a prescription record?
ORS 689.508

- Date of transaction
- Dispensed medication: Brand name OR generic name and manufacturer
- Manufacturer's name

What items must be included in a refill log?
Pharmacist identifier
Patient name
Medication name
Refill date
Quantity dispensed

What items must be included in a drug administration record?
OAR 855.019.0265, OAR 855.019.0290

Think	Item
Who	Patient identifier (for vaccine this includes patient name, address, phone number, gender, DOB)
Who	Pharmacist Identifier
What	Drug or Device and strength (for vaccine, include dose, manufacturer, lot, and expiration date
Where- Vaccine	Route and site of administration
Where- Pharmacy	Pharmacy address
When	Date AND TIME of administration (although for vaccines, date only is required)

What must be documented after an MTM session? — *PROVIDER COMMUNICATION*
Whatever you think necessary for accountability purposes. In this you must include documentation of your communication with other healthcare providers. *① COMMUNICATION WITH PROVIDER(S)*
OAR 855.019.0250

How long must I keep patient records?
3 years.

How long do I have to keep inventory records?
3 years.

How long do I keep records of immunizations I have given at my pharmacy?
3 years. ALL records are kept for at least 3 years in OR.

Got it. How long do I keep Hormonal Contraception Self-screening questionnaires?
Ok, you got us there. This is the ONE record you must keep for **5 years.**

OREGON PHARMACY LAW PART 2: LICENSES, REGISTRATIONS, OPERATIONS

You are a pharmacist licensed in Washington state only. Can you practice as a pharmacist in Oregon?
No.

What if your OR license is pending, you already passed the MPJE?
Still no.

What if you only do work as if you were a pharmacy technician?
No.

Then what can you do?
Only what a clerk can do! Nothing more!

What are the requirements to become a PIC?
OAR 855.019.0300
One year of licensed pharmacy practice OR Board approved PIC training course
Training course must be completed before or within 30 days after PIC apt.
Training course provides 3 CE's, including 1 in medication error and 1 in law
Complete inspection of pharmacy within 15 days of becoming PIC
Complete inventory of all CS within 15 days before or after effective PIC date

What are the requirements to become a pharmacy preceptor?
OAR 855.031.0045
Actively practicing pharmacist for 1 year
Apply for license with BOP and renew license biennially
Complete school-specific training courses
Note: you must advise the school if you precept students from more than 1 school at the same time
Verify intern is licensed with BOP

Who is responsible for verifying the intern is licensed appropriately with the BOP?
The precepting pharmacist

Who is responsible for verifying the precepting pharmacist is appropriately licensed with the BOP?
The intern

Does a pharmacist have to supervise all of a SRI's rotational hours?
No. Must supervise the MAJORITY of hours, but not necessary to supervise all hours.

What are the CE Requirements for pharmacist license renewal?
OAR 855.021.0005-0016

30 hours (3CEUs) every 2 years. Hours must include		
2 hours LAW	2 hours MED ERROR or PATIENT SAFETY	7 Hours PAIN MANAGEMENT within the first 24 months of initial license renewal, of which 1 hour is specific to Oregon provided by the pain management commission.

What is a CEU?
A CEU, or continuing pharmacy education unit, is the way pharmacist continuing education is measured.
In Oregon:
1 CEU = 10 contact hours
1 Contact hour = 50 minutes of continuing education

Does all CE have to be ACPE accredited?
No. CE accredited by the OR BOP but not by ACPE is still valid.

When do you have to renew your pharmacist license?
June 30th of odd years

Does a pharmacist practicing in a pharmacy outside of Oregon, but which provides services to Oregon patients, need to be licensed in Oregon?
It depends. The PIC of the pharmacy must be licensed in Oregon, but a non-PIC pharmacist can complete prescription evaluation, verification, and even counseling without being licensed in Oregon.
OAR 855.019.0100

Are there requirements to obtain a license as a nuclear pharmacist?
Yes, a pharmacist has to complete a nuclear pharmacy training program, complete six months of on-the-job training, and obtain BPS certification in nuclear pharmacy.
OAR 855.019.0160

What equipment is mandatory to operate a pharmacy?
OAR 855.041.1035

One updated pharmaceutical reference
Oregon Revised Statutes, Chapters 689 and 475, Oregon Administrative Rules Chapter 855, and last three years of BOP newsletters
Official Poison and Exempt Narcotic Register (if poisons and exempt narcotics are sold or distributed at the location)
The CDC reference "Epidemiology and Prevention of Vaccine-Preventable Diseases" (if vaccines are administered at your pharmacy)
Refrigeration
Sink with hot and cold water
Equipment and supplies as determined by PIC
Computer and software capable of and accessing etc. filed prescriptions

How often does the temperature of the refrigerator and/or freezer used for medications need to be recorded?
The temperature should be continuously monitored by a centrally placed thermometer, but also needs to be documented with either an automated system that provides a history of temperature readings OR by manually documenting the temperature at least twice daily.

If the refrigerator or freezer houses vaccines, are there any special requirements that must be followed?
Yes, if vaccines are being stored the temperature monitoring system MUST be automated. Data from the system must be downloaded on a weekly basis and the system must be validated on a quarterly basis.

Does a hospital pharmacy need any additional equipment?
No, but they need a copy of the drug formulary approved by the hospital.

Does a pharmacy need any additional equipment if vaccines are administered at the location?
Yes, the pharmacy must also have an emergency kit if vaccines are administered as well as a copy of the CDC reference, "Epidemiology and Prevention of Vaccine-Preventable Diseases".[9]

What must be in the emergency kit?
Three doses of epinephrine for both adult and pediatric use, 2 doses of Benadryl for both an adult and child, and supplies (i.e. Resuscitation masks).[9]

Can the medications in an emergency kit be multi use vials?
Yes. Epinephrine (EPI) can be in the form of multi-dose vials (MDV) or single dose vials (SDV), 1:1000 EPI vial with syringes, or auto-injectors

What if intra-muscular (IM) Benadryl is unavailable?
Serious question. Shortages are real. If this happens hydroxyzine is ok.

Note that in addition to above supplies you can also have ammonia capsules for fainting, but these are not required

As a pharmacy, are there any signs that I am legally obligated to post?
Yes. Even if you are a closed pharmacy (i.e. Not open to the public) you must post a sign that states: "This pharmacy may be able to substitute a less expensive drug which is therapeutically equivalent to the one prescribed by your doctor unless you do not approve". This statement must be typed in block letters with 1-inch font.
ORS 689.515

Do I have to put my pharmacist license on the wall of the pharmacy I work at?
Yes. Any personnel licensed by the board (including pharmacists, technicians, interns) must have their license displayed where they are working.
ORS 689.615

Besides a pharmacy, what other business must be registered with the BOP?
Any business that handles controlled substances, prescription medications, or nonprescription medications, whether manufacturing, delivering, or dispensing. Practitioners may or may not be registered with the BOP depending on their scope of handling and dispensing medications.
ORS 475.125, 689.305, OAR 855.062.0020, 855.080.0031

When confronted with questions regarding BOP and DEA registration, it will be important to think about the medication supply chain, or any business involved either the manufacture, distribution, or dispensing of controlled substances, prescription medications, or nonprescription medications. Each entity is expected to verify that the other entities they do business with are appropriately registered, and each is responsible for appropriately handling adulterated or misbranded products, and not passing any adulterated or misbranded products further along the medication supply chain. When discussing controlled substances specifically, each of these entities must be registered with the BOP and the DEA.

How often must businesses renew their registration with the BOP?
Annually.

What out-of-state pharmacies must register with the Oregon BOP?
Any pharmacy that provides services or medications to Oregon residents must register with the OR BOP. These are referred to as "Non-resident pharmacies".
OAR 855.041.1060

Do any pharmacists working in the non-resident pharmacy need to be licensed in Oregon?
Only the PIC must be licensed in Oregon, and this pharmacist must be present in the non-resident pharmacy for at least 20 hours a week.
OAR 855.041.1060

For what actions may the BOP consider disciplinary measures, for either licensees or registrants? ORS 689.405, OAR 855.006.0020, 855.019.0310, 855.041.1170
Unprofessional conduct
Gross negligence
Impairment of licensee, where licensee cannot practice safely (think: substance abuse, mental health condition)
Business does not allow adequate staffing and/or breaks to allow pharmacist to complete duties (DUR, counseling) or take uninterrupted breaks
Violation of federal or state pharmacy laws
Felony charges
Defrauding the BOP, refusing to allow BOP inspection (OAR 855.001.0040)
Practicing pharmacy without appropriate license or helping someone do so. This includes pharmacist and technician.
Discipline by another state on a licensee

What actions may the BOP take as disciplinary measures?
Suspending, restricting, or revoking, or refusing to renew a license
Applying a civil penalty for either an individual or drug outlet
Subject licensee to probationary period
ORS 689.445

Is there a program in place to assist pharmacists that are impaired due to drug abuse or mental health ailments?
Yes, it is called the Health Professionals Service Program.
OAR 855.011.0005

Does a pharmacist have to be referred to the Health Professionals Service Program to participate?
No, pharmacists may refer themselves or they may be referred by the BOP.
OAR 855.011.0020

How long must a pharmacist participate in the program?
At least two years, but potentially longer.
OAR 855.011.0050

Are quality assurance programs required? *QUARTERLY GOALS + ASSESMENTS*
Yes, your pharmacy must have a quality assurance program and a quality assurance policy and procedure.

How often must I review the quality assurance program?
You must set goals and determine progress within the program on a quarterly basis.

QUARTERLY GOALS + ASSESMENTS

OREGON PHARMACY LAW PART 3: GENERAL REGULATIONS

Who is on the Oregon State Board of Pharmacy?
ORS 689.115

9 Board Members		
5 licensed pharmacists	2 licensed techs	2 members of public
Must have 5 years of practicing in OR	Must have 3 years of practicing in OR AND be currently working	Cannot be in any way involved in pharmacy

How long are terms for BOP members?
4 years.

Who appoints BOP members?
Governor.

How often does the BOP meet?
Every 3 months.
OAR 855.010.0005

Who is on the Public Health and Pharmacy Formulary Advisory Committee?
ORS 689.649, OAR 855.020.0105

7 Committee Members				
2 Physicians	2 Advanced-Practice Registered Nurses	3 Pharmacists		
		1 Community-based	1 Health Systems-based	1 from anywhere

How long are terms for public health and pharmacy formulary advisory committee?
2 years.

Who appoints the members of the public health and pharmacy formulary advisory committee?
Governor.

What is the Public Health and Pharmacy Formulary Advisory Committee?
A committee that reviews and approves the protocols and medications that pharmacists may prescribe and dispense.
ORS 689.649, OAR 855.020.0105

Oregon Pharmacy Law Exam

Objectives
- This is a 120-question exam that mimics the Oregon pharmacy portion of the MPJE exam.
- Use these questions as a supplement to test your self-study learning and go back to review questions missed. There will be material covered in the questions not covered in the text above so use the questions as a supplement for further learning.
- Ensure to time yourself at 1 hour and 45 minutes to complete the questions in one sitting.
- Answers can be reviewed after the federal pharmacy law exam section.
- If you do not get above a 75% score, it's prudent to review the laws discussed in the previous chapters

GOOD LUCK!

1. Match the activities to the time period.

Activity	Answer	Time period
Report misconduct of nurse practitioner	10	15 days
Obtain off-site records for BOP inspection	3	10 days
Change in pharmacy name	15	30 days
Provide BOP with Plan of Correction after inspection	30	3 days

2. Which of the following activities can a clerk complete?
I. Stock medication on shelves
II. Pull medication off shelves for filling
III. Pull outdated medication off shelves

A. I and II only
B. II and III only
C. I and III only
D. I, II and III

3. Which activities must be completed only by a pharmacist? (INTERNS CONSIDERED)
I. DUR check
II. Final Verification
III. Administer Immunizations

A. I only
B. II only
C. III only
D. II and III only

4. Which activities can a technician complete?
I. Accept a refill from a provider for Zanaflex
II. Enter allergies into a patient's electronic chart
III. Bypass an electronic alert for duplicate therapy

A. I and II only
B. II and III only
C. I and III only
D. I, II and III

5. You receive an electronic prescription transmitted by a provider's agent for a product containing dextromethorphan for a patient that is 16 years old. You:
A. Refuse to fill the prescription
B. Call the providers office to get a hard-copy prescription
C. Tell the patient you can only dispense this medication to a parent or guardian over 18 years old.
D. Dispense the medication to the patient as written.

6. There is an authorized checking technician at your location. What of the following can they check?
I. Anaphylaxis kit NOT EMERGENCY KITS
II. Suture kit
III. Restocks for the Family Care Unit automated dispensing cabinet

A. I and II only
B. II and III only
C. I and III only
D. I, II and III

7. Which of the following is true in regard to counseling?
I. Only a pharmacist can accept a refusal for counseling
II. A pharmacist may document counseling with a log with a check box for either accept or refuse
III. A pharmacist must counsel on a refill for levothyroxine with a change in dose

A. I and II only
B. II and III only
C. I and III only
D. I, II and III

8. Which of the following personnel ratios are required?
A. Three technicians to every one pharmacist.
B. Two technicians to every one pharmacist.
C. Two SRIs to each one pharmacist.
D. Two TPIs to each one pharmacist.

9. The pharmacy is holding an immunization clinic and would like to have immunizing interns participate. How many immunizing interns may a pharmacist supervise?
A. One immunization certified TPI.
B. Two immunization certified TPIs, as long as only one is doing the immunizations.
C. Two immunization certified interns.
D. Three immunization certified SRIs.

10. You receive a prescription from an optometrist office for Paracaine eye drops, with the name of the office under the patient name and directions listed "for Office Use". You:
A. Fill the prescription as written.
B. Call the prescriber back and request specific patient names for the medication.
C. Fill out an invoice for the office for Paracaine.
D. Fill out a DEA 222 form for Paracaine drops.

11. Which of the following providers are not allowed to prescribe CII's in Oregon?
A. ND
B. RDH
C. OD
D. DVM

12. Which of the following would be illegal to fill?
A. NP without DATA Waiver prescribing Suboxone for treatment of pain control.
B. PA with DATA Waiver prescribing Suboxone for treatment of opioid abuse.
C. DO without DATA Waiver prescribing Suboxone for treatment of opioid abuse.
D. MD with DATA Waiver prescribing Subutex for treatment of pain control.

13. In what situation would a provider's office have to be registered as a DPDO?

A. A physician's office wishes to dispense 3 tablets of Entresto samples to a patient.
B. A physician's office wishes to dispense 2 tablets of Norco samples to a patient.
C. A podiatrist's office wishes to dispense 1 tube of a Lotrimin sample to a patient.
D. A physician's office wishes to dispense 4 tablets of Cozaar samples to a patient.

72°
(3 DAYS)

14. Which of the following prescriptions may a pharmacy legally process?
A. Refills for a prescription written by a provider that passed away 6 months ago.
B. A new prescription from an internet provider.
C. A new prescription from a provider practicing within their scope in Montana.
D. A new prescription from a provider practicing within their scope in Canada.

15. Order the following prescriptions by expiration date, starting with the soonest expiration to the latest expiration.
A. Azithromycin with directions "For EPT, take as directed", quantity of 4 — 1 MONTH
B. Dilaudid, take 1 tablet every 4 hours as needed, quantity of 12 — FOREVER
C. Xanax, take 1 tablet twice daily as needed, quantity 60 — 6 MONTHS
D. Zanaflex, take 1 tablet three times daily as needed, quantity 30 — 1 YEAR

A C D B

16. A patient comes in to your CVS pharmacy and requests her prescriptions for Tenormin and Klonopin be transferred from a CVS pharmacy in California. You review the prescription logs and note that two months ago you transferred the prescriptions to the CVS pharmacy in California. What do you tell the patient?
A. The patient will have to contact her provider to obtain new prescriptions.
B. If there are refills available you can dispense the Tenormin today but not the Klonopin.
C. If there are refills available you can dispense both the Tenormin and Klonopin.
D. If there are refills available you can dispense the Klonopin but not the Tenormin.

SHARED REAL-TIME DATABASE

17. A patient requests a refill that was originally written on 12/20/2018 for Amaryl Take 1 po daily, #30, PRN refills. On 6/10/2019 you see the prescription was filled on 12/21/2018 #30, 1/18/2019 #30, 2/15/19 #30, 3/25/19 #30, 4/23/19 #30, and 5/17/19 #30. The patient requests the remaining quantity of the prescription today. You:
A. Tell the patient to contact the provider for a new prescription.
B. Dispense #30 to the patient.
C. Dispense #150 to the patient.
D. Dispense #184 to the patient.

"PRN" = 365
− (6 × 30)

18. A patient that is new to your pharmacy brings in the following prescriptions, all with 11 refills:
Zoloft 10mg 1 daily #30 days
Abilify 20mg 1 daily #30 days
Prilosec 20mg daily #30 days

> PSYCHOTHERAPEUTIC / CONTROL

The patient requests that you provide the entire quantity of each of the prescriptions today. You:
A. Fill the entire quantity of Prilosec only, but only #30 of the Abilify and Zoloft.
B. Fill the #360 of Zoloft, Abilify and Prilosec.
C. Fill only #30 of Zoloft, Abilify and Prilosec.
D. Fill #360 of Zoloft and Prilosec, but only #30 of Abilify.

19. A patient has signed up all applicable prescriptions to be auto-refilled. In March she picked up her Glucophage her refills of Basaglar or Lyrica. She comes in in April and asks why the Lyrica and Basaglar weren't automatically refilled. You explain:
A. Lyrica and Basaglar are not eligible for the auto-refill program; she must request refills every month.
B. As Basaglar and Lyrica were not picked up in March they were automatically removed from the refill program and cannot be added back to the program.
C. Lyrica is not eligible for the auto-refill program and refills must be requested individually every month.
D. As Basaglar and Lyrica were not picked up in March they were automatically removed from the refill program but can be added back to the auto-refill program if she requests it.

20. A patient comes in and states she wants "everything refilled". You overhear this and see the technician put through refills for all medications in the patient's profile. You:
A. Verify all refilled medications
B. Verify all refilled medications except for her Ambien
C. Verify all refilled medications except for her Prilosec, whose directions state for patient to take as needed
D. Call patient and review each medication that needs refilled

21. It is 6PM on Friday night and your pharmacy receives a prescription for Tamiflu liquid. The pharmacy just ran out, but you have Tamiflu capsules in the same concentration and at the same strength as the prescription. The provider's office is closed at this time, but the patient says they are ok with receiving the capsules instead of the liquid. You:
A. Notify the patient that since you cannot get in touch with the provider you cannot fill the prescription for capsules.
B. Call an emergency room provider to obtain an emergency prescription for capsules.
C. Document that you have changed the prescription to capsules and fill the prescription with capsules instead.
D. Fill the prescription for capsules and fax the provider a prescription to sign off and return to the pharmacy within 7 days.

22. Which of the following is not an allowable substitution?
A. A levothyroxine product that is AB rated in the orange book.
B. A diltiazem product that has BC rating in the orange book
C. A levothyroxine product that costs more than the originally prescribed thyroid product.
D. A diltiazem product that costs less than the originally prescribed diltiazem product.

23. What is true about the substitution for biologic substances?
I. The provider must be notified within 3 business days after the initial fill and each refill.
II. The substituted biosimilar is listed as interchangeable with the prescribed biologic in the Purple Book.
III. DAW must be absent from the prescription.

A. I and II only
B. II and III only
C. I and III only
D. I, II and III

24. Which of the following prescriptions requires a DUR?
I. A new prescription for Azithromycin for "Partner 1" with directions "For EPT, take as directed", quantity of 4
II. A refill of Robaxin, take 1 tablet every 8 hours as needed, quantity of 30
III. A refill of Fiorinal, take 1 tablet as needed as directed, quantity of 10, that was transferred in to your pharmacy.

A. I and II only
B. II and III only
C. I and III only
D. I, II and III

25. Which of the following must not be dispensed to the patient?
A. A 35 year old patient requesting a 10 pack of syringes. ✓
B. A 17 year old patient with a prescription for a product containing dextromethorphan. ✓
C. A faxed prescription for Sudogest with a stamped signature from the provider. ✗
D. An electronic prescription for Cheritussin AC sent by the provider for a patient that is 16 years old. ✓

26. There is a shortage of oxycodone 10mg tablets. You notify the provider, who asks you to change the medication to Percocet 10mg instead, but he can't get you a hard copy script until tomorrow. You:
A. Document a verbal order from the provider for an emergency prescription.
B. Change the medication to Percocet.
C. Tell the patient they will have to wait until tomorrow when you receive a hardcopy prescription.
D. Tell the provider to fax an emergency prescription.

27. A pharmacist receives an electronic prescription on 2/12/19 for Duragesic. The prescription is dated 2/12/19, but states "Do not fill until 2/20/2019". Janet, a nurse from the prescriber's office calls and states the prescription was misprinted and asks if we can change the "Do not fill until" date to 2/12/2019. You:
A. Tell Janet that you need a new hardcopy prescription.
B. Tell Janet you will need to talk to the prescriber directly about this.
C. Tell Janet thank you for calling, you will document the change and fill the prescription right away.
D. Tell Janet to electronic submit a revised prescription.

28. Your pharmacy receives a prescription for hydrocodone/acetaminophen solution. The pharmacy just ran out, but you have hydrocodone/acetaminophen tablets in the same concentration and at the same strength as the prescription. The patient is ok with receiving tablets. You:
A. Notify the provider's agent to quickly send you a revised electronic prescription.
B. Notify the providers office, and when the providers nurse, Janet, says the provider has approved the change, change the prescription.
C. Notify the providers office and let Janet know you will need to talk to the provider directly before changing the prescription.
D. If you have not been able to reach the providers office, tell the patient you cannot fill the prescription.

29. A patient brings in a hard copy prescription for Marinol but there is no patient name listed, just a date of birth. You:
A. Notify the patient the prescription is not valid and they will need to notify the provider to send a new prescription.
B. Call the provider and add the patient's name after talking to the providers agent, Janet.
C. Call the providers office and notify Janet that you will have to get the patient's name directly from the prescriber. → ONLY IF CII,
D. Document the correct name after speaking with the patient.

30. A pharmacist licensed in Idaho has moved to Oregon and their Oregon pharmacist license application is pending. They have already taken and passed the MPJE. Which of the following activities can they participate in?
I. Pull medications from shelves for filling prescriptions
II. DUR checks under the supervision of an Oregon licensed pharmacist
III. Pull outdated medications from shelves

A. I only
B. II only
C. III only
D. I and III only

31. A provider has written a prescription for Percocet, and in the directions has included "Must return Norco in order to obtain Percocet". You:
A. Accept the remaining Norco back upon dispensing the Percocet.
B. Tell the patient to return the Norco to his provider before dispensing the Percocet.
C. Ask the patient to destroy and throw away the medications in front of you, but not in the pharmacy.
D. Have the patient destroy the medication in front of you and accept the destroyed medication to put in your expired/destroy bin.

32. Which items can be changed on a hard copy prescription for Avinza?
I. A name written as A Smith, birthday 2/22/1948
II. The date of issue, which was originally post-dated. — NEVER LEGAL
III. Addition of a prescribers DEA

A. I and II only
B. II and III only
C. I and III only
D. I, II and III

33. You receive a prescription for Provigil, written as "Take 1 daily, #365". With this prescription you may:
I. Dispense #365 → STILL GOOD! 6 MONTHS IS LIMIT SCRIPT ITSELF IS VALID
II. Dispense #180
III. Dispense #30

A. I and II only
B. II and III only
C. I and III only

D. I, II and III

34. A patient comes in with a prescription for Quillichew, #30. You have 10 tablets in stock and the patient would like as many as you can supply her now, and to pick up the rest later. You:
A. Tell the patient you cannot partial this medication, she must come back when you can provide her the full quantity.
B. Provide her 10 tablets now and the remaining supply in 10 days. [crossed out, 72°]
C. Provide her 10 tablets now and the remaining supply within 3 days. 72°
D. Call the provider to change the prescription to Ritalin, which you can supply 30 tablets of today. → CAN'T CHANGE CII DRUG NAME

35. Which of the following emergency medication refills may you provide?
A. A 30 day emergency supply of metazolone. ONLY 72°
B. A 48 hour emergency supply of Viibryd.
C. A 48 hour emergency supply of Vimpat. → NO CONTROLS
D. A 96 hour emergency supply of Vimpat.

36. A patient comes to pick up her EPT prescription as well as the EPT prescription written for her partner. You:
A. Explain that she can only pick up her EPT prescription, her partner will have to come in to pick up theirs.
B. Verbally counsel the patient on both prescriptions.
C. Verbally counsel the patient on both prescriptions and provide written patient information for both prescriptions.
D. Verbally counsel the patient on both prescriptions and provide written patient information for the partners prescription.

37. How do you complete a DUR on an EPT prescription?
A. You do not have to complete a DUR on an EPT prescription, as you have no information for the partner.
B. Inform the patient dropping off the prescription that you will need to contact the partner to obtain more information before filling the prescription.
C. Ask the patient that drops off the prescription if the partner has any allergies or concurrent medications. ATTEMPT MUST BE MADE
D. The extent that you can complete a DUR is just to ensure that the prescription is written correctly and appropriately, as you have no other information.

38. Which of the following is true regarding immunizations
I. A pharmacy that provides immunizations must have "Epidemiology and prevention of Vaccine – Preventable Diseases" on hand to reference.
II. Report of vaccinations given must be sent in to OHA Alert
III. A pharmacist may only immunize patients under the age of 7 when authorization is given by the Oregon Board of Pharmacy → GOVENER

A. I and II only
B. II and III only
C. I and III only
D. I, II and III

39. A patient experiences an adverse reaction to a vaccine. You immediately report it to:
I. MedWatch
II. VAERS
III. The patients primary care provider

A. I and II only
B. II and III only
C. I and III only
D. I, II and III

40. Which follows appropriate order for vaccination protocol?
A. Provide the patient with the vaccine information sheet, confirm the patient has no questions about the vaccine, immunize the patient, and notify the patients' primary care provider.
B. Confirm the patient has no questions about the vaccine, immunize the patient, provide the patient with the vaccine information sheet, and notify OHA Alert.
C. Provide the patient with the vaccine information sheet, confirm the patient has no questions about the vaccine, immunize the patient, and notify OHA Alert.
D. Confirm the patient has no questions about the vaccine, immunize the patient, provide the patient with the vaccine information sheet, and notify the patients' primary care provider

41. Under Oregon statewide protocol, a pharmacist may prescribe and dispense naloxone to:
I. A patient on opioid therapy
II. A person completing overdose training
III. A patient not on opioid therapy

A. I and II only
B. II and III only
C. I and III only
D. I, II and III

42. Which of the following is true regarding pharmacist prescribing of naloxone?
I. A pharmacist must complete a training course before they are allowed to prescribe naloxone.
II. A pharmacist must counsel on new naloxone prescriptions
III. A pharmacist may provide any supplies needed to use naloxone along with the medication.

A. I and II only
B. II and III only
C. I and III only
D. I, II and III

43. A 17 year-old female patient would like you to prescribe oral contraceptives. She last saw her provider 18 months ago. She has previously been on Seasonique that you last filled at your pharmacy 3 months ago. The prescription is expired. You:
A. Tell her you cannot prescribe her birth control until she is over 18.
B. Tell her you cannot prescribe her birth control because she last saw the provider more than a year [3 YEARS] ago.
C. Tell her you can only prescribe her Seasonique at this time, after she fills out the self-screening assessment questionnaire.

D. Tell her she must fill out the self-screening assessment questionnaire, and that you will be able to prescribe her appropriate birth control based on her responses and your assessment.

44. Which of the following is true regarding pharmacist prescribing of birth control?
I. The patient may be asked to make an appointment with the pharmacist.
II. The pharmacist may not prescribe birth control to their immediate family.
III. The pharmacist may not provide birth control to a patient if the standard procedural algorithm states the patient must be referred to their provider.

A. I and II only
B. II and III only
C. I and III only
D. I, II and III

45. The record of a patients filled out Birth Control Self-Screening assessment questionnaire must be kept for ___ years.
A. 2
B. 3
C. 4
D. 5

46. To which of the following people may a pharmacist prescribe epinephrine?
A. An EMS trainee who presents with an Authorization to Obtain Epinephrine certificate, issued one year ago and showing one previous dispensing of epinephrine, and an Epinephrine approval form.
B. An EMS trainee who presents with an Authorization to Obtain Epinephrine certificate, issued two years ago, showing one previous dispensing of epinephrine, and a Statement of Completion.
C. An EMS trainee who presents with an Authorization to Obtain Epinephrine certificate, issued four years ago, showing one previous dispensing of epinephrine, and an Epinephrine approval form.
D. An EMS trainee who presents with an Authorization to Obtain Epinephrine certificate, issued four years ago, showing four previous dispensing's of epinephrine, and an Epinephrine approval form.

47. Which of the following is true regarding a Chief Pharmacy Officer and a Pharmacist in Charge in a hospital pharmacy setting?
A. The Chief Pharmacy Officer may also be the Pharmacist in Charge when the institution has only one pharmacy.
B. The Chief Pharmacy Officer must be a different person than the Pharmacist in Charge, even when the institution has only one pharmacy.
C. The Chief Pharmacy Officer may also be the Pharmacist in Charge of all pharmacies, even if the institution has two or more pharmacies.
D. The Chief Pharmacy Officer must be a different person than the Pharmacist in Charge when the institution has two or more pharmacies, but the Pharmacist in Charge may supervise the pharmacy operations of all of the institution's pharmacies.

48. Which of the following is true for pharmacy practice in a hospital setting?
A. Areas in the hospital that are used to store medications must be inspected monthly.
B. Any trained nurse may be allowed to access the pharmacy after hours.
C. Areas in the hospital that are used to store medications must be inspected every two months.
D. No one may access a hospital pharmacy without a pharmacist present.

49. Emergency kits in a hospital setting must have the following components:
✓ I. Tamper-evident seals
~~II. A list of medication kept inside the drawer~~ with the medication.
✓ III. A label indicating the kit is for emergency use and containing the expiration date.

A. I and II only
B. II and III only
C. I and III only ← ANSWER IN BACK IS WRONG
D. I, II and III

50. Which of the following is true regarding medication orders in a hospital setting?
A. Verbal orders ~~may be used routinely,~~ provided the pharmacist receiving the order immediately reduces the order to writing and confirms the order through a read-back.
B. Written orders must include the name, strength, ~~and quantity~~ of the medication ordered
C. DUR checks are not required before the use of medication in the treatment of emergency needs OR IF PHARMACY CLOSED
D. A provider must sign written orders, ~~but does not need to sign off on verbal orders~~

51. A hospitalized patient with cancer would like to use a supplement he takes at home that was recommended by his oncologist. You explain:
✗ A. Patients may not take medication brought in from home.
B. If the patient can show you a labeled bottle of medication, he may keep it by his bedside and take it as he would like.
C. The patient should talk to the attending provider, as the attending must write an order stating the patient may take the medication.
✗ D. As long as the attending writes an order for the patient's supplement, the patient may bring in and take the supplement ~~without any further inspection~~ of the medication by the attending provider or pharmacist.

52. Which of the following is true for the storage and distribution of controlled substances in a hospital setting?
I. Suboxone may be used as floor stock as long as proper documentation is kept.
~~II.~~ Halcion may be kept in a robotic distribution system.   CII's CAN'T   CIII-V CAN
III. Quantities of Roxanol kept in the pharmacy must be tracked using a perpetual inventory.

A. I and II only
B. II and III only
C. I and III only
D. I, II and III

53. A patient is being discharged from the hospital for a COPD exacerbation, and he is to continue using a new inhaler that was started in the hospital. You would like to send the patient home with the inhaler he has been using in the hospital, as there are still 23 doses left. You:
A. Notify your PIC, who informs you that unfortunately you cannot legally provide the inhaler to the patient.
B. Provide the inhaler to the patient with the hospital label but with written counseling instructions that contain the directions on how to use the medication.
C. Put an outpatient label on the medication, and counsel the patient on taking the medication.

D. Put an outpatient label on the medication and provide it to the patient. The patient does not need to be counseled as he has already been using the medication in the hospital.

54. A pharmacist in Montana works in a Central Fill pharmacy that processes prescriptions for Oregon patients. Which of the following is true?
I. Both the pharmacist processing prescriptions and the PIC of the Central Fill pharmacy must be licensed in Oregon.
II. Only the PIC of the Central Fill pharmacy needs to be licensed in Oregon
III. As long as the PIC of the Central Fill pharmacy is licensed in Oregon, the Central Fill Pharmacy itself does not need to be registered with the Oregon Board of Pharmacy.

A. I only
B. II only
C. II and III only
D. I, II and III

55. An Oregon pharmacy uses a Remote Processing Drug Outlet located in Idaho to handle its prescription processing. Which of the following is correct?
A. Only a pharmacist licensed in Oregon may provide counseling to Oregon patient's on prescriptions processed by the RPDO.
B. If owned by different entities, there must be a shared pharmacy services agreement between the Oregon pharmacy and the RPDO.
C. The prescription label should contain the information ~~of both~~ the primary Oregon pharmacy ~~and the RPDO~~.
D. The records kept at the primary pharmacy ~~only~~ need to show the functions of prescription filling or processing ~~performed at the primary pharmacy~~. ALL FUNCTIONS

56. As a consultant pharmacist, you are responsible for the following:
I. Providing the facility with Policies and Procedures regarding the storage of medication.
II. Completing a DUR on each medication when it is prescribed within the facility. DURs ARE USUALLY FULL MEDICATION REVIEWS
III. Assisting the nurses in appropriate documentation of administered medications.

A. I and II only
B. I and III only
C. II and III only
D. I, II and III

57. Which of the following Beyond Use Dates (BUD) is appropriate, if no additional BUD testing is completed?
A. BUD of ~~14 days~~ for a medium-risk compound kept in the refrigerator. 9 DAYS
B. BUD of ~~18 hours~~ for a high-risk compound kept at room temperature. 24°
C. BUD of 1 hour for a low-risk compound designed for immediate use.
D. BUD of ~~30 days~~ for a medium-risk compound kept in the freezer. 45 DAYS

58. Match the compounds to their appropriate beyond use date:

Compound	Annotation	BUD	Annotation
Single-volume transfer of a sterile hazardous substance	MED (30)	48 hours at room temperature	Low
Single-volume transfer using preservative free gentamycin	HIGH (3)	1 hour at room temperature	IMMED
Transfer of three sterile substances into one container prepared appropriately for use tomorrow on the inpatient ward	(48)	3 days refrigerated	HIGH
Transfer of three sterile substances into one container prepared in the emergency room for use within 15 minutes.	(1°)	30 hours room temperature	MED

59. Which items are appropriately matched to their mandated cleaning schedule when in an ISO Class 7 environment?
- A. Work surfaces- ~~each shift~~ DAY
- B. Floors- ~~Weekly~~ DAY
- C. Walls- ~~Weekly~~ MONTH
- (D.) Ceilings- Monthly

NO "WEEKLY"

60. Which of the following statements regarding the Pharmacist in Charge (PIC) are correct?
- ✓ I. A person may be the PIC of two pharmacies at one time.
- ✓ II. The PIC of a nuclear pharmacy must be a recognized nuclear pharmacist.
- ~~III.~~ A person may be the PIC of ~~two~~ nuclear pharmacies at one time. ONLY ONE

A. I and II only
B. I and III only
C. II and III only
D. I, II and III

61. Which of the following patients may receive medications from a Charitable Pharmacy in Oregon?
- A. An Oregon resident who does not have health insurance and has ~~proof of previously receiving Cozaar~~ for high-blood pressure. VALID SCRIPT
- B. An ~~Idaho resident~~ OREGON ONLY who is temporarily in Oregon who is enrolled in an Oregon public assistance program and has a prescription for Trajenta (linagliptin).
- C. An Oregon resident who is enrolled in an Oregon public assistance program and has a prescription for ~~clozapine.~~ → (REMS)
- D. An Oregon resident who does not have health insurance and has a prescription for Buspar.

62. Which of the following is true regarding emergency kits located in Long-Term Care Facilities (LTCF)?
- I. An emergency kit becomes the property and responsibility ~~of the LTCF~~ PHARMACY when they sign that they have received the kit.
- II. Only a designated nurse may remove medications from an emergency kit.
- ✓ III. An emergency kit may contain medication that may be used in an emergency as well as medications routinely prescribed for a new admission.

EMERGENCY FOR LTCF = PHARMACY CLOSE/FAR AWAY

A. I only
B. II only
C. I and II only
(D.) II and III only

63. Which of the following is true regarding medications dispensed from a Dispensing Practitioner Drug Outlet (DPDO)?
A. Medications may be kept in a physicians' desk drawer, as long as the drawer remains locked.
B. A 60g tube of Eucrisa must be labeled, but the label does not need to contain a physical description. [unit dose]
C. A 60g tube of Eucrisa must be labeled, but the label does not need to include cautionary statements.
D. A record of dispensing Eucrisa that is kept in the patients' electronic chart alongside treatment notes is adequate to fulfill the record requirements for dispensing prescriptions. [not separate, combinable record]

64. Practitioners that dispense the which of the following medications are exempt from registering as a Dispensing Practitioner Drug Outlet
I. Homeopathic medications
II. Natural thyroid supplements
III. Medications obtained from a Medication Assistance Program

A. I and II only
B. I and III only
C. II and III only
D. I, II and III

65. Which of the following is true regarding the reporting of lost medications?
I. A pharmacist must report a significant loss to the Board of Pharmacy within 1 business day.
II. If medication is lost in transit from the supplier to the pharmacy, the pharmacy is still responsible for reporting it.
III. If medication is lost in transit from a central fill pharmacy to a patient, the central fill pharmacy is responsible for reporting it

A. I and II only
B. I and III only
C. II and III only
D. I, II and III

66. Your pharmacy stores applicable records off site to save space in the pharmacy. The BOP comes in for an inspection, and requests to see the records you keep on-site. You show him:
A. The records for the last 365 days that are kept onsite and notify him that the remaining two years of records can be retrieved within 3 business days.
B. The records for the last 120 days are kept onsite and notify him the remaining 2.5 years of records can be retrieved within 3 business days.
C. The records for the last 365 days are kept onsite and notify him the remaining two years of records can be retrieved in 5 business days.
D. The records for the last 120 days are kept onsite and notify him the remaining 2.5 years of records can be retrieved in 5 business days.

67. Which of the following medications may not be accepted back from a patient for disposal?
A. A patient has been affected by a recall of his irbesartan, and has brought his bottle of medication back to the pharmacy to return.
B. A patient discovers that the expiration date on the box of Imitrex she received from the pharmacy today expired last month, and brings it back in.

C. A patient brings his bottle of Xanax, dispensed today, back into the pharmacy because he noticed there are two different types of medication inside. You confirm that there are both Xanax tablets as well as another medication mixed in his bottle.
D. A patient brings his bottle of Xanax, dispensed today, back to the pharmacy because the prescription was written by an urgent care provider and violates his pain contract, and the patient didn't realize until he got home.

68. Your pharmacy has decided to host a take-back program and you have notified the BOP. You have a couple of interns available to help you during the take back program. You may ask them to do the following:
I. Count the number of tablets of Schedule II substances that are collected during the program.
II. Help clean out the expired storage area in the pharmacy and put these medications into the take back receptacle
III. Interview patients as they are coming in on their perceived value of the take-back program.

A. II only
B. III only
C. I and II only
D. II and III only

69. How long are you required to keep physical copies of controlled and non-controlled hard copy prescription received by the pharmacy?
A. Both controlled and non-controlled prescriptions must be kept in hard copy form for 365 days.
B. Both controlled and non-controlled prescriptions must be kept in hard copy form for 120 days.
C. Non-controlled prescriptions must be kept in hard copy form for 365 days, and controlled prescriptions must be kept for at least 3 years.
D. Non-controlled prescriptions must be kept in hard copy form for 120 days and controlled prescriptions must be kept for at least 3 years.

70. Which of the following review items and timelines are matched incorrectly?
A. An outpatient pharmacy must complete an inventory of Schedule II substances quarterly.
B. A CDTM agreement must be reviewed annually.
C. The pharmacy policy on returned medications must be reviewed annually.
D. A PIC inspection must be completed annually by February 1st.

71. Which of the following events and reporting deadlines are matched incorrectly?
A. A report of a natural disaster, which has destroyed part of your medication stock, must be provided to the BOP in 3 days.
B. The board has found some problems on their inspection, and the PIC is required to submit a correction within 30 days.
C. A felony charge on a pharmacist must be reported to the BOP within 15 days.
D. A change in PIC must be communicated to the BOP within 15 days.

72. Which of the following items does not need to be kept in a patients record in outpatient pharmacy?
A. The fact that the patient is a diabetic.
B. The brand of test strips a patient receives from your pharmacy on a monthly basis.

C. The type of insulin the patient receives from a different mail order pharmacy, as mandated by his insurance.
D. The patient's allergy to latex.

73. Which of the following items is matched incorrectly to the length of time it needs to be kept on file?
A. Invoice record for Schedule II prescriptions must be kept for 3 years.
B. Vaccine administration records must be kept for 3 years.
C. Hormonal Contraception Self-screening questionnaires must be kept for 3 years.
D. Records of birth control prescribed by the pharmacist must be kept for 3 years.

74. Which of the following cannot become PIC of a pharmacy, starting today?
A. A pharmacist that has 1 year of experience as a pharmacist but has not completed the PIC training course.
B. A pharmacist with two months of experience as a pharmacist and who is scheduled to complete the PIC training course 10 days after becoming PIC.
C. A pharmacist with two months of experience as a pharmacist and who is scheduled to complete the PIC training course in 60 days.
D. A pharmacist that has eight months of experience as a pharmacist and who completed the PIC training course 60 days ago.

75. A pharmacist takes a position as the PIC of the pharmacy on March 1st. Which of the following is true?
A. They must complete an inventory of all controlled substances within the next month, as well as a pharmacy inspection.
B. They must complete an inventory of all controlled substances within the next 15 days, as well as a pharmacy inspection.
C. They must complete an inventory of all controlled substances within the next 15 days, but do not need to repeat the pharmacy inspection as it was just completed on February 1st.
D. They do not need to complete an inventory of all controlled substances, as the retiring PIC completed it on February 1st, but they need to inspect the pharmacy.

76. Which of the following are true regarding becoming a pharmacist preceptor?
I. There are no additional CE requirements for pharmacist preceptors.
II. A pharmacist must be licensed as a preceptor and may apply for a license after practicing as a pharmacist for one year.
III. A pharmacist preceptor is not required to supervise all of the hours an intern completes under them.

A. I and II only
B. I and III only
C. II and III only
D. I, II and III

77. How many CEs must a pharmacist complete in each renewal cycle?
A. 30 total, 3 of which must be on pharmacy law.
B. 30 total, 2 of which must be on pharmacy law.
C. 20 total, 3 of which must be on pharmacy law.
D. 15 total, 2 of which must be on pharmacy law.

78. Which of the following equipment is mandatory to operate a pharmacy?
A. Oregon Revised Statues, Refrigeration, Sink with cold water, and an updated pharmaceutical reference.
B. Oregon Administrative Rules Chapter 855, Refrigeration, sink with hot and cold water, and an updated pharmaceutical reference.
C. Oregon Revised Statues chapters 689 and 475, Oregon Administrative Rules Chapter 855, Refrigeration, sink with cold water, and an updated pharmaceutical reference.
D. Oregon Revised Statues chapters 689 and 475, Oregon Administrative Rules Chapter 855, Refrigeration, sink with hot and cold water, and an updated pharmaceutical reference.

79. What are the refrigerator requirements for a pharmacy that has refrigerated vaccines?
I. The temperature must be on an automated monitoring system.
II. If the temperature is manually recorded twice daily, it does not have to be automated.
III. The temperature log must be downloaded weekly.

A. I and II only
B. I and III only
C. II and III only
D. I, II and III

80. What items must be present in a pharmacy?
I. Licenses of the pharmacists only must be clearly displayed
II. All personnel must wear name badges that have their name and position
III. A sign that states the pharmacy may be able to substitute a less expensive medication that is therapeutically equivalent, unless the pharmacy is not open to the public.

A. II only
B. III only
C. I and II only
D. II and III only

81. Which of the following entities must be registered with the Oregon Board of Pharmacy?
I. A Central-fill pharmacy located in Idaho that processes prescriptions for Oregon patients.
II. A pharmaceutical distributor located in Oregon.
III. A common carrier that a central-fill pharmacy uses to deliver dispensed medications to Oregon patients.

A. II only
B. III only
C. I and II only
D. II and III only

82. Which of the following is true regarding the Health Professionals Service Program?
A. This is a program for pharmacists only, and a pharmacist must be referred by the Oregon BOP in order to participate.
B. A pharmacist that refers themselves to the program may participate for only one year.
C. Any pharmacist participating in the program must participate for a minimum of two years.

D. The Health Professionals Service Program is only for pharmacists that have been diagnosed with Substance Abuse disorders.

83. Which of the following is the correct regarding the make-up of the Oregon Board of Pharmacy?
A. 7 total members, including 3 pharmacists, 2 technicians, and 2 members of the public
B. 7 total members, including 3 pharmacists and 2 technicians that must have at least 5 years practicing in Oregon.
C. 9 total members, including 5 pharmacists, 2 technicians, and 2 members of the public
D. 9 total members, including 5 pharmacists and 2 technicians that must have at least 5 years practicing in Oregon.

84. Which of the following is correct regarding the Oregon Board of Pharmacy?
A. Members of the Oregon BOP serve 2 year terms after their initial appointment by the governor.
B. Members of the Oregon BOP serve 2 year terms after their initial appointment by the Oregon Health Authority.
C. Members of the Oregon BOP serve 4 year terms after their initial appointment by the governor.
D. Members of the Oregon BOP serve 4 year terms after their initial appointment by the Oregon Health Authority.

85. Which of the following is correct regarding the composition of the Oregon Public Health and Formulary Advisory Committee?
A. 7 total members, including 2 Physicians, 2 advanced practice nurses, and 3 pharmacists.
B. 7 total members, including 2 pharmacists from a community setting and 1 pharmacist from a hospital setting.
C. 9 total members, including 3 physicians, 3 advanced practice nurses, and 3 pharmacists.
D. 9 total members, including 1 community based pharmacist, 1 hospital based pharmacist, and 1 consultant based pharmacist.

86. Which of the following is correct regarding the Oregon Public Health and Pharmacy Formulary Advisory Committee?
I. Members of the committee serve 2 year terms
II. The committee takes protocol recommendations from pharmacists not on the committee
III. Members of the committee are appointed by the Oregon Health Authority

A. I and II only
B. I and III only
C. II and III only
D. I, II and III

87. Which of the following activities can a technician complete?
I. Reconcile the inventory of Schedule II controlled substances
II. Fax requests for prescription refills to a provider
III. Fill prescriptions that the pharmacist has already processed while the pharmacist has stepped away from the pharmacy for a brief meeting.

A. I and II only
B. I and III only
C. II and III only

D. I, II and III

88. A patient brings in a prescription for Linzess and Lomotil. After reviewing the prescriptions, you note that the patient is the providers' daughter. You tell the patient:
A. You cannot fill either prescription.
B. You can fill the prescription for Linzess but not for Lomotil.
C. You can fill both prescriptions by the end of the day.
D. You have to get verification from a second provider before filling either prescription.

89. You receive a hard copy prescription from a patient that was just in the emergency room. The prescription contains three different medications; Norco, Ketorolac, and Septra DS, with directions and quantities for each. The prescription is hand signed by the provider. You:
A. Tell the patient you cannot fill this prescription.
B. Tell the patient you may fill the Ketorolac and Septra DS, but not the Nucynta ER.
C. Fill all three prescriptions and file the hardcopy prescription in your CII files only.
D. Fill all three prescriptions and file the hardcopy prescription in the CII files, but a copy of the prescription in your files for legend medications.

90. A patient would like to fill her prescription for methotrexate through an online pharmacy and has come to ask you for advice. She tells you she has found two internet pharmacies she can send a prescription to, and the one located in Canada is offering her a much better price. You tell her:
I. Unfortunately there are no valid internet pharmacies.
II. There are no pharmacies in Canada that are validated to dispense medications to Oregon patients.
III. She should ensure that the online pharmacy is verified. If it is, it will have VIPPS accreditation on its website.

A. I and II only
B. I and III only
C. II and III only
D. I, II and III

91. You receive a hardcopy prescription from a providers' office that has both Diflucan and Nucynta ER with complete directions and quantities. The prescription has been signed by the providers' agent. You tell the patient:
A. You may not fill either the Diflucan or the Nucynta ER.
B. You may fill the Diflucan but not the Nucynta ER.
C. You may fill both the Diflucan and the Nucynta ER after verifying both medications with the provider.
D. You may fill both the Diflucan and Nucynta ER without any further verification.

92. A prescribers' agent calls in a prescription for Nembutal. She explains that this is an emergency situation. You tell her:
A. If this is truly an emergency you may take a verbal order from her for the Nembutal, as long as she sends a hard-copy prescription to your pharmacy postmarked within 7 business days with the providers signature.
B. If this is truly an emergency, you may take a verbal order from the prescriber for the Nembutal, as long as a hard-copy prescription is sent to your pharmacy, postmarked within 7 business days with the provider's signature.

C. If this is truly an emergency, she must fax you a hardcopy prescription written and signed by the prescriber, and send the hard-copy to your pharmacy, postmarked within 7 business days.
D. Unfortunately, even if this is an emergency situation, you will need a hard copy prescription presented to the pharmacy before filling the medication.

93. Which items do you have to document on a prescription transferred into your pharmacy?
I. Prescription number at the transferring pharmacy
II. Dates of each time the prescription was filled at the transferring pharmacy.
III. The number of refills authorized on the original prescription.

A. II only
B. III only
C. I and II only
D. II and III only

94. A provider with MD credentials electronically sends three prescriptions for Tamiflu to your pharmacy. The prescriptions are for both family members and the Cuddles, the family cat. You:
A. Fill all prescriptions as written.
B. Fill the prescriptions for the two humans only.
C. After verifying with a local veterinarian that a can may take Tamiflu, fill all prescriptions as written.
D. After verifying that the prescriber has a patient-provider relationship with both humans and the cat, fill all the prescriptions.

95. You receive a faxed prescription for Enbrel. The prescription has the signature of the providers' agent and was faxed by the prescribers' agent. The prescription states "Brand Only". You:
A. Call the providers office and explain the prescription must be signed by the provider themselves in order for you to fill the prescription.
B. Call the providers office and explain that "Brand Only" is not a valid DAW notation, but you can mark the prescription DAW after speaking with the provider directly.
C. Call the providers office and explain that "Brand Only" is not a valid DAW notation, but you can mark the prescription DAW after speaking with the providers' agent.
D. Fill the prescription as written.

96. Which of the following is true regarding prescriptions for controlled substances?
I. The prescription does not need to have the DEA of the prescriber written, as long as you can look up the prescribers DEA.
II. Prescriptions for Schedule II Controlled substances do not expire.
III. You may not fill prescriptions for Schedule II Controlled substances from out of state providers, even if they are practicing within their scope.

A. II only
B. III only
C. I and II only
D. II and III only

97. A retired pharmacist would like to go back to practicing pharmacy part time. Their license was last active 4 years ago. In order to reinstate their license, the retired pharmacist must:
A. Complete 30 CE's and pay the licensing fee for the year they are reinstating their license.

B. Complete 60 CE's and pay the licensing fee for the year they are reinstating their license.
C. Complete 30 CE's pay the licensing fee for the year they are reinstating their license and pass the MPJE again.
D. Complete 60 CE's, pay the licensing fee for the year they are reinstating their license, and pass the MPJE again.

98. There is a wildfire in Northern California that displaces many residents and is declared a natural disaster. A patient comes into your pharmacy in Oregon and states he is a resident of that area. He regularly takes Keppra and needs an emergency refill as he has run out this morning. He has brought in his bottle of medication labeled from his pharmacy in California. You:
A. Tell the patient that you cannot provide him an emergency refill as your pharmacy is not in the natural disaster area.
B. Tell the patient you can only provide him with a 72hour emergency refill of this medication.
C. Tell the patient you may provide him with a 30 day emergency refill of this medication but will need a provider to authorize additional refills.
D. Tell the patient you can only fill this medication if he obtains a new prescription, which he can do by going to the local emergency room and speaking with a provider there.

99. Which of the following is true regarding the dispensing of controlled substances?
I. A faxed prescription for a controlled substance is only valid if it contains the hand signature of the provider.
II. A patient that is 12 years old may pick up a controlled substance for his mother.
III. You may not require a patient to present an ID in order to dispense a controlled substance.

A. I and II only
B. I and III only
C. II and III only
D. I, II and III

100. Which of the following activities may a clerk complete?
I. Accept refill request from a patient who has their prescription numbers.
II. Inform a patient of a change in manufacturer when a patient is picking up a medication refill.
III. Create a new patient profile and fill in the patient name, address, and insurance information.

A. I and II only
B. I and III only
C. II and III only
D. I, II and III

101. Which of the following constitute valid prescriptions?
I. A verbal prescription transmitted by a prescribers' agent for Sudogest.
II. A hard copy prescription signed by the providers' agent for Brintellix.
III. A faxed prescription signed by the provider for Androgel, brought into the pharmacy by a patient.

A. I and II only
B. I and III only
C. II and III only
D. I, II and III

102. A nursing home has single-dose blister-packed medications for a patient that no longer resides in the facility. The nurse is wondering what her options are for these medications. You explain that she may:
I. Return them to the pharmacy where they were obtained, provided that she can account for proper storage and handling of the medications and the medications remain in sealed blisters.
II. Keep the medications in the nursing home as floor stock.
III. Donate them to a charitable pharmacy as long as there are no controlled substances and the medications remain in sealed blisters.

A. I and II only
B. I and III only
C. II and III only
D. I, II and III

103. A patient's agent comes in to your pharmacy to pick up a prescription for Azithromycin 500mg tablets, quantity of 4, take 4 tablets by mouth once. The prescription requires counseling. You:
A. Tell the patients' agent that you need to talk to the patient regarding this prescription and dispense the medication along with a number the patient can reach you at.
B. Tell the patients' agent that you need to talk to the patient regarding this prescription, and therefore must dispense it to the patient themselves.
C. Counsel the patients' agent as you would the patient themselves and dispense the medication to the patients' agent.
D. Dispense the medication to the patients' agent without counseling, but with written information on the medication.

104. A provider writes a prescription for Kadian, "Take 1 tablet by mouth every 6 hours as needed, #120. Please dispense a one week supply at a time." A diagnosis of Stage 4 breast cancer is written on the prescription. You have verified with the provider previously that this is a terminal diagnosis. You:
A. Call the providers office and explain that you must provide the entire quantity at one time.
B. Dispense the entire quantity to the patients' agent and explain they must only supply the patient with a one-week supply at a time.
C. Dispense #28, document on the prescription the number dispensed and the number remaining and tell the patient's agent that they must refill the remaining quantity within 30 days.
D. Dispense #28, document on the prescription the number dispensed and the number remaining and tell the patient's agent that they must refill the remaining quantity within 30 days.

105. You a providing partial fills for a nursing home patient for Xtampza ER. The following are correct procedures when partial filling this medication:
I. You must document the date and the quantity dispensed for each fill.
II. You must document the remaining quantity after each fill.
III. You may continue to partial fill the medication for 30 days from the date the prescription was written.

A. II only
B. III only
C. I and II only
D. II and III only

106. Which of the following statements regarding Oregon's Prescription Drug Monitoring Program (PDMP) are true?
I. A pharmacy must transmit the necessary information to the PDMP within 48 hours after filling a controlled substance.
II. The PDMP only tracks the dispensing of medication in schedule II-IV.
III. The provider is required to register with the PDMP but is not required to check it when writing a prescription.

A. II only
B. III only
C. I and II only
D. II and III only

107. A patient and a policeman present to your pharmacy, each asking for a copy of the patient's PDMP record. You:
A. Provide both the patient and policeman with a copy of the patient's record.
B. Explain to both that they need to request their record from the Oregon Health Authority.
C. Provide the patient their PDMP record but explain to the policeman that she must make a request to the Oregon Health Authority.
D. Provide the policeman with a copy of the patients PDMP record but explain to the patient he must make a request to the Oregon Health Authority.

108. Which of the following statements are true regarding compounding pharmacies?
I. A compounding pharmacy may compound a commercially available medication if they can make it cheaper than the commercially available medication.
II. Mixing two or more commercial, non-sterile products is not considered compounding.
III. Compounding pharmacies must adhere to the guidelines presented in USP 795 but not to those in USP 797.

A. II only
B. III only
C. I and II only
D. II and III only

109. Which of the following is true regarding prescription labeling in an outpatient setting?
I. If the medication is for an animal, it must include the animals' species
II. If the medication is a generic, it must also include the manufacturer
III. The expiration date listed must be no greater than one year from the date of filling

A. II only
B. III only
C. I and II only
D. I, II and III

110. Which of the following statements regarding health care providers is true?
A. An expanded-practice dental hygienist may prescribe Keflex for a patient.
B. A midwife may prescribe ondansetron for a patient.

C. An optometrist may prescribe Percocet for a patient.
D. A chiropractor may prescribe ibuprofen 800mg for a patient.

111. Which of the following is true regarding counseling when a new medication is being delivered to a patient?
A. The pharmacist must make a reasonable effort to reach the patient to offer counseling, and document this.
B. New medications may not be delivered to patients because the patient must be counseled.
C. The pharmacist must provide written counseling information to the patient when new medication is delivered.
D. The pharmacist must provide written counseling information to the patient as well as a contact number to reach the pharmacist if the patient has any questions when a new medication is being delivered.

112. A complete drug utilization review (DUR) for a prescription may include:
I. Review of contraindications between the medication and the patients' disease states
II. Review of contraindications between the medication and the patient's other medications listed in the pharmacy profile.
III. Review for drug abuse

A. II only
B. III only
C. I and II only
D. I, II and III

113. Which of the following may be completed by a trained pharmacy intern?
I. An intern may accept a refusal to be counseled.
II. An intern may immunize patients.
III. An intern may accept a verbal prescription for a Schedule III substance.

A. II only
B. III only
C. I and II only
D. I, II and III

114. Which of the following must be on the label of a unit-dose medication designed for inpatient use?
I. The medication name and manufacturer
II. An expiration date
III. The manufacturer's lot number

A. II only
B. III only
C. I and II only
D. I, II and III

115. Which of the following is true regarding pharmacist practice?
A. A pharmacist practicing medication therapy management may change a dose of insulin under the prescriber's name.
B. A pharmacist practicing under a collaborative practice agreement may change a dose of insulin under the prescriber's name.
C. A pharmacist practicing medication therapy management may change a dose of insulin under their own name.
D. A pharmacist practicing under a collaborative practice agreement may change a dose of insulin under their own name.

116. A pharmacy must transmit information regarding controlled substance prescriptions to the Oregon PDMP within _____, but if a breach of security is suspected must notify the Oregon Health Authority within _____.
A. 48 hours, 24 hours.
B. 72 hours, 48 hours.
C. 48 hours, 48 hours.
D. 72 hours, 24 hours.

117. Which of the following is true regarding the labeling of intravenous medications in a hospital setting?
I. The label must contain a beyond-use date
II. As long as the label was electronically generated, it does not need to include the information of the verifying pharmacist
III. The label must include a rate of infusion

A. II only
B. III only
C. I and II only
D. I and III only

118. An IV is sent back from the inpatient ward as the patient for whom the IV was originally intended was switched to oral medication. The beyond-use date listed on the IV is not until tomorrow. You:
A. Properly dispose of the medication for no further use.
B. Remove the medication label and store appropriately for potential use within the next day.
C. Remove any patient identifier on the label and store appropriately for potential use within the next day.
D. Re-label the medication with a beyond use date in 1 hour.

119. Pharmacists must renew their license _____ on _____.
A. Annually, February 1st.
B. Annually, June 30th.
C. Biannually, February 1st.
D. Biannually, June 30th.

120. What must be present in a vaccine emergency kit?
I. Resuscitation mask
II. Epinephrine auto injectors or vials
III. Diphenhydramine injection

A. II only
B. III only
C. I and II only
D. I, II, and III

ANSWERS TO OREGON PHARMACY LAW EXAM

1.
Report misconduct of nurse practitioner- 10 days
Obtain off-site records for BOP inspection- 3 days
Change in pharmacy name- 15 days
Provide BOP with Plan of Correction- 30 days

2. C, I and III only. A clerk is not allowed to pull medications for filling because this could impact the outcome of the prescription.[2]

3. B, II only. Only a pharmacist can do the final verification of a prescription. DUR checks and immunization administration can also be completed by a properly trained pharmacy intern.

4. A, I and II only. A technician may accept a refill from a provider Zanaflex (tizanidine), which is not a controlled substance, as long as there are no changes. A technician may enter allergies into a patient's chart because this does not require professional judgment by the technician. A technician may not bypass any DUR checks, which would include duplicate therapy alerts.

5. D. While sale of over-the-counter dextromethorphan is restricted to patients aged 18 or older, this does not apply to prescription medication sales. There is no age restriction on dispensing medication and there is no reason you would need a hard copy prescription for this medication, even if it were for a controlled substance. As dextromethorphan is not a controlled substance, it is ok that an agent of the provider transmitted the prescription. ORS 475.380

6. B, II and III only. Technician checkers cannot check any emergency kits, such as an anaphylaxis kit. They can check non-emergent kits, such as a suture kit, and they can check stock to go into automated dispensing cabinets. OAR 855.041.5055

7. C, I and III only. Only a pharmacist may accept a refusal to be counseled, and counseling must be completed on new prescriptions, any refills that contain changes such as dosing changes. Counseling must be documented with more than just "accept", and therefore II is incorrect. OAR 855.019.0230

8. C. There is no pharmacist to technician ratio. A pharmacist may supervise only one TPI at a time but may supervise two SRIs at a time. OAR 855.031.0026

9. C. A pharmacist may supervise two immunization certified interns at a time during immunization clinics, regardless of if the intern is a TPI or SRI. OAR 855.031.0026

10. C. Providers are not allowed to write prescriptions "for Office use". A pharmacy can provide office use medications to providers via invoice or DEA 222, if the substance requested is a CII. Paracaine drops (proparacaine) is an anesthetic and is not a controlled substance. While the prescriber could provide you with specific patient names for this medication, and you could take a verbal order for them, the BEST answer in this situation is to fill out an invoice for the office.

11. B. RDH, registered dental hygienists, even if they are certified for expanded practice, are not allowed to prescribe CII substances. NDs (naturopathic physicians), ODs (optometrists), and DVMs (Veterinarians) are all allowed to prescribe CII's, although OD's are limited to hydrocodone combination products.[4]

12. C. A DATA Waiver is what providers complete to obtain their X DEA number. A DATA Waiver, or X DEA is required to prescribe buprenorphine products (Subutex and Suboxone) for treatment of opioid abuse but is not required for prescribing buprenorphine products for pain control. Midlevel practitioners may obtain a DATA Waiver and prescribe buprenorphine produce for opioid abuse in Oregon. In A, a midlevel practitioner is prescribing a buprenorphine product for pain control, and so an X DEA (or DATA Waiver) is not needed. In B, a midlevel practitioner has the X DEA and is prescribing the product for opioid abuse, which is legal. In D, the DATA Waiver isn't necessary because the provider is treating pain, not opioid abuse. C is the only option that is not legal, as the provider is treating opioid abuse but does not have a DATA Waiver.

13. D. Practitioners may dispense up to 72 hours of medication to a patient, unless the product is in a unit of use container. As long as the practitioner is following appropriate laws, they may dispense controlled substances to a patient. While the provider is dispensing more than a 72 hour supply of medication in both C and D in the above examples, in C the provider is dispensing a unit of use container, and therefore does not have to be registered as a DPDO. OAR 85.042.0510, OAR 855.042.0505

14. C. As long as a provider is writing within their scope in that state, and all other applicable laws are followed, prescriptions from other states are legal to process. A pharmacist may not process prescriptions from Canada. A pharmacist may not process a prescription from an internet provider, as this does not meet the state requirement for practitioner-patient relationship. Option A is somewhat subjective, however once a provider dies or retires there is no longer an appropriate provider-patient relationship and therefore even refills of the prescription are not legal. In this situation you would use your professional judgment; if the provider passed away more recently, you may consider providing an emergency refill to the patient to give the patient time to obtain a new prescription from a valid provider.[6] OAR 855.019.0210, ORS 689.525

15. Order should be A -> C-> D-> B. EPT prescriptions (A) expire 30 days from date of issue, CIII-CIV prescriptions (C) expire 6 months from date of issue, non-controlled prescription (D) expire 12 months from date of issue, and CII prescriptions do not have an expiration date. ORS 475.185, OAR 855.041.1125, OAR 855.041.4005

16. C. Non-controlled substances can be transferred as long as there are refills left on the prescription, but CIII-V substances can only be transferred once. However, if the pharmacies share a real-time database, CIII-V substances can be transferred more than one time. Assuming that two CVS pharmacies share a real time database, both prescriptions can be transferred again, regardless of the pharmacies being located in different states. OAR 855.041.2115

17. D. PRN refills indicates that the prescription is good for one full year of refills on a non-controlled prescription. It is easiest to translate that into 365 days. Therefore, add up the number of days the patient has received and the difference between the date of fill and the date the prescription was written, and note the difference between that number and a full 365 days. That will result in 184 that

you can still dispense to the patient. Remember, you must notify the provider when you combine all of the fills in this case. OAR 855.041.1125

18. A. You can fill the entire quantity of Prilosec (combine refills) although you must notify the provider that you have done so. You cannot combine refills into one fill for psychotherapeutic substances or controlled substance prescriptions. Therefore, you can only provide the patient with #30 of either Zoloft or Abilify. OAR 855.041.1120

19. C. As Lyrica is a controlled substance it cannot be part of an auto-refill program. Basaglar is eligible to be part of an auto-refill program, but if a patient does not pick up an auto-refill medication it is automatically removed from the program. It can be added back to the program if the patient requests it. OAR 855.041.1120

20. D. A patient is not allowed to request that "everything" be refilled. They must request medication specifically by name or prescription number. It does not matter if the medication is a controlled substance or not, or what the directions say. OAR 855.041.1120

21. C. You may substitute a liquid for a tablet or a tablet for a liquid, and you can make this substitution without the providers approval if you have made a reasonable effort to reach the provider and have been unable to, and if the medication does not have a unique delivery system. This situation does not meet the requirements for a new emergency prescription, and while it is good practice to notify the provider of the change after it has been made, it is not necessary to get any new prescription signed because of the change made in the prescription. OAR 689.515

22. C. You may not substitute a product that costs more than the prescribed medication. You may substitute a medication without an AB rating in the orange book if, in your professional judgment, the medication is still therapeutically equivalent. ORS 689.515

23. B. The provider must be notified within 3 business days after the INITIAL fill only, not on subsequent refills. The product must be listed as interchangeable in the purple book and DAW must be absent from the prescription in order to substitute a biologic product. In addition, the patient must be notified about the substitution. ORS 689.522, OAR 855.014.1105

24. D. ALL prescriptions require a DUR check, whether new or refilled, no matter what the medication is.

25. C. While pseudoephedrine is a controlled substance requiring a prescription, the faxed prescription must be hand signed by the provider. Syringes do not require a prescription. While you may not sell dextromethorphan to a patient under 18 years of age, it is ok to dispense dextromethorphan to a patient of any age if they have a prescription. An electronic prescription for a controlled substance is allowed as long as it is transmitted by the provider. ORS 475.525, ORS 475.380 and .390, OAR 855.019.0210

26: B. In the case of a medication shortage, you may substitute the medication prescribed as long as it is properly documented. There is nothing in the question to indicate this patient meets the requirements for an emergency oral authorization or fax of a CII substance.[3, 4, 6]

27. B. This is an allowable change, but only if you obtain this change directly from the prescriber and not the prescriber's agent. The change can either be in the form of a new prescription electronically

submitted by the provider (not Janet), or by verbal confirmation from the prescriber. There is no need for an actual hardcopy prescription, CIIs may be electronically transmitted.

28. C. The dose form can be changed on a prescription, but authorization must come from the provider themselves, not the provider's agent. If you cannot reach the providers' office, it is legal to substitute the medication for a therapeutically equivalent medication with a different dosage form, so D is incorrect. You could make this switch with proper documentation.

29. B. In this case you must know that Marinol is a CIII substance. For a CIII substance, it is ok to get a verbal authorization from the providers agent, as in this case you are basically getting a verbal order from the provider's agent for the medication. If this was a CII substance talking to the provider directly wouldn't matter, as you cannot add a name only change the name. If this was not a controlled substance you would want to verify with the providers office before filling in the name, so D would not be correct no matter what the medication was.

30. C. Until a pharmacist is actually licensed in Oregon, they cannot participate in any activities that require a license in an Oregon pharmacy. This includes duties of a technician, intern, or pharmacist. They can only act as a clerk until they are licensed. The only activities in the above list that a clerk may complete are pulling outdated medications from the shelves.[2]

31. C. Unless the pharmacy is licensed as a reverse distributor and is appropriately registered to take back CII substances, you may not accept the Norco under any circumstances. The most you may do in this situation is to ask the patient to destroy and dispose of the medication in front of you, without allowing either the intact or destroyed medication back into the pharmacy.

32. C. A name written A Smith may be updated to Adam Smith with a call and verification from the provider that wrote the prescription. A prescribers DEA number can be added to the prescription without calling and clarifying with the provider. A backdated prescription is not a legal prescription and therefore changing the date would not have any bearing on the prescription.

33. D. Although this is a CIV medication, and the prescription expires after 6 months, the provider may legally write the above prescription. It is up to your professional judgment to determine if you will dispense the entire quantity or a lesser quantity.

34. C. As a CII substance, you may partial the medication as long as the remaining supply is dispensed to the patient within 72 hours. As a CII substance, you cannot obtain a verbal prescription from the provider and you may not change the name of the medication, even with the provider's approval.

35. B. A 48 hour supply of Viibryd is the only option in the list that meets the requirement to be essential therapy, less than a 72-hour supply, and not a controlled substance. While Vimpat is essential therapy, as a controlled substance, you may not provide an emergency supply to a patient. OAR 855.041.1120

36. C. The law states that written information must be provided for each EPT prescription, and this would include the patient themselves.

37. C. You must always complete a DUR. You must ask the patient either when they drop off the prescription or when you are dispensing the prescription about any allergies or concurrent medications

the partner may have. You must attempt to obtain this information, and if the patient does not know this information you would essentially follow option D. You do not need to contact the partner.

38. A. The CDC reverence "Epidemiology and prevention of Vaccine –Preventable Diseases" is considered a required reference if vaccines are provided by the pharmacy. Vaccinations must be reported to OHA Alert within 15 days. Option III is incorrect because vaccinating patients under 7 is only allowed when the Governor, not the BOP authorizes it. OAR 855.019.0270, 855.019.0280, ORS 689.645

39. B. Adverse reactions to vaccines must be reported to VAERS and the patients' primary care provider. MedWatch is used to report adverse drug reactions. OAR 855.019.0270, 855.019.0280, ORS 689.645

40. C. The VIS must be given to the patient and the patient must be able to review it before the vaccine is given. Once the vaccine is administered, it must be reported to OHA Alert. The patients' primary care provider only needs to be notified when the patient experiences an adverse reaction to a vaccination.

41. D. A pharmacist may provide naloxone to any person seeking it under current Oregon law. This includes persons completing overdose training, and even patients that are not currently on opioid therapy. ORS 689.681, 689.682, OAR 855.019.0450-0460

42. B. Naloxone prescriptions are not exempt from counseling requirements, and when prescribing and dispensing, the pharmacist may also provide the patient with any supplies needed to use the naloxone. There is not currently any training course a pharmacist must take before prescribing naloxone therapy. ORS 689.681, 689.682, OAR 855.019.0450-0460

43. D. Although this patient is under 18, a pharmacist may prescribe birth control for patients that have previously been on a self-administered patch or oral contraceptive and to patients that have seen their provider within the last three years. This patient meets both of those criteria, so you may prescribe her birth control based on her responses to the questionnaire and your assessment using the standard procedural algorithm. There is no reason you would only be able to prescribe this patient Seasonique.

44. B. A patient may not be required to make an appointment to receive birth control prescribed by the pharmacist. The other two options are correct statements. ORS 689.689, OAR 855.019.0400-0435

45. D. This record must be kept for 5 years.

46. B. A person wishing to obtain epinephrine without a prescription from a pharmacy must present with an Authorization to Obtain Epinephrine dated within the last three years, along with a Statement of Completion. The person may use the Authorization to Obtain Epinephrine four times within a three-year period. OAR 855.041.2320

47. A. The Chief Pharmacy Officer is someone in charge of supervising all pharmacy operations in a hospital setting. The Chief Pharmacy Officer may be the same person as the Pharmacist in Charge when the institution only has one pharmacy. When the institution has more than one pharmacy, the Chief Pharmacy Officer may still be the Pharmacist in Charge of one of those pharmacies. This rules out option B and C. D is also incorrect because supervision of pharmacy operations is the definition of the job of the Chief Pharmacy Officer.

48. C. Medication storage areas must be inspected every two months. This is the best answer for this question, although options B and D are close possibilities. B is incorrect because there must only be ONE nurse, and it must be the nurse supervisor that can access the pharmacy. D is incorrect because the law does allow one trained nurse supervisor to access the pharmacy after hours.

49. A. Emergency kits must have tamper-evident seals and be labeled. The label must note that the kit is for emergency use, have the kit's expiration date, and also include the name, strength, and quantity of the medication contained inside. This label must be on the outside of the kit, not in the drawer with the medication. OAR 855.041.6420

50. C. There are three circumstances when a DUR check is not required before medication administration. In emergency situations, when the medication is used for the treatment of emergency needs, whether the medication comes from an emergency kit or not, and when medication is being dispensed from a medication cabinet when the pharmacy is closed and there is no pharmacist present. Therefore, C is correct. Verbal orders must not be used often, and when they are used a provider must sign off on the order. Written orders must include the name and strength of the medication, but do not need to include a quantity. OAR 855.041.6500, OAR 855.041.6510

51. C. A patient may use their own medication while hospitalized IF the attending provider writes an order for the medication. Furthermore, even with the order written, the medication must be in a labeled container, be identified by the prescriber or pharmacist, and be detrimental to the patient if they don't have it. In this question A is clearly incorrect, and D is clearly incorrect because the medication does need further inspection in order to meet the identification requirement. B is almost correct, because this option suggests the bottle is labeled and the pharmacist will inspect the medication, but it also suggests that no further actions are needed, when we know that there must also be an order from the provider. C is the only option that is a correct statement and does not suggest that this is the only requirement for the patient to take this medication.

52. D. Controlled substances may be kept as floor stock as long as proper documentation is kept and the substances are kept in locked compartments, CIII-V substances may be kept in robotic distribution systems, and CII substances must be kept on a perpetual inventory. Therefore, option I is correct regardless of the medication's schedule. Option II does depend on the medication's schedule. Halcion (triazolam) is a schedule IV substance, and so it can be kept in a robotic distribution system. Option III also depends on the medication schedule. Roxanol is a schedule II substance and therefore must be tracked with a perpetual inventory.

53. C. A patient may be provided with medication upon hospital discharge. Any medication provided must comply with outpatient labeling standards, and therefore hospital labeling (as noted in option B) is not appropriate as it does not contain all the necessary information for outpatient dispensing. Patient counseling is required upon hospital discharge for any medication the patient is sent home with.

54. B. The PIC of a Central Fill pharmacy must be a licensed pharmacist in Oregon, but the other pharmacists processing prescriptions do not need to be licensed in Oregon. Therefore, I is incorrect. Any pharmacy that completes any part of prescription processing for Oregon patient's must be licensed with the Oregon Board of Pharmacy, so III is also incorrect.

55. B. Pharmacists in a RPDO may counsel Oregon patients, even if they are not licensed in Oregon as long as the facility is registered with the Oregon Board of Pharmacy, the PIC is licensed in Oregon and

the pharmacist is licensed in the state the RPDO is located in. The primary pharmacy and the RPDO must either share an owner or have a shared pharmacy services agreement specifying the activities and responsibilities of each entity. The prescription label only needs to contain the information of the primary pharmacy. Records kept at both the primary pharmacy and the RPDO need to show who performed each task involved in the processing and filling of a prescription, whether this occurred at the primary pharmacy or RPDO.

56. B. A consultant pharmacist must provide the facility with policies and procedures on storage, security, and distribution of medications and guidance on appropriate documentation of medication administration. A consultant pharmacist is not routinely responsible for completing DURs, unless this is part of the duties the facility specifies. In addition, DUR checks typically comprise of a regular medication review for each patient, rather than completing a DUR for each medication when it is ordered. OAR 855.019.0240

57. C. Immediate-use compounds must be administered within 1 hour of compounding. Otherwise, use the following table:

Category 3 (Low Risk)	48hrs at room temp, 14 days refrigerated, 45 days frozen
Category 4 (Medium Risk)	30hrs room temp, 9 days refrigerated, 45 days frozen
Category 5 (High Risk)	24hrs room temp, 3 days refrigerated, 45 days frozen

58. Single-volume transfer of a sterile hazardous substance- 30 hours room temperature (Medium-risk compound due to use of hazardous substance)
Single-volume transfer using preservative free gentamycin (High-risk compound due to use of preservative free components)
Transfer of three sterile substances into one container prepared appropriately for use tomorrow on the inpatient ward- 48 hours at room temperature (Low-risk compound)
Transfer of three sterile substances into one container prepared in the emergency room for use within 15 minutes - 1 hour at room temperature (Immediate-use compound)

59. D. Work surfaces and floors are to be cleaned daily. Walls, ceilings and shelving are to be cleaned monthly.

60. A. A person may be the Pharmacist-in-Charge (PIC) of two pharmacies without obtaining additional approval from the Oregon Board of Pharmacy. However, a may only act as a PIC to one nuclear pharmacy at a time. The PIC of a nuclear pharmacy must be a nuclear pharmacist. OAR 855.042.0015

61. D. In order to receive medication from an Oregon Charitable Pharmacy, a patient must be an Oregon resident, must either not have adequate health coverage or be enrolled in an Oregon public assistance program, and have a valid prescription for the medication. This rules out options A and B. In addition, a charitable pharmacy may not dispense any medications that are controlled substances, under an FDA REMS program, require refrigeration, etc. (see references). Therefore, while the patient in option C may receive medication from the Charitable Pharmacy, the patient has a prescription for clozapine, which cannot be dispensed by a Charitable pharmacy. That leaves option D. There are no reasons that a Charitable Pharmacy cannot dispense Buspar. OAR 855.044.0030, OAR 855.044.0050

62. D. An emergency kit remains the property and responsibility of the pharmacy that provided the kit. Only a designated nurse may remove medications from the emergency kit and medications may only be removed after a prescriber's order has been received. An emergency kit may contain any medications

deemed necessary to meet the immediate need of a patient when it is likely that that pharmacy will not be able to provide these medications to the LTCF by the time they are needed. For example, when patients are transferred to a LTCF they are often in need of medication for pain control, and it is likely that it will not be possible for an off-site pharmacy to provide this in adequate time. Therefore, it would be reasonable to stock medication for pain control in an emergency kit in a LTCF. OAR 855.041.7060

63. B. Although the review did not cover DPDO, it did provide some general guidance. No matter what outlet, medications must be stored and secured appropriately, they must be labeled, counseling is required, and everything must be documented. Without reading through the rule on DPDO's you may not be able to answer this question confidently (which is why you should read the rules!), but you should be able to reason it out. A is incorrect, because it is unlikely that the physicians desk drawer meets appropriate storage or security requirements for medications. B is correct because we know that medications must be properly labeled, and that any unit-of-use medications do not need a product identification label (PIL), or physical description of the product. C is incorrect because a label must always contain cautionary statements. D is incorrect because the dispensing record must be a unique and separate record at a DPDO site. You may reason this out if you think of how the BOP would inspect this outlet. Would it be reasonable to assume the BOP would comb through patient charts to obtain records of dispensing, or are they likely to want a separate dispensing record to review? OAR 855.043.0505-0555

64. D. Practitioners that only dispense the homeopathic medications, natural thyroid supplements, or medication assistance program medications do not need to register as a Dispensing Practitioner Drug Outlet. OAR 855.043.0510

65. B. A pharmacist must report any significant loss to both the DEA and the Board of Pharmacy within 1 business day. Loss occurring in transit must also be reported. The general guideline is until the medication has arrived at its destination, and is officially received, it is considered the responsibility of the supplier when it comes to reporting a loss. So, in option II the supplier is still responsible as long as the pharmacy has not taken custody of the medication, whereas option III is written correctly, the central fill pharmacy, as the supplier, is still responsible for reporting the loss.

66. A. Records can be moved to an off-site location after 1 year and must be retrieved within 3 business days.

67. D. Any medication, including controlled substances, that were dispensed from the pharmacy in error, such as a medication that is damaged, deteriorated, misbranded, or adulterated, may be returned to the pharmacy for disposal. In this question, this includes option A, B, and C. A is likely adulterated based on a recall, B is adulterated because it is expired, and C is misbranded and dispensed in error as there are two different medications in his bottle, which should just be Xanax. There is one additional caveat; that if the medication dispensed could actually cause patient harm, you may accept it back. In option D the medication is not adulterated, misbranded, nor could it cause patient harm, and so you cannot take the medication back.

68. B. During a take-back program the receptacle must be placed in front of the counter, and medications put in the receptacle may not be counted, inventoried, or sorted in any way. Therefore, interns would not be allowed to count the tablets of Schedule II substances collected. Stock medication from the pharmacy, expired or not, may not be put into the receptacle, so II is also not appropriate. The only option listed that the inters would be able to do is interview patients.

69. D. Non-controlled prescriptions must be kept in hard copy form for 120 days before they can be destroyed and kept only in their electronic format. However, controlled substance prescriptions that are received as hard copy prescriptions must be kept indefinitely. The rules state they must be kept as long as you keep the prescription records. As the BOP requires prescription records to be kept for 3 years, option D is the best answer. OAR 855.041.1160

70. B. Review the Regular Reviews table in the guide for further review of this information. All policies and procedures must be reviewed annually, however a CDTM arrangement only needs to be reviewed every 2 years.

71. C. A felony charge must be reported within 10 days. See the Dates and Deadlines table for further review.

72. C. Chronic diseases, list of medications, and allergies should all be included in a patient's record. The caveat is that the list of medications only needs to cover the medication the patient receives from your pharmacy. Therefore, you do not need to have the type of insulin the patient receives from a different pharmacy in the patient's record at your pharmacy.

73. C. Hormonal Contraception Self-screening questionnaires must be kept for 5 years. This is the only record that must be kept longer than 3 years.

74. C. To become PIC you must have either 1 year of experience as a licensed pharmacist or you must complete the BOP approved PIC training course beforehand or within the 30 days after becoming PIC. The only pharmacist that does not meet these requirements is in option C. OAR 855.019.0300

75. B. When a pharmacist becomes PIC of the pharmacy, they must complete both a pharmacy inspection and an inventory of all the controlled substances within 15 days. If the retiring pharmacist had completed the inventory within the last 15 days, it would be ok for the incoming PIC to review and sign the inventory without completing the inventory themselves. OAR 855.019.0300

76. D. There are no additional CE requirements once a pharmacist becomes a preceptor, although a pharmacist may be required to complete additional training courses for the school for which they precept. A pharmacist may apply for a pharmacist preceptor license after being licensed as a pharmacist for one year. A pharmacist is not required to supervise all of an interns' hours, only a majority of them.

77. B. A pharmacist must complete 30 CEs in each renewal cycle. Two of these hours must be on law and 2 hours must be on medication errors or patient safety.

78. D. This is the most complete and accurate list of required equipment listed. The sink must have both hot and cold running water. In addition to these supplies, a pharmacy must also have computer and software capable of completing the duties of prescription processing completed at the pharmacy, and any additional equipment determined necessary by the PIC. OAR 855.041.1035

79. B. If the refrigerator holds vaccines, the temperature must be on an automated monitoring system that should be downloaded weekly and validated quarterly. If the refrigerator does not house vaccines, an automated system is not necessary but in this case the temperature must be manually documented twice a day.

80. A. Licenses of ALL licensed personnel must be displayed, and this would include pharmacists, technicians, and interns. All personnel must wear name badges that have their name and position, and the sign regarding substitution must be present at all pharmacies, even ones that are not open to the public (such as closed pharmacies that serve long-term care facilities.) ORS 689.515, ORS 689.615

81. C. Any out of state pharmacy that handles prescriptions, whether filling or processing, designated for Oregon patients must be registered with the Oregon Board of Pharmacy. In addition, any entity in the pharmaceutical supply chain (manufacturers, distributors, pharmacies) located in Oregon must be registered with the Oregon Board of Pharmacy. Common carriers that handle medications after they have been dispensed do not need to be registered with the Oregon Board of Pharmacy. ORS 475.125, 689.305, OAR 855.062.0020, 855.080.0031

82. C. The Health Professionals Service Program is for all health professionals in Oregon, including pharmacists, doctors etc. The program is to help health professions with EITHER substance abuse disorder or dependency as well as health professionals with a mental-health disorder. Pharmacists may refer themselves to the program. Any pharmacist participating in the program must participate for at least two years. Participation in the program does not mean a pharmacists' license will be automatically revoked or suspended. The Oregon BOP will review the pharmacists' case and determine in what capacity, if any, the pharmacist may continue to practice. OAR 855.011.0020

83. C. The Oregon BOP is made up of 9 members, including 5 pharmacists, 2 technicians, and 2 members of the public. Participating pharmacists must have 5 years of pharmacist experience in Oregon, and technicians must have 3 years of technician experience in Oregon and be currently practicing as technicians. The members of the public cannot have any connection to or be involved in pharmacy practice. ORS 689.115

84. C. Members of the Oregon BOP are appointed by the governor and serve 4 year terms. ORS 689.115

85. A. The Public Health and Pharmacy Formulary Advisory Committee is made up of 2 physicians, 2 advanced practice nurses, and 3 pharmacists. Of the pharmacists on the committee, one must be based in the community and one must be based in a health system. The third pharmacist may be practicing in any environment.

86. A. The Oregon Public Health and Pharmacy Formulary Advisory Committee is charged with reviewing and approving the protocols that pharmacists may prescribe under, such as the immunization protocol. Pharmacists that are not on the committee may make protocol recommendations to the committee for review. Terms for committee members are only 2 years, and members are appointed by the governor.

87. A. A technician me reconcile an inventory of Schedule II controlled substances but may not resolve any discrepancies found during the reconciliation. A technician may also initiate refill requests made to a provider. A pharmacist must always be present while a pharmacy is in operation, and a pharmacist must supervise all activities completed by non-pharmacist personnel. Not only would a technician not be able to be present in the pharmacy while a pharmacist is away, but the act of filling prescriptions must be supervised.

88. C. You may fill both prescriptions. In Oregon, providers may write prescriptions for their family members. Prescriptions may be for controlled or non-controlled substances. There is no need to verify

the prescriptions with a second provider. If you feel the prescriptions raise suspicions about the provider, you should contact the board that governs that provider.

89. D. Providers may write more than 1 prescription on a hardcopy, even when one of the medications is for a Schedule II Controlled substance (Nucynta ER). However, when filing the prescription, you must include a copy in both your CII and legend prescription files, and the files must reference each other.

90. C. There are valid, legal online pharmacies that process prescriptions. However, there are no pharmacies in Canada that are registered with the Oregon Board of Pharmacy, and so there are no Canadian based pharmacies that may legally process prescriptions for Oregon residents. Verifiable online pharmacies will have the VIPPS symbol displayed on their website. [6]

91. B. Multiple prescriptions may be written on a hardcopy prescription, and the prescribers' agent may sign hard copy prescriptions for non-controlled substances. Nucynta ER, however is a Schedule II controlled substance. Without the providers' hand signature, the order for Nucynta ER is not valid. As a Schedule II controlled substance, you will also not be able to take a verbal order for the medication even after speaking to the prescriber.

92. B. Nembutal is one of the three barbiturates that is a Schedule II controlled substance. Therefore, if this is an emergency situation only, you may accept a verbal prescription from the provider only, provided that the hard copy prescription is sent to your pharmacy and postmarked within 7 days.

93. B. You do not need to document the prescription number at the transferring pharmacy. You also do not need to document each fill completed at the transferring pharmacy, only the last fill. You do need to document the number of refills authorized by the provider.

94. B. A Medical Doctor may not write prescriptions for animals. Therefore, regardless of verifying the prescription is accurately written for a cat, or if the provider has a relationship with the cat, you may not fill the prescription for the cat. Poor cuddles.

95. D. There are no issues with this prescription. "Brand Only" would meet the Oregon BOP guidelines for no substitution, as it would be reasonably considered to mean you cannot make substitutions on this prescription. If Brand Only was not on the prescription and the provider wished to add it, you may add this to the prescription after talking to either the provider or the providers' agent. A providers' agent may fax a prescription, and the providers agent may even sign the fax for the provider for a non-controlled substance such as Enbrel.

96. D. Prescriptions for controlled substances MUST have the providers' DEA number written on them. If the providers DEA is not on the prescription you may write it on the prescription yourself without verifying the DEA with the provider. Prescriptions for Schedule II controlled substances do not expire. You may fill any prescriptions from out of state providers that are practicing within their scope, even if the prescription is for a Schedule II Controlled substance.

97. D. Note that this was not covered in the review section. But we will cover it briefly here. A pharmacist who has retired may reinstate their license after they pass the MPJE again, certify that they have completed ALL CE's required since they retired, and pay the licensing fee. At 30CEs per two-year renewal cycle, you may assume that the pharmacist would have to complete 60 CE's as well as pass the MPJE in order to reinstate their license. OAR 855.019.0170

98. C. There are two types of Emergency prescriptions, as discussed in the review. In this case, the emergency prescription is being generated due to a natural disaster. Oregon rules state that a patient affected by the area of the natural disaster may be provided with an emergency refill, even if your pharmacy is not in the natural disaster area. In these situations, you may provide up to a 30-day emergency refill of a prescription but need to tell the patient that a provider will need to authorize additional refills. While the patient may obtain a new prescription from an emergency room provider, this is not required in this situation. If the patient were attempting to obtain an emergency refill of a controlled substance, they would have to have a valid prescription. Review the emergency prescription section for further information. OAR 855.007.0090

99. A. A faxed prescription for a controlled substance must contain the hand signature of the provider. There is no age requirement to pick up controlled substances, so a 12 year old may pick up a controlled substance prescription. You may require ID to pick up controlled substances, and you may require other patient verification information (such as date of birth, etc.) for a patient to pick up a controlled substance prescription. Oregon law however does not require either of these things. As a pharmacist you should use your professional judgment in determining what information a patient must present with to pick these medications up from your pharmacy.

100. D. A clerk may only accept refill requests when a patient makes the request using their prescription number. A properly trained clerk may inform a patient of a manufacturer change when the patient is picking up a refill. A clerk can also enter non-medical information into a patient's chart, which includes the patients name, address, and billing information.[2]

101. A. A prescribers' agent may verbally transmit a prescription for CIII-V substances, which would include Sudogest. A prescribers' agent may sign for the prescriber for non-controlled substances, such as Brintellix. While option III appears to be a valid prescription, as it is for a CIII substance and has been signed off by the prescriber, a faxed prescription may only be transmitted to a pharmacies' fax machine or to their electronic portal. It may not be faxed to the patient or to anywhere that is not a pharmacy and remain a valid prescription. Therefore, option III is not valid. OAR 855.006.0015

102. B. Medications packaged for use in a nursing home are acceptable for return to the pharmacy, as long as they were handled by trained personnel that kept them properly stored and they are in tamper evident packaging. They may also be donated to a charitable pharmacy if they the medication has been packaged in single-dose blister packs. Nursing homes may NOT keep these medications as floor stock.

103. C. You should counsel the patients' agent as you would counsel the patient themselves. You may also provide information to the patient in the form of written material, or a number at which the patient may reach you should they have questions when they receive the prescription, however this is not necessary and doesn't preclude the necessity for counseling.

104. D. A patient with a terminal diagnosis may receive partial fills of a CII prescription for up to 60 days after the date the prescription was written.

105. C. You may partial fill a CII medication (Xtampza ER, oxycodone) for a nursing home patient. Each time the medication is partialed you must document on the prescription your initials, the date, the quantity dispensed and the quantity remaining on the prescription. You may continue to partial the prescription until either the quantity written for runs out or 60 days after the prescription was written.

106. D. A pharmacy must transmit necessary information within 72 hours of filling a controlled substance. Oregon PDMP does not track Schedule V substances. Providers are required to register with the PDMP but are not required to check it.

107. B. All requests to obtain a copy of a patient's PDMP record must be made to the Oregon Health Authority. You may not provide a patient or a policeman a copy of a patient's PDMP record at the pharmacy! OAR 333.023.0820

108. A. Under no circumstances may a compounding pharmacy compound a commercially available medication, no matter how much the cost difference. Mixing two or more non-sterile commercial products is not considered compounding. Compounding pharmacies do not have to adhere directly to either USP 795 or 797, as long as the pharmacy is following the "spirit" of the guidelines. OAR 855.045.0200, 0210, 0250

109. C. Medications for animals must include the animals' species on the prescription label. If a generic medication is dispensed it must include the manufacturer. The label must have an expiration date for the medication, however there is no reason the expiration date must be within one year. The expiration date must be what the pharmacist feels is appropriate. If the medication is dispensed in the manufacturers original packaging (such as for an inhaler), it may be appropriate to list the expiration of the inhaler listed on the manufacturer's package, which may be greater than one year from the date of filling.

110. A. Expanded-practice dental hygienists may prescribe fluoride products, antibiotics, proton-pump inhibitors, and NSAIDs. Midwives do not have prescriptive authority and are only allowed to administer a limited number of medications. Optometrists may prescribe combination hydrocodone products only, not Percocet. Chiropractors do not have prescriptive authority.

111. D. When a prescription requires counseling but will be delivered to a patient the pharmacist must include written documentation that offers counseling to the patient along with contact information for the patient to reach the pharmacist. Written information must also be included about the medication being delivered.

112. A complete DUR for a prescription may include a review of the patients' allergies, comorbidities, other medications as listed at your pharmacy, the appropriateness of the prescription itself, medication abuse, and using too much or too little of a medication. Therefore, all of the options are appropriate components of a DUR.

113. D. A properly trained intern may complete all of the listed activities. The only activity an intern may not complete is the final verification of a medication.

114. C. The label of a unit dose medication must have the medication name, manufacturer, and strength. It must have an expiration date. It must have a lot number but it does not have to be the manufacturer's lot number. It may be a pharmacy designated lot number if the pharmacy created the unit-dose package.

115. B. Medication therapy management does not allow a pharmacist to change medication doses, although a pharmacist may recommend dose changes to a provider. A pharmacist practicing under a

collaborative practice agreement may change medication dosages, but any new prescription generated must be under the prescriber's name. Pharmacists do not have prescriptive authority under collaborative practice agreements.

116. D. Data must be transmitted to the OR PDMP within 72 hours after filling a prescription, but if a breach of security is detected it must be reported to the Oregon Health Authority within 24 hours.

117. D. The label must include a beyond-use date, a rate of infusion, as well as the initials of the verifying pharmacist. A label does not need to be electronically generated.

118. C. Intravenous medication may be relabeled for use by another patient if it was not used for the original patient, was properly stored, and is still within its beyond-use date. Any patient identifier must be removed from the label if you are going to put the IV back into the pharmacy stock. There is no reason to change the beyond use date. You do not want to just remove the medication label, as then the medication is not identified and the IV is misbranded.

119. D. Pharmacists must renew their license biannually in odd numbered years on June 30th.

120. D. Each of these items must be present in a vaccine emergency kit. For further information see reference 9, or the most recent Immunization Protocol for Pharmacists written by the Oregon Health Authority.

OREGON PHARMACY LAW REFERENCES

1. National Association of Boards of Pharmacy. (2019). *NABP Candidate Application Bulletin.* [PDF file]. Retrieved from https://nabp.pharmacy/wp-content/uploads/2019/03/NAPLEX-MPJE-Bulletin-March-2019.pdf

2. Oregon Board of Pharmacy. (2013) *Non-Licensed Personnel- Clerks.* [PDF file]. Retrieved from https://www.oregon.gov/pharmacy/Imports/Compliance/Non-LicensedPersonnelDuties7.13.pdf

3. Oregon Board of Pharmacy (2014) *Prescription Requirements of Controlled and Non-Controlled Drugs.* [PDF file]. Retrieved from https://www.oregon.gov/pharmacy/Imports/Compliance/PrescriptionRequirements.pdf

4. Oregon Board of Pharmacy (2014) *Prescriptive Authority- State of Oregon.* [PDF file]. Retrieved from https://www.oregon.gov/pharmacy/imports/prescribers.pdf

5. Oregon Board of pharmacy (2015) *Prescription Changes for CII Controlled Substances.* [PDF file]. Retrieved from https://www.oregon.gov/pharmacy/Imports/CSAddsChangesChart.pdf

6. Oregon Board of Pharmacy. (2016) *Oregon Board of Pharmacy Frequently Asked Questions).* [PDF file]. Retrieved from https://www.oregon.gov/pharmacy/Imports/Compliance_FAQ.pdf

7. Oregon Health Authority. (2015) *Expedited Partner Therapy (EPT) for Sexually Transmitted Diseases.* [PDF file]. Retrieved from https://www.oregon.gov/oha/PH/DISEASESCONDITIONS/HIVSTDVIRALHEPATITIS/SEXUALLYTRANSMITTEDDISEASE/Documents/EPT/EPTProtocolFeb2015.pdf

8. Oregon Health Authority. Death with Dignity Act. Retrieved from https://www.oregon.gov/oha/PH/PROVIDERPARTNERRESOURCES/EVALUATIONRESEARCH/DEATHWITHDIGNITYACT/Pages/index.aspx

9. Oregon Health Authority. Pharmacy Protocols. Retrieved from https://www.oregon.gov/oha/PH/PREVENTIONWELLNESS/VACCINESIMMUNIZATION/IMMUNIZATIONPROVIDERRESOURCES/Pages/pharmpro.aspx

Like the book? Help us help you more!

- Please help positively (5/5) rate this book on Amazon.com if you liked this book, search title **"Oregon Pharmacy Law"**, find our book and rate us under customer reviews

- Access our website for more guides at or to make recommendations/suggestions: www.rxpharmacist.com

- Find a mistake in this guide? You may get a monetary reward! Help your pharmacy profession in giving back to ensure these guides continue to serve our fellow pharmacists and graduates. Please contact help@rxpharmacist.com

- Want to share feedback? We would love to hear! Send us a recommendation and any comments/suggestions to: help@rxpharmacist.com

Made in the USA
Columbia, SC
11 February 2021